SIMON POORE 1992   £2-50

GW00459136

Gregor McLennan

NLB

Marxism and the Methodologies of History

British Library
Cataloguing in Publication Data

McLennan, Gregor
    Marxism and the methodologies of history.
    1. History—Philosophy
    I. Title
    901   D16.9

    ISBN 0-86091-045-8 Cloth
         0-86091-743-6 Pbk

Verso Editions and NLB,
15 Greek Street, London W1

Typeset in Garamond by
Preface Ltd,
Salisbury, Wilts

Printed and bound by
Unwin Brothers Limited
The Gresham Press, Old Woking, Surrey

Contents

Preface

This book is about the relationship between philosophical assumptions and historical writing, and suggests the need to dismantle some of the barriers dividing the two. Ultimately, this issue is inseparable from the question of the ideological or political implications of historiography.[1] However, while I also try to give support to that view, my object of analysis is the logic of historical work more than its wider political context. It may seem paradoxical that I do not discuss the substantive question of the politics or history of history (including Marxism), since Marxism is my special focus. Indeed, some historical materialists would argue that reflection on the presuppositions of historians is itself an excessively philosophical task.

It is true that philosophers are often inexcusably prescriptive, and that substantive, 'really useful' knowledge is the condition for and goal of theoretical work. It does not follow, though, that there is no place and no use for projects that try to throw light on the conceptual structure of historical debates. History books are not just stores of information or expressions of personal interests: they embody explanations and arguments that structure and support empirical conclusions. And just because they are also artefacts, the production of which has ideological and political effects, the epistemological dimension *is* connected to more 'concrete' problems.

I mainly deal with issues of Marxist historiography and their connection to the problem of whether there can be a distinctive Marxist philosophy. As a matter of fact, I think it can be shown that there has always been a *nexus* of philosophy, history, and politics in historical materialism. Some Marxists,[2] and with justice, have spoken out against the increasingly academic nature of modern Western Marxism, in particular against its obsession with philosophy. But there is nothing new in that obsession—in fact it could be argued that socialists today are possibly *less* philosophically minded than they once were. The problem is rather that the philosophy is more academic and specialist than in previous eras. In fairness, that is a general, and historical, problem, and cannot be put down wholly to philosophy.

The context of the book is the so-called crisis of Marxism, which reveals itself on the intellectual level in several ways. One tendency is that Marxists become hesitant about the force of historical materialism, either withdrawing its substantive claims altogether and pronouncing it dead, or softening its assertions into 'methodological' guidelines. Alternatively, Marxism can be reaffirmed under pressure either as a theory of history or as materialist philosophy. There are options within options, too. For example, Marxist philosophy might be re-cast as 'structural causality' or as 'realism'; and the question is posed whether historical materialism is a mode of empirical research instead of a general theory of history.

These options are somewhat overstated here, but each touches on an important consideration. The first two chapters discuss the main philosophical positions in the Marxist tradition, and suggest that clarity on the precise role of philosophy has proved difficult to attain. Misrecognition of that role has been associated, in a variety of ways, with important theoretical weaknesses in Marxism. I argue that the philosophical premisses of the latter are *realist* in character, involving no special notions of 'dialectic' or 'materialism'. But realism does not *uniquely* justify Marxism any more than 'dialectical materialism' does, and historical materialism neither provides nor requires *elaborate* philosophical doctrines of any kind. This is partly because detailed historical issues cannot be directly resolved by philosophical criteria alone.

Chapter 3 engages some important debates about the character of historical, as opposed to dialectical, materialism, though there is no clean separation between the two. I support the view that the former embodies a theory of history, and that its general propositions are of a 'functional' kind. This, however, raises problems to do with the very generality of those propositions (such as the explanatory primacy of 'material life'). How do they bear on more specific questions about causality in particular societies or eras, about the analysis of politics or ideology? Whilst these questions can never be fully resolved, it is important that causal and functional explanations complement each other, both in Marxism and in general.

I then move from debates located essentially within Marxism to problems at the interface between Marxist and non-Marxist theoretical frameworks. My doubts about how rigorous Marxist explanation is in practice are shared by many analytical philosophers. Obviously, these doubts would seem to be strengthened by the recent 'opening-up' of classical Marxism (to which, I suppose, this book contributes). Consequently, philosophers (like Karl Popper) who in the past have sought to expose the allegedly speculative and unscientific character of historical materialism are now joined by those (like Leszek Kolakowski) who think that a more open Marxism, being open, says nothing.

It seems important, then, to consider the criteria adopted by the analytical philosophy of history, and to what extent they are challenged or satisfied by a 'broad' Marxism. Chapter 4 proposes that a purely 'analytic' account of historical practice is untenable. The rest of the book, being about historians, provides grounds for this claim. But it is also supported by recent developments in philosophy of science, which itself is now a more open arena of debate and whose guidelines philosophy of history generally follows. Moreover, classic confrontations between positivism and idealism in philosophy of history now seem to be less polarized, in spite of the currency of what I term 'the new idealism'. In this context the prospects are bright for a lasting realist contribution in this area.

The second part of the book 'descends' slightly, into the realm of historical methodology. I consider the general methodological statements or 'manifestos' of some well-known historians (chapter 5), and try to show that despite a common view amongst practitioners that they do not take up philosophical (or ideological) positions, this view is wrong. Whether in statements about general historical methodology or in claims for the importance of particular historical specialisms, historians do take up such stances. The notion that history is, or ought to be, outside philosophical wrangles is itself a philosophical attitude, usually empiricist. It is true, and significant, that 'hard' empiricist views of this kind are breaking down. One false alternative, however, is the return to positions that hold that history is inherently value-relative, subjective, qualitative, or literary. These continuing dichotomies are especially felt in two important fields: social history and feminist history.

The story gets complicated here (chapter 6), because, first, these contributions have been responsible in part for the decline of empiricist and particularist historiography. Also, social history has been influenced by Marxism. The view that social history just *is* historical materialism (perhaps without the theoretical preambles) is rejected in favour of a conception of social history as a 'domain'. Some Marxist social historians have argued eloquently against Marxism-as-system and in defence of history. I examine E. P. Thompson's arguments in this context, finding them valuable but unconvincing. Another complication is that feminist history too provides a partial critique of both social history *and* Marxism, from a political and theoretical point of view. Indeed, feminists have forced many Marxists to re-think the very concepts of socialism and socialist history. The vexed question of the relation between materialism and feminism in historiography is discussed, but not conclusively.

Of other influential bodies of work requiring discussion as methodologies critical of traditional historiography but distanced from historical materialism, I consider (chapter 7) the *Annales* 'school'. I argue that there is no single methodology of the 'school', and, on the basis of available translations in English, distinguish between its protagonists. Marc Bloch and Fernand Braudel are particularly interesting here, both in their own right and in relation to realist assumptions and Marxist theory. The relationship is, in my view, one of theoretical convergence, though not of underlying identity. The appendix to this chapter is important, first because its subject—the debates on the transition from feudalism to capitalism—is classic ground for my theoretical concerns. Second, it takes us over the rather artificial division between methodology and historiography.

The third part returns to Marxist historiography in the light of the first two parts. Marx's and Engels's more historical writings are reviewed in chapter 8, where some of the problems outlined in Part 1 are rediscovered. Chapters 9 and 10 look in detail at two key historical debates in which the varieties of Marxism and the issues between Marxist and non-Marxist historians are displayed. The French revolution is familiar territory for that confrontation. I argue that the work of the prominent Marxist historian of the revolution, Albert Soboul, is fraught with problems. This is because, in his hands, a general theory of history in which the concept of *productive forces* figures conflicts with more appropriate causal attribution and classification. A reminder that Marxism must respect the play of different levels of abstraction is pertinent here.

Some historical theories within Marxism are not wholly dependent on the primacy of the productive forces, but convey a similar principle, namely the 'logic of capital'. The theory of the labour aristocracy in nineteenth-century Britain is a more specific location of the problems taken up in the book. I outline two versions of the theory, their relative merits, and their relation to non-Marxist accounts. The Marxist theory of the labour aristocracy is viable, and is of a realist complexion. But it is not, just on that score, adequate. Here again there are difficulties in combining historical specificity and general theoretical ambition. Indeed, that problematical relationship is the subject, in various ways, of the book as a whole, which closes with a summary discussion of causal pluralism.

The book covers a wide range of issues in an effort to persuade philosophers and historians of their common interest in the alliance of philosophical realism and historical materialism. Consequently, some questions are presented in outline only, whilst others—perhaps inevitably—remain open-ended. Still, I would hope that both in outline and in detail, the positions advanced here are basically sound, and that they may serve as a resource for further research and discussion.

I would like to express my appreciation for the help of many friends. Without Suzanne Battleday's constant and critical encouragement, the work upon which this book is based might have been left to the 'gnawing criticism of the mice'. It is not her fault if it should have been! My interests and opinions are in good part the product of collaboration with members of successive 'history' groups at the Centre for Contemporary Cultural Studies, with Stuart Hall, Bill Schwarz, and (especially) Richard Johnson. Since none of the above, I am sure, would endorse everything in the book, I must add that its errors are mine.

Part One

Philosophy

Mr Lowe criticizes my approach
. . . on the ground that it is formal in character. I feel that he is
confusing here two things: analysis
of the formal structure of a theory
and 'starting from' a priori postulates in creating or expounding a
theory. While my chapter began
with the former, it proceeded explicitly to repudiate the latter.

MAURICE DOBB

Dialectical Materialism and Its 'Historical' Conversions

In Marxism more than in other historiographical traditions, the principles of historical analysis have been justified by recourse to tenets concerning the general relation between knowledge and the world. This chapter will outline some problems that beset the traditional concept of 'dialectical materialism'. Those problems have led some writers to the view that Marxism-as-philosophy is untenable, and that since it is inherently philosophical, Marxism should be abandoned. Others have argued that Marxism can be defended, but as *historical* method instead of epistemology. I will discuss some of these arguments in turn, since each has an important bearing on Marxism-as-history. I remain as sceptical about views that hold that Marxism does not require an epistemological basis as I am about those that maintain that there is a unique Marxist philosophy. The second chapter will examine, in a little more detail, two recent re-statements of the philosophical status of Marxism.

1. Dialectical Materialism

Until the onset of 'Western Marxism', the most common interpretation of Marxism-as-philosophy was 'dialectical materialism'. Marxist historical principles were held to be a subset of more general scientific principles. The justification of historical materialism thus depended on the explication and defence of dialectical laws. Stalin's pamphlet *Dialectical and Historical Materialism*[1] set out the arguments schematically, including a sequence of historical stages in which distinct sets of property relations accommodated the progressive and necessary development of the forces of production (science, technology, and labour-power). It is true that Soviet 'diamat' has been characterized by a mechanical yoking together of the principle of materialism and 'dialectic', to the point that component terms became but slogans with which to denounce ideological foes. But it is important to see that the openness of dialectical materialism to pragmatic mobilization and to a variety of theoretical interpretations neither begins nor ends with Stalin.

The tradition itself has never satisfactorily demonstrated the *unity* (dialectical or otherwise) of the 'materialism' on the one hand and the 'dialectics' on the other. For a materialist, 'dialectical' relations need only be construed as causal interaction. This is compatible with saying, for example, that some sets of interactions (material ones) are of *fundamental* importance whereas others, however important, are not. A dialectician may take material or social causality for granted, yet maintain that, *essentially*, all things are logically interrelated and so equivalent. The debate between the 'founders' of dialectical materialism, Josef Dietzgen and G. V. Plekhanov (Marx never having used the term), was of this kind. Plekhanov took the materialist option (Marxism was *Feuerbach* 'corrected'[2]), and consequently also flirted with a technological theory of history. Dietzgen posited a monism whereby thought and things, nature and history, being internally connected, were part of the same universal substance.[3]

There are two main possibilities within each of the materialist and dialectical approaches. 'Materialism', as in Plekhanov, comes close to being 'Feuerbachian'—that is, it upholds the metaphysical assertion that *matter* is primary. Or, it could consist of the weaker claim that what counts is knowledge of material (determinate and causal) *relationships* in nature and society. Here, science—not philosophy—tells us what 'material' things and relations are. On the dialectical side, we can ask, is 'dialectics' a universal logic or does it refer to the particular nature of human and historical relations? What kind of *historical* theory Marxism is depends on how history is thought of in the variant positions. No single theorist fits snugly into any one of these conceptual boxes. Engels, Lenin, and Bukharin sustain quite complex discourses. But the problems are persistent and international in character. In Britain, for example, the same sets of questions that exercised T. A. Jackson or the scientists in the 1930s are subjects of controversy amongst Marxists in university philosophy departments today.[4] For the moment, let us try to shed some light on the meaning of dialectical materialism, leaving to a later section the notion of a *specifically historical* dialectic. Does it, for example, involve the notion of special laws, or is it more a general heuristic principle?

The general principles of dialectical materialism can be stated in such a way that most Marxists would subscribe to it. One might say, for example, that all things in nature have material determinations; that no thing or process is discrete; and that each thing or relation is internally composed of 'contradictions', between elements of stasis and change, action and conditioning, essence and attribute, and so forth. In spite of the quantity of literature in Anglo-Saxon philosophy making nonsense of dialectical materialism, the general principle attracts surprisingly little dissension.[5] The 'bourgeois' critics of Marxism mostly acknowledge that if dialectical materialism is about the scientific concern for, and recognition of, determinate change, then it may be a true doctrine—though probably trivially so. For Marxists and critics alike, no great furor arises if 'diamat' is expounded as sensible generalizations. Rather, it is when Marxist notions of 'contradiction' and 'laws', and their 'application' in other fields, are regarded as of special cognitive status that hackles are raised. For example, even today a Soviet textbook characterizes *historical* materialism as the 'objective logic of world history'.[6] The idea is that the growth of the productive forces is the basis of historical development, and so the 'dialectical' relation between forces and relations of production, material and social interaction, etc., forms the stages of that growth: the modes of production. Moreover, this is the scientific or natural basis for the deduction of social forms. In many ways, Kelle and Kovalson's book is a clear and intelligent defence of general principles, which themselves cannot aspire 'in any complete sense' to form a detailed theory of history.[7] But it is a typical work of 'diamat' in that its changes of emphasis almost amount to contradictions. The sequence of modes of production is still regarded as logical; with the appearance of historical materialism 'mankind is ripe for self-cognition', and 'the full triumph of the socialist cause' is therefore 'inevitable'.[8] It is these elements that encourage refutations of Marxism as contradictory, or as claiming to predict the future. A barrage of pejoratives—'dogma', 'doctrine', 'metaphysics', etc.—is regularly hurled at Marxists. Indeed, 'diamat' is taken by some to be a curious cultural phenomenon more appropriately treated by anthropologists than philosophers.[9] But within Marxism too, the *forced* character of diamat (rather than its humble truths) is the subject of fundamental theoretical and political dispute.

What, then, are dialectical laws, and do they involve an 'alternative' science or logic? If 'dialectic' is more than a principle of interaction that can as well be stated in other terms, can it be materialist? The second question can be illuminated by consideration of the recent debate between Lucio Colletti and Roy Edgley. For the first question, we must turn to Engels. Engels's dialectical 'laws' are: the transformation of quantity into quality; the interpenetration of opposites; and the negation of the negation. It is difficult to simply affirm or deny Engels's claims, but allowing for the

Darwinian context of his thought,[10] Engels does seem to argue that his laws are fully *scientific*. They 'constitute the science of universal interaction'.[11] Consequently, they must apply to all things; for example, to butterflies and history, barley and calculi.[12]

Contemporary philosophers of science have some difficulty in saying exactly what a scientific law is. But even so, Engels's definitions do not entail the specification of determinate conditions, and the latter would seem to be part of the meaning of 'law'. The first dialectical law 'fits' cases of 'qualitative' change (a famous example is the kettle boiling), but it has no bearing on establishing at what point in particular processes the said changes occur. That is the job, still, of natural laws in the ordinary sense. The question is, does dialectics *replace* science?

Engels's impressive knowledge of, and respect for, science would suggest that this is not so. By 'higher' laws, Engels does not appear to mean those that *justify* scientific propositions. Rather, in accordance with the conception of philosophy expressed in the *German Ideology*, Engels seems to hold that dialectical laws are compact philosophical generalizations synthesizing scientific practice. Against Dühring, for example,[13] Engels rejects the Hegelian idea that philosophy *is* constitutive. But Engels is seldom free of ambiguity. The status of his 'philosophical' generalizations still requires clarification. Does 'interpenetration of opposites' mean logically connected 'contradictory unities'? Or does it just refer to the necessary natural connections of various kinds between some things and other things? Engels's comments do not, in my view, give a clear-cut answer. The tendency of all philosophy is to be prescriptive, and there is a strong impulse in Marxism to defend science against idealism (whatever the scientists say). These, together with Engels's many 'constitutive' propositions—about the dialectical unities in electric fields or mathematics for example[14]—mean that the idea of dialectic as the logical or metaphysical *foundation* of science is never cleanly rejected. The tendency in Soviet developments of the doctrines to invoke science as *evidence* for a foundational cosmology has confirmed the metaphysical cast of 'diamat'.[15]

Applied to history, 'diamat' grew into 'histomat'. Here again, the appeal to Engels and (less so) to Marx resolves very little. Despite his renowned declaration that Marxism is but a guide to study,[16] Engels did hold that the laws of dialectic 'apply' to history, too.[17] If modes of production are thought to negate one another, or revolutions to be transitions from quantity to quality, then Engels must take his share of the blame. It is not that these *descriptions* are 'outrageous'. Rather, it is the a priori character of the sequences of necessary contradiction and synthesis that is dubiously metaphysical. As in Hegel, the sense of an inexorable conceptual development tends to divest the parts of the historical process of their specificity. At the same time, the *basis* of contradictory movement remains, in diamat, firmly 'materialist'. In the best book of its kind, the Bolshevik N. Bukharin[18] spent 143 pages on nature and the forces of production before mentioning social relations. A 'rationalist' conception of science and history, therefore, need not be strictly idealist; but the strong sense of Hegelian 'dialectic' is retained in 'diamat'.

It may be that it is only the axiomatization of dialectical and historical materialism that is at fault. The principles of materialism and logical interaction, perhaps, do not *require* mechanical formulation and 'application'. Moreover, historians need not appeal to the philosophy directly to utilize its categories for more concrete purposes. This rejoinder has some force. The debates on the transition from feudalism to capitalism, for instance, are not about proving the validity of the entire Marxist worldview. On the other hand, participating historians sometimes invoke as the very fundament of their case the notion that the material development of a historical system is revealed by a grasp of its primary internal contradictions. It is only in recent years that the historian's practice has been thought to represent a challenge to the philosophical axioms of Marxism. In any case, the problem with the systematic exposition of the latter relates not so much to *Soviet* dogma or 'mechanism' as to the false sense of certainty the axioms encourage. The crucial question is seldom posed: do the materialist and dialectical axioms cancel each other out rather than form a 'dialectical synthesis'?

Lenin's work is one important location of the main features of dialectical materialism. But only the most devoted follower could argue that, at face value anyway, the different strands in his writings mutually support one another. In his polemic against empirio-criticism, Lenin ambiguously defended materialism. On the one hand, matter is primary; it is what our thoughts and percepts 'copy' if they are to be correct. On the other hand, Lenin sometimes uses 'matter' only to signify whatever is 'objectively' arrived at by science.[19] Anton Pannekoek, the Dutch socialist, criticized the first sense as being 'bourgeois' materialism.[20] Louis Althusser has defended Lenin's objective partisanship in philosophy on the basis of the second argument.[21] In any event, Lenin himself was later (in his *Philosophical Notebooks*) to give his ideas a more dialectical cast by incorporating more of Hegel. Althusser has also tried to present the earlier and later Lenin as the same in every respect. Here again, the convenient notion of a 'synthesis' or 'contradictory unity' compounds rather than illuminates the issues.

The recent debates about contradiction exhibit less obligation to defend major figures of Marxist politics. They consequently form an appropriate context in which to assess more closely the general problems that have been at the heart of Marxist philosophy from the outset. Two main questions can be asked. Is 'dialectic' a *logical* principle? Are Marxists committed to an account of the *essential* properties of things (an 'ontology')?

Roy Edgley[22] has characterized Lucio Colletti's denial of 'contradictions in reality' as a return to idealism. This is because Colletti restricts the logical sense of 'contradiction' to relations between propositions. Edgley, by contrast, defends the idea that Marxist dialectic goes beyond purely formal logic. Rather, it ties logic to a materialist ontology. Things and thoughts can still be both dialectically *and* materially connected.[23] Much of the heat of the debate is generated by the supposition by each side that the other is essentially non-Marxist. 'Dialecticians' tend to accuse 'Kantians' of endorsing bourgeois logic, and thus of ignoring the material basis of the latter. The other side accuses the dialectical ontologists of resurrecting the Hegelian mysteries of Being. But we should not think that Edgley or Fisk dispute the validity of formal logic any more than Colletti denies the existence of real oppositions. Here—as in Engels and Plekhanov—there is a point at which the significance of the argument can elude us. Neither of those earlier thinkers saw dialectical contradiction as incompatible with logical contradiction in every respect. And yet there is a sense in both the classical formulations and their modern analogues that formal logic is inferior because undialectical, that it is a partial *substantive* doctrine rather than an indispensable tool for any clear thinking. For example: 'thinking in accordance with the rules of formal logic . . . is a particular instance of dialectical thinking.'[24] And: 'dialectic is based on the doctrine of Nature.'[25] For Engels, the law of identity in formal logic 'has been refuted by natural science bit by bit in each separate case, but theoretically it still prevails and is still put forward by the supporters of the old in opposition to the new.'[26] These ideas suggest that dialectical logic, being founded on the real nature of things, is alternative and superior to formal logic, and not simply that the latter is a necessary but quite limited condition of thinking.

My own view is that the second way of putting the issue is less confusing: dialectic is more a general way of thinking than, in and of itself, a 'logic'. Similarly, logic cannot be dispensed with, but being *formal* it cannot be other than 'limited'. Neither the classics nor the current disputants seem to be content with this fairly straightforward resolution. Colletti's view, I think, can be supported provided that we leave aside the confusing twist in the argument whereby 'alienation' is held to render (capitalist) reality *logically* contradictory. The fact that real oppositions are not strictly logical does not mean that the interactions and oppositions in nature are inaccessible to ontological generalization. Thought is also a natural phenomenon, so it can be treated according to whatever relations hold between other things. But none of this establishes that real contradiction is the same as logical contradiction, even if the term 'dialectical contradiction' conforms now to the one, now to the other emphasis.

Edgley and Fisk do not establish anything different. To be sure, the notion of natural necessity that bridges an over-simple division between the 'purely' logical and the 'merely' empirical is important. Similarly, the 'dialectical' claim that there is a tension or opposition between the essence (natural kind) and the attributes of a thing is an important advance on those who would deny ontology altogether. But ontology must depend on natural science, not an a priori metaphysics, and here Fisk is perhaps clearer than Engels was: 'These theses try to remain neutral on the issue of how changes occur.'[27] Moreover, on the question of dialectical logic, Edgley does not *refute* Colletti, at least as I have construed the argument: 'It's true that many real oppositions or conflicts are not contradictory or logical oppositions. But it's also true that a contradictory or logical opposition can be a perfectly real conflict: as, for instance, when on that question of whether the Earth moves, Copernicus and Galileo contradicted the Church.' From this, Edgley reasons that 'Kant's distinction between "real" and "contradictory" oppositions, which Colletti relies on, must be rejected.'[28]

But that does not follow. It may be true that the distinction referred to has been and is often mobilized for ideological purposes. And great thinkers who contradict official doctrines are in real opposition to authority. Yet it is a further step again to say that real oppositions are contradictory *in the sense that* they involve the simultaneous existence of logically contradictory states of affairs.[29] Philosophers have been quick to disallow the ontology of 'complexes', or the idea of 'natural' necessity (and may well have been ideologically motivated in doing so). However, the defence of those doctrines by Engels or Fisk does not entail the *identity* of logical and dialectical contradiction.[30]

It is hard to conclude that the ontology so ably defended by Fisk and others is a *Marxist* dialectic. Dialectical materialism is best regarded as the series of general statements I referred to earlier as arousing little opposition from non-Marxist philosophers. In fact, disagreements do persist, and they largely turn on the question of whether those realist principles are 'true but trivial' or 'true and fundamental'.

2. Rejections of Marxism-as-Philosophy

One of the main arguments of its critics is that because the strong philosophical pronouncements of Marxism are problematical, no suitable restatement of its theses is possible. Leaving aside the fact that this opinion is frequently mounted on wilful caricature, the charge of vacuity is often markedly rhetorical. Popper, for example, takes the view that 'the "moderate position" of Marxism destroys the whole Marxist argument.'[31] In his exchange with G. A. Cohen—who defends a classical historical materialism—H. B. Acton notes that Marxism has become increasingly flexible since his *Illusion of the Epoch*.[32] However, like Popper, and in spite of the fact that some *Marx* texts were rediscovered in the meantime, Acton illogically concludes that his refutation of Marxism has in due course been corroborated by Marxism itself.

The most recent significant example of this kind of 'refutation' is Leszek Kolakowski's massive *Main Currents of Marxism*. There are many useful insights in Kolakowski's three volumes, and much of the exposition is untainted by his increasingly polemical judgements. But here too there is a pattern to the critique: a dubious inference can be supported, ultimately, only by gross caricature. According to Kolakowski, historical materialism, if interpreted loosely, is a mere truism: 'Considered as a theory explaining all historical change by technological progress and all civilization by the class struggle, Marxism is unsustainable. As a theory of the interdependence of technology, property relations, and civilization, it is trivial.'[33]

John Plamenatz[34] also presents the doctrine as being about *technology*, about *all* change, and all civilization. And Acton too might (wrongly) assume that all theories of 'interdependence' must be essentially the same, allowing of no dominant causal relations. But more than most critics, Kolakowski knows that this demolition is somehow too facile. The doctrine is trivial, but Marx 'has profoundly affected our understanding of history'. For example, Kolakowski thinks it makes 'an essential difference' to think of Christianity as having material determinations, rather than being (only) 'intellectual struggle'.[35] Again: 'Historical materialism . . . has enriched our understanding of the past. True, it has been argued that in a strict form the doctrine is nonsense and in a loose form it is a commonplace; but if it has become a commonplace, this is largely due to Marx's originality.'[36] The argument has to be put starkly, because Kolakowski's book is widely regarded not only as a knowledgeable survey of Marxism, but also as a nail in its coffin. Now, once again accepting that there are problems with the 'strict forms' of dialectical and historical materialism, Kolakowski's conclusion is manifestly a *non sequitur*. How can a trivial or truistic doctrine make 'an essential difference'? And many 'commonplaces' (the term is conveniently vague) are no less true and important for being common (the laws of gravity, for instance). To take the analogy favoured by philosophers since Kant (and the one Althusser is keen to apply to Marx), if Kolakowski's view was right, it would apply, term for term, to Copernicus.

I am not saying that a full dialectical materialism is defensible, nor that a restatement is in every respect illuminating. My argument is merely that what is serviceable in the tradition of Marxist philosophy should be seen to be defensible. This is important, since some Marxists, holding out too much hope for a full and definitive Marxist science, tend to vacate the ground of historical materialism altogether. The work of Barry Hindess and Paul Hirst[37] is an important example of this tendency. Their complaints are based on sharp criticism of the substantive concepts that 'diamat' encourages— for example, a rigid historical sequence of modes of production based on the primacy of the productive forces. But they are also aware—and rightly so—that merely to add 'dialectic' to 'materialism' is not necessarily to produce a 'unity' adequate to history.

Their case has, roughly, the following shape. Economistic variants of Marxism hold that societies display features reducible to a single causal factor. The essential unit of society and history centres on the productive forces, and is given by the concept 'mode of production'. The latter is rationalistically instantiated in social formations. But softer or dialectical Marxisms cannot help here: the primacy of the relations of production as developed by Althusser, for example, still requires that diverse social elements and practices continue to be regarded as forming a necessary inner unity bound by Marxist causal principles. The 'relative autonomy' of the superstructures does not displace the already given and hierarchical relationship between economic causes and their effects. To recast this relationship in terms of a structure and its effects (Althusser) succeeds only in reproducing problems associated with the philosophical figure 'essence/ appearance'. In any case, the cause-effect model of historical materialism is but one form of the essence/manifestation couplet.

The charge here is that Marxism in any form cannot escape the inherent dogmas of *all* philosophy. Hindess and Hirst's argument is therefore of a status different from that of the philosophical critics referred to earlier. Though they share substantive ground, Hindess and Hirst refuse to return to empiricism or indeed to any other philosophical problematic. The very

idea of a necessary totality that can be grasped according to special principles of reason (diamat, structural causality) is, for Hindess and Hirst, a
fallacy of epistemology. For Marxists genuinely to escape philosophy, they
must abandon the epistemological fallacy. Yet since classical Marxism, on
this view, could not do without basic concepts and privileged reasoning,
which maps the essential features of social reality, classical Marxism must
collapse. 'Relative autonomy' is nothing more than a stalling operation,
preventing full acknowledgement that there are many discourses and that
discourses cannot be judged by reference to epistemological categories.

Three sets of points can be made against these fundamental criticisms.
First and most substantively, the argument hangs on a rather loose concept
of determination and 'relative autonomy'. These are said to be heterogeneous concepts violently pulled together by Marxists. However, it is
gratuitous simply to define 'determination' as necessarily reductive. It is
simply not the case that x's being determined by y deprives x of causal
status in its own right, including the propensity to substantially affect the
determining conditions. It may be that Marxists have not followed this
insight convincingly, and the terms adopted may sometimes beg the question. Further, there are no set rules for what the nature and degree of the
determination is. But these reservations do not constitute a logical point
against the concept of causality available to historical materialism.

Second, Hindess and Hirst's argument is really about epistemology,
since they include Marxism only as one (important) case of the epistemological fallacy. All epistemologies, they argue, construct an a priori core of
concepts to which rival theories, by definition, must fail to measure up.
Since epistemologies claim to specify the conditions of all knowledge, their
own conditions of validity must therefore be assumed, not demonstrated.
Thus every epistemology is inherently dogmatic and circular: it dismisses
rival positions solely by reference to the basic principles thought to ground
them. This argument is difficult to assess. If the charge is that all epistemological argument is necessarily dogmatic because it condemns views
by reference to the principles that unavoidably ground those views, then
the criticism is circular, too. Epistemology is condemned by Hindess and
Hirst in exactly the same manner in which they say epistemology operates.
If, on the other hand, arguments can become dogmatic because they rely
too directly on fundamental premisses, then the point is fair but weaker. It
is not a necessary feature of arguments that rely at some higher level on
epistemological principles that they are reliant in just that way. Unless, of
course, we take dogmatic argument to *mean* 'having premisses at some
remove', whence epistemology becomes a mere synonym for that equation.

But that equation would abolish any distinction between reductive (dogmatic) and causal arguments. Some of Hindess and Hirst's points against Marxism suggest that they are attracted by this view—but it is hardly a convincing one.

The preferred concept of 'discourse' is deliberately mobilized by Hindess and Hirst against philosophical constructions. My third objection to their critique is that this alternative has not been established. Hindess and Hirst continue to refer to what is non-discursive, especially economic and political states of affairs. Does that mean that they have not succeeded in 'bracketing off' epistemological and ontological questions? Hirst has rebutted this charge[38] by arguing that the epistemological aim of a presuppositionless philosophy is not his problem. Discourses *do* have referents, but they are not in a realm somehow independent of discourse. In other words, the question of the *really* non-discursive does not arise outside of philosophical neurosis.

It is true nevertheless that even this view of Hirst's has a distinguished philosophical pedigree. Stephen Gaukroger's work is one recent example in the philosophy of science, and Hindess and Hirst have acknowledged it.[39] Gaukroger's argument is, roughly, that the entities of a discourse are constructs of the discourse, and as a consequence that discourses do not 'compete for reality'.[40] If this means that even apparently competing discourses, employing theoretically different conceptions *of* reality, are not compared term for term with a theory-independent world serving as arbiter, then the point is well made. However, it does not seem to me contrary to that point to argue that the comparison of theories contains *some* element of independent empirical asssessment which, together with criteria of theoretical power and range, confers on successful theories a realistic status. Gaukroger seems to deny this; but in that case his open refusal of idealism must appear problematical. Hirst is also keen to say that the objects of discourse are not purely discursive: 'What is subject to calculation in our position is certainly not purely discursive.'[41] However, it *is* true that 'the potentiality of *difference* in the constructs of practices and the referents discourses speak of explodes the "non-discursive" as a unitary category.'[42] As it stands, this view is still not logically untenable, although further pedantic investigation into the meaning of 'potentiality' or 'unitary category' might render the thesis trivial rather than radical.

The general point is that the term 'discourse' is embroiled in as many epistemological problems as 'problematic' or 'premiss'. And Hirst's rather loose usage does not make his anti-epistemology more effective. For example, there seems to me no point in speaking of 'epistemological discourses' as such. If it has a clear sense, the term refers as much to the kind of enterprise Hirst is engaged in as it does to his objects of analysis. There are substantive discourses, some of which employ epistemological premises; and there are discourses *within* epistemology. There are also discourses about epistemology that strive to make some general theoretical and not directly substantive point. Nearly all discourses could be regarded from this discursive angle, though they may not be exhausted by an epistemological approach. There are probably many other senses of the term 'discourse', and I have set down only some meanings of 'epistemological discourse'. Hirst's position does not help a great deal here. My argument has been to defend the possibility of a Marxist historiography, but the notion of *any* determinate knowledge of history that is not just the product of discursive and political preferences is also at stake, and it is worth defending. Despite their sensationalistic argument about the absurdity of the concept of real history in *Pre-capitalist Modes of Production*,[43] the conclusion that 'objectivity' is illusory was not embraced. Hindess and Hirst remained faithful to Marxism, and so the earlier book was markedly inconsistent in both objective and conclusions. Having now abandoned Marxism, they argue for a purge of ontological conceptions of 'the world' or 'the past'. Though much of their diagnosis of rationalism in history is interesting and politically relevant, the idea that history is a knowable, if complex, process has not been decisively refuted.

3. Marxism as Method

One attractive alternative to a philosophically-based Marxism has been the idea that it is principally a *method* rather than a theory. This option is appealing because it suggests a middle road between a full-blown materialist cosmology and the abandonment of Marxism altogether.

The classic exponent of the Marxism-as-method view is Georg Lukács. If research disproved all Marx's theses *in toto*, he argued, the 'orthodox' Marxist would find no cause for concern, since 'orthodoxy refers exclusively to method'.[44]

This formulation is intended to counter or evade the charges levelled by non-Marxists against the empirical predictions of Marxism: the falling rate of profit, the immiseration of the proletariat, the timing of the transition to socialism, and so on. In addition, the emphasis on method seems to free us from the clutches of a 'speculative' Marxism, be it in the form of Soviet 'diamat' or Althusserian structuralism. Certain key clarifications or caveats in Marx, Engels, and Lenin can be marshalled to justify this perspective. For example, Marxism is not an 'a priori construction', a 'lever for construction', or a 'compulsory philosophical schema of history'. It is rather a guide to study and action, or a hypothesis about specific historical phases: what else is this but the dialectical method?[45]

However, the assertion that dialectical method is not only distinct from, but also a safeguard against, philosophical a priorism and a general theory of history is problematic. Quotations alone will not establish the point, since many formulas implying just such a trans-historical schema are scattered throughout the texts of the classics, often on the very same page as the 'favourable' references cited above. And in any case there is something strange about the idea that Marxism is no more than a doctrine-free methodological tool. In fact, an examination of the claims for 'method' uncovers an inextricably interwoven mesh of substance and heuristic. (This would seem to be part of what is meant by 'dialectic'.) There is something prima facie unacceptable about absolving a methodological stance from the unfavourable consequences of its 'application'.

Of course, as soon as Lukács advanced his quotable claim on behalf of method, he tied it irrevocably to the very movement of history: 'It might appear as if the dialectic relation between parts and whole were no more than a construct of thought as removed from the true categories of social reality. . . . If so, the superiority of dialectics would be purely methodological. The real difference, however, is deeper and more fundamental.'[46] It seems, after all, that dialectic and the provability of substantive theses are intimately connected. What Lukács is really doing in *History and Class Consciousness* is to knit the internal bonds between dialectic, history, and revolutionary consciousness such that to state an empirical objection to the theory is necessarily no more than to express a misunderstanding. This is because the protest requires a division between fact and value or inner movement—a distinction that is abolished, definitively, from 'the standpoint of the proletariat'. History (with a capital *H*) is the dialectical unfolding of the special bonds between its inseparable component parts.

In short, Lukács's claims for Marxism as method are certainly as philosophical, and indeed trans-historical, as the orthodoxy he sought to supplant.

A modern analogue of the Lukacsian standpoint is put forward by some social historians, fired by the opinion that the Althusserian concern for philosophical elaboration within historical materialism has been a disaster. For example, Gavin Williams and other contributors to the *History Workshop Journal* debate on theory in history seem to object to any separation of the elements of historical process.[47] Distinctions between the economic and cultural spheres, or between theoretical and historical emphases, are held to be artificial, even 'bourgeois'. This view is akin to Lukács's in two senses. First, the historians suppose that analytical separations are tantamount to the 'reification' of the social totality. Second, they fear that conceptual analysis gives undue prominence to philosophy and determinism, both of which in Marxism are merged, they argue, in Stalinism. However (and this is a third sense in which their views resemble Lukács's), they manifest little awareness of the metaphysical pedigree of the concept of an undifferentiated 'totality'. And despite, for example, the paradox of Williams's espousal of the theory of value, the historians seem complacent about the real possibilities of historical *indeterminism* that attend their protest against analytical priorities.

The main influence behind the 'historical' reaction to philosophical imperialism is E. P. Thompson. I will discuss Thompson's work later, but some points should be made here. For one thing, it must be said that Thompson is well aware[48] that Marxian economics cannot dispense with analytical and causal hierarchies. The theory of value is both *abstract* and entails the (relative) separation of social spheres. Thompson himself dislikes the prospect of historical truncation, which he sees implied in that abstractness. He therefore challenges value theory as well as epistemology. Thompson has, therefore, less need to develop an account of the logical equivalence or inseparability of social elements than some of his followers appear to require. However, as we shall see, Thompson's theory of 'experience' generates similar difficulties. As for the rejection of philosophical Marxism in his book *The Poverty of Theory*, it is clear that Thompson is caught in a dilemma. On the one hand, he appears to decisively refute the claims of epistemology on history. On the other hand, he defends the 'epistemological legitimacy' of history in a way that depends upon philosophical criteria.[49] Indeed, it is not so much epistemology *per se* that Thompson despises (for he offers his own 'interactionist' version), but epistemological *rationalism*. But it is difficult to tar all Marxist philosophy with the one brush.

Another way to try to oust philosophy is to assert that Marxist theory is not a philosophy of History, but a critique of capitalism. Karl Korsch took this view, arguing that Marxism, like all theories, has historical conditions of existence to which alone it is relevant. Korsch believed that Marxism's association with philosophical materialism could only be damaging. Similarly, for Korsch, no generalizations should be made even in propositions concerning 'base-and-superstructure', a notion about which he was sceptical.[50] Marxism is to be seen as a critique of both bourgeois society and philosophical abstraction with the specific aim of transforming the two.

Korsch's outlook is therefore radically historical for a Marxist philosopher. Yet he continued to argue for the importance of philosophy and other intellectual practices as realities in their own right.[51] Again, while he abhorred 'economism', Korsch would not accept 'sociologism' as a consequence of his views: the idea of the interaction and equivalence of all spheres of social life.[52] However, Korsch's important and fertile positions are also, I think, inconclusive. Marxism is said to provide theoretical tools for the critique of capitalist ideology and of philosophical abstraction. Yet Korsch is ambiguous about virtually all those 'tools': materialism, 'laws', the primacy of the economic. In short, it is difficult to place Korsch's sense of historical specificity alongside any general theoretical arguments (especially since he clearly rejected empiricism). Korsch was certainly honest enough to express his doubts about some of Marx and Engels, most of Lenin, and even, latterly, about the Hegel whose influence can be seen in Korsch's earlier 'revisionist' perspective.[53]

I have introduced Korsch because he seems to me the 'limit' case of the argument against philosophy and for empirical method. Obviously, to fully establish this interpretation of Korsch would require a more extended treatment of his work. But the general position seems worth stating schematically, for Korsch too has contemporary parallels. For example, Derek Sayer and Philip Corrigan *et al.*[54] have developed a view of Marx's method that shares many of Korsch's concerns. I would also suggest that the rational core of the points made by historians tempted by Lukács is probably encompassed by the sort of arguments advanced by Sayer *et al.*

That position may be characterized as follows. Marx's objects of explanation are particular social forms. While it is true that very general transhistorical categories (like 'production') are required to make sense of change and continuity, those categories have no independent content. In addition, there can be no meaningful separation between forces and relations of production in Marxism, and thus no overarching, technologically-inclined theory of history. Each historical epoch has both specific social forms of production and social relations within which it takes place. Consequently, Marxism places a premium on *historical* as opposed to analytic modes of thinking, and *social* rather than merely economic relations. It is therefore also empirically open-ended: an a posteriori methodology, not an a priori doctrine.

There is much to applaud in this view, as we will see in the following chapter. But there are difficulties with it as well. One enduring problem (as with most texts on 'what Marx really meant') is that although the position squares well with parts of Marx, it clearly is not the whole story. Those writers who favour the 'productive forces' view are equally entitled—and perhaps equally unjustified—in invoking the 'real Marx'.[55] Substantively, it is very difficult not to end up with a concept of 'social relations' that lacks any theoretical content. If social relations are themselves productive forces and if the notion of superstructures is illegitimate, then everything is a 'social relation'. But there is also something worrying about considering the latter category historically variable, or empirically open-ended. In reference and scope, concepts like 'social relations' could conceivably receive any interpretation, and be satisfied by fairly random empirical evidence.

Marxism-as-method is not, in my view, a tenable solution to the problem of the relation between epistemology and historical materialism. Each proponent discussed holds a stronger view than can be encompassed by the idea of 'method'. Lukács marks a return to a dialectical philosophy of history. Historians who criticize philosophy often unwittingly play into the hands of philosophical dialecticians. Where they do not, they advocate a concern to *historicize* philosophy in a legitimate non-epistemological sense. Sayer's view is linked to his realism. Korsch raises the problem of the relation between the theory of capitalism and the theory of history. My own view needs to be elaborated in the light of further discussion of these questions, though I think my perspective is clear by now. The defence of a substantive (if 'minimal') Marxism cannot be supplanted by claims for Marx's method. In a fine book, G. D. H. Cole acknowledges that, despite his advocacy of 'method', Marx's 'method will fail us only if his whole analysis was on the wrong lines'.[56]

4. Dialectic as History

I suggested that Lukács's claim on behalf of method was no less philosophical than the orthodox Marxism he sought to replace. I want now to distinguish two ways in which history might be brought back into the forefront of Marxism at the expense of the pretensions of dialectical materialism. The first approach may be termed dialectical philosophy of history, and it might include Lukács and his followers, Jean-Paul Sartre, and other continental dialecticians. The second aims at applying historical materialism to philosophy itself. The key difference is that in the former position, but not in the latter, knowledge of human history is justified purely by philosophical arguments.

My remarks on dialectical ontology were restricted to the idea that the dialectic was a general *material* category. Dialectical philosophers of history are more tempted by the idea that Hegel's system and the dialectic cannot be doctrines of *nature*. Rather, dialectic concerns the necessary features of *human* consciousness and the historical mode in which consciousness exists. Marxism, from this standpoint, is a theory about and an expression of the consciousness-history relation. Dialecticians frequently advocate the theory of alienation. Here, the alienation that characterizes class societies, and the reification (the reduction to thinghood) that marks science and consciousness within those societies, are thought to be artificial or unnatural amputations of the 'totality' of human existence. On the other hand, the movement from states of alienation to renewed totality is itself a dialectical, totalizing movement. It follows that history is inherently dialectical and that the historical consciousness is *critical*; it is never fixed or completed. Such incompleteness is ontological, not just a matter of time and accuracy: consciousness can express or reflect the larger totality of which it is a necessary part, but it can never, so to speak, capture and exhibit the whole.

The categories of totality, negation, mediation, and transcendence are thus common to dialectical philosophers, and play a crucial role in their world-view. The problem with a merely 'external dialectic' (for Sartre), with the 'bourgeois antinomies' (for Lukács), or with 'basic principles' (for Theodor Adorno) is that each attempts to state and describe moments of a total process as if they were separable things. For dialecticians, things are never fixed or isolated from their human context, except by distortion. Thus historical knowledge is not only *different* from natural-scientific knowledge and its mechanistic philosophies (including diamat); it is also a superior form of knowledge, one that corresponds in its ever-incomplete dialectic to the real dialectical movement of human-historical praxis.

These sentences are, of course, very general. But it is a characteristic of dialectical humanism to evade crisp and clear formulation or summary. Part of the central idea is that while dialectic is critical, it is not in any orthodox philosophical sense 'rational', because rationality is a feature of reified thought, and is therefore constrained by the limitations of its (bourgeois) conditions of existence. The more Marxist-inclined dialecticians tie this critical disposition to the worldly history of class struggles. Here Lukács and Sartre[57] are undoubtedly closer to classical Marxism than, say, Ernst Bloch or Adorno. Bloch, for example, offers a dialectic of Man-in-general: Marx's theory, Bloch suggests, is that 'the whole world is an open system of enlightenment developing dialectically. Its focal point is humanity objectively alienated'.[58] Adorno, for his part (and here he is typical of the Frankfurt 'school'), is concerned to show the ceaseless critical power of the concept of 'negation'. However, his major work, *Negative Dialectics*,[59] grows from a philosophical critique into an aesthetic monologue, because 'negation' and 'transcendence' themselves become *instances* of absolute or fetishized concepts, and so also have to be negated. Hence the need, stylistically exemplified by Adorno, for a constantly shifting, creative vocabulary and meaning.

Dialectical philosophy of history is not, it seems to me, necessarily connected to historical materialism. To be sure, Marxism gives some support to the general theses, but the terms that are privileged in dialectics have a wider reference than the ideas of Marxism, and the latter could be stated in concepts other than negation, mediation, totality, and the like. Faced with this problem, dialecticians who are Marxists tend to argue that the essence of Marxism is just dialectics. Despite Bertell Ollman's careful attempt to claim Marx for the 'philosophy of internal relations',[60] the logic of dialectic is inescapably Hegelian, its relation to determinate material and historical propositions tenuous. As regards *content*, dialectical philosophy of history is a general humanism. Lukács's 'standpoint of the proletariat'—however invested by teleology—has been the most important attempt to afford the dialectical categories a *historical* basis. Sartre is another major writer in this respect: the *Critique of Dialectical Reason* has a rich smattering of historical examples. But we may be forgiven for thinking that they are examples to support a 'totalizing' philosophy about the human project, wherever and however it may be instantiated. In less capable hands than Sartre's, the paucity of specific argument is evident. In *Marx's Theory of Alienation*, for example, István Mézáros maintains that the essence of man as such is revealed through the ontological notion of *mediation*, and asserts without further ado that this is the core of Marxism itself.[61] There is no necessary link between a general dialectical humanism and historical specificity, and those Marxists who espouse the view cannot in all seriousness claim that Marx's historical theories rely on or entail the kind of full-blooded theodicy embodied in the following quotation from Henri Lefebvre: 'Consciousness expresses therefore both the finitude and infinitude of man. Herein lies his inner contradiction, which forces him to deepen and transcend himself. Herein too lies his drama, his misfortune— and also his greatness. From out of his limitation man produces a determinate and human infinite, which envelops and liberates and overcomes the indefinite given in natural existence; this infinite might be called: the power of man, knowledge, action, love, Mind, or quite simply, the human.'[62] Philosophically, more moderate dialectical views, such as Lucien Goldmann's, tend to reproduce the epistemological division between the natural and human sciences. As I will argue later, Marxists, as epistemo-logical realists, have no obligation to defend this view. Substantively, Goldmann's work[63] is stimulating, but it is no accident that his principal concept—that of a 'world-vision'—is logically close, too close, to a Weberian 'ideal type'.

It is possible, I think, to historicize philosophy without embracing a dialectical philosophy of history, though some work (such as Christopher Caudwell's[64]) has been marked by a combination of those two possibilities. Philosophy is, after all, a superstructure and a social product. The kinds of ideas it presents, and even the forms the disquisitions take, should surely be open to Marxist historical explanation. This kind of enterprise is impor-tant, though surprisingly it has rarely been given extended treatment. Alfred Sohn Rethel and (especially) George Thomson are exceptions. They analyse the historical conditions of existence of philosophical thought, an exercise one intention and effect of which is to demystify philosophical abstraction. These writers reject the posture of philosophy above other disciplines. Abstract thought, they argue, is no less historical for appearing to avoid historical references. Specifically, philosophy, with mathematics, is the product of the generalization of commodity exchange. Above all, philosophy is, for Sohn-Rethel and Thomson, the result of the division of hand and brain as a consequence of commodity exchange. Their point recalls Marx's suspicion of philosophy in the *German Ideology*, that with the split between manual and mental labour, 'Philosophy can flatter itself that it *really* represents something without representing something real.'[65]

In *The First Philosophers*, Thomson's remarkable research into ancient society is brought to bear in his equation between the labour process, language structures, and abstract thought. He argues that the Greek philo-sophers raise, in a speculative manner, the questions and variant solutions later to become those of bourgeois science. And it is the prefiguration of the capitalist system in the Greek market and coinage that explains this parallel. The very universality inherent in the way in which commodities are measured and exchanged lies behind scientific theory and its philo-sophical handmaiden. Thomson sticks closely to the bounds of his case-study, but he clearly thinks that philosophy in general functions as abstrac-tion only because it is 'socially necessary false consciousness' linked to the real abstraction from concrete labour that characterizes exchange-value. So while its role in class societies may be inevitable, philosophy will have no place in a society where the mental/manual labour division has been healed.

This view, which we might call radical historicism, is an impressive return to the historical domain at the expense of philosophy.[66] The cognitive structure of science and philosophy is seen to have its necessity in social forms. Philosophy itself represents the very justification of an apparent divorce between abstract thought and its material basis. How far, on this account, does the concept of philosophy have to be abandoned by Marxists as necessary illusion?

The relation between philosophy and society here is functional, but pitched at quite a general level, in two ways. First, neither Thomson nor Sohn-Rethel suggests that science is false consciousness, even though its forms be homologous to and derivative from the abstractions of the market economy. In other words, that science is shaped socially does not mean that it is untrue to nature. These writers are particularly keen to refute the role of philosophy in science. In so far as philosophy is partially, and sometimes no more than, 'theoretical ideology', the argument is a valid reminder of philosophy's superstructural character, and of the need to examine it accordingly. But the role of philosophy, not as metaphysics, but as generalizations from science and its concepts, takes on a 'scientific' aspect that stands or falls not with ideology but with science itself. There are features of the natural world and of human conduct that cannot be *exhausted* by, even though they are explained by, historically specific conditions.

The second factor that renders radical historicism fairly general is the strategic role of market relations in the doctrine. Sohn-Rethel in particular derives scientific laws and philosophical illusions directly from exchange-value, which represents the purely formal in reality itself. So, with the return of production for use-value under socialism, the need for abstract thought distinct from particular contents will vanish. George Thomson is more careful than Sohn-Rethel about this generalization, for he keeps his own historical limits—ancient society—sharply in focus. The derivation referred to is a general parallel more than a causal deduction, and is therefore less than universal but more than historically specific. Market society is not just capitalism, for example, and covers a considerable time-span. Accordingly, the exact force and logic of radical historicism is unclear to me at least. It need not warrant any detailed account of thought under socialist relations of production, and the 'illusions' of philosophy in societies where head and hand are divided seem to be neither false consciousness in any total sense, nor structurally evitable.

Radical historicism can be endorsed as an approach to the *transitive* dimension of science or philosophy,[67] that is, as an account of the social conditions and effects that shape the theoretical formation and ideological significance of concepts. But does not follow that a philosophical elaboration of the *intransitive* aspect of knowledge (its illumination of real structures) is thereby rendered inappropriate. Historicists are often drawn to this plausible but unfounded conclusion. For example, Antonio Gramsci offered an important account of the *function* of philosophy. For Gramsci, the systematic character of philosophy is a necessary adjunct to both science and political analysis,[68] for it represents the critique of common sense. Yet common sense too can have critical aspects, and philosophy, not being science, is related to common sense directly as part of a cultural and ideological field. Gramsci's ideas thus enable us to stress the historical conditions of philosophy, its transitive dimension. However, this useful distinction of Gramsci's does not commit us to his notion of *absolute* historicism,[69] especially when we recall Gramsci's idealist notion that the existence of the external world is dependent upon human cognition.[70]

2
Marxism, Realism, and Epistemology

I suggested in chapter 1 that the strengths of Marxism are not necessarily bolstered, nor its weaknesses overcome, by an appeal to 'higher' principles. Nevertheless, the temptation to abolish epistemological considerations altogether must be resisted. There are versions of Marxist philosophy that strive to avoid the dilemmas of 'diamat' and seek to assist historiographical analysis. But before discussing these, two over-arching problems are worth stating at the outset.

First, there is the question of Marx's own contribution to these issues. Especially since Althusser, there has been an ironic tendency amongst academic Marxists confidently to present what they think is the essential, the *real* Marx, as if the great man himself was nodding approvingly over the author's shoulder. Frank Parkin and E. P. Thompson have wittily constructed a scenario of a tenured Marxist intelligentsia virulently squabbling over the right to claim legitimate descent.[1] This rightly (if sometimes a little cheaply) draws attention to the need for socialists to be serious about *their own* contribution, even while remaining aware of its real limitations. I will discuss Marx at the end of my account of Marxist philosophy, for his work is notoriously suggestive rather than definitive. Exegetical disputes are connected to contemporary debates more than disinterested scholarship: I do not claim that my views are Marx's.

The second problem is a paradox. 'Structural causality' and 'realism' significantly advance the discussion about Marxist philosophy. But in my view both develop philosophical considerations that go beyond Marxism. I uphold a (broadly) realist epistemology, and argue that realism is indispensable for a Marxist approach to historiography. But realism no more *uniquely* justifies Marxism than does diamat or historicism, and where it strives to do so, it merits criticism, for detailed historical questions cannot be resolved directly by a realist or any other philosophical criterion.

1. Epistemology and Rationalism

If it is true that historical materialism can explain philosophical movements as cultural phenomenon, then the possibility of an epistemology
appropriate to the explication of Marxist concepts, though curtailed in
importance, remains real. The harder forms of dialectical materialism and
dialectical philosophy of history are ill-suited candidates for this role, and
dissatisfaction with these positions as traditionally conceived has been a
general feature of recent Marxist reflection on philosophy. Louis Althusser
and Lucio Colletti have been highly influential in offering criteria by which
the contending poles of dialectical materialism can be jointly subjected to
criticism. Colletti's and Althusser's contributions are substantially similar,
though neither theorist seems to have said so overtly.[2]

Both condemn the Hegelian tradition in Marxist philosophy, because it
is their view that a dialectical ontology obscures the specific and determinate character of scientific knowledge. Colletti, we have seen, counterposes
the distinction between real and logical contradictions to the dialectical
alternative. Scientific thought is abstract and deductive, that is, 'a process
from which reality emerges as the result of a sifting and a selection carried
out by thought'.[3] Accordingly, materialism is the doctrine that reality is
independent of thought, not the claim that it is a particular kind of
substance. This is held to be sufficient to refute idealism, because science
discovers and recognizes reality through 'determinate abstractions': the
liaison between reason and reality is never a pre-established harmony, as it
is in dialectical idealism.

For Colletti and his mentor, Galvano Della Volpe, this stipulation is the
epistemic precondition of any scientific-materialist enterprise. In a manner
similar to Althusser, they criticize both *purely* ontological and purely epistemic philosophies. Common to these Marxists is the view that a purely
ontological approach is intrinsically idealist, obliterating the distinction
between being and thought whilst undermining the need for an independent account of the nature and production of scientific concepts. Diamat,
on this view, performs a reduction of concepts to what is in fact a hypostatized, conceptual vision of 'being'. Thus Colletti: 'The absolute and
irremediable theoretical insignificance of "dialectical materialism" is all
here: it has mimed idealism, thinking that it was being materialist; it has
underwritten Hegel's liquidation of the "intellect" and the principle of
non-contradiction, without comprehending that this meant liquidating the
very independence of the finite from the infinite, of being from thought.'[4]
At the same time, opposition must be expressed to the characteristic reduc-

tion in bourgeois epistemology: that because of the constitutive role of the subject, criteria for *knowledge* can be drawn up, but we cannot have independent means of knowing how things are, or even that they exist 'objectively'.

There are important differences between Althusser and Colletti. As we will see, the former employs a materialist nomenclature for the transitive dimension of science; but its historical impulse may be questioned. The Della Volpeans are probably more deeply committed to the critique of hypostatized concepts in social science and Marxism.[5] Moreover, they retain a more central place for induction or experiment as the final phase in the projected model of scientific practice (concrete-abstract-concrete) than does Althusser.[6] Again, to cite Colletti:[7] The '*actual* passage from the abstract to the concrete is not a passage "within the abstract", but goes from the latter to the concrete of reality (or is the conversion of deduction into induction); so that here one is dealing not with the relationship of "thought-being" *within*, but rather with the relationship *between* thought and reality.'[8] This final move out of thought is less clearly invoked by Althusser.

Althusser's strategy is to assume that there is a knowledge process with distinct characteristics, but also to assume that it is knowledge *of* an independently existing world. So there is no 'problem of knowledge'. But neither need we pre-empt science by stating that the knowledge produced and the form of production involved must reveal the necessary forms of being itself. The task of epistemology, in Althusser's scheme, is to elaborate the differential mechanisms of knowledge. And *Marxist* epistemology is central here, because Marx himself contributed to, and clarified, the nature of a scientific theoretical break from its non-scientific origin.

If this sketch is accurate, the proposals of Althusser and Colletti may be classed within the 'materialist' side of the dialectic, while they also shun any ontology of 'material things'. Both are aware that the legacy of Hegel's dialectic encourages the idea that a special *logic* is available to Marxists that somehow guarantees the fit between thought and reality, Marxism and history. On the other hand, the reductionism some dialectical *materialists* perform on scientific concepts or social superstructures is also opposed by Colletti and Althusser, who insist that these be ascribed a certain autonomy. In philosophy, for example, epistemology is given priority over ontology. Colletti's distinction between real and logical contradiction and the Della Volpean emphasis on the centrality of 'determinate abstraction' render the correspondence of concepts to things indirect. Althusser sees no problem of correspondence at all: Marxist epistemology simply assumes that the sciences' internal criteria of validity and theoretical adequacy suffice. Moreover, the *materialist* hallmark of epistemology is not so much the reference of concepts as the *production* process through which they are forged. Althusser offers an elaborate system whereby scientific concepts are produced in a 'theoretical practice' whose structure entails movement from abstract to concrete 'Generalities', and back.[9]

Fundamentally, Althusser was striving towards a better account of causality in science and history than he believed was available to previous Marxist philosophy. The apparently indulgent and intricate detour through a preconceived 'science' was held to be necessary: if *historical materialism* is to be given its proper place, then (paradoxically) Marxist *philosophy* must hold the centre of the stage.[10] An account of the mechanisms of scientific knowledge has to be provided to explain how Marxist (and other) theories are able to register real complexity fully whilst retaining principles of determinacy.

In order for this to remain *Marxist* philosophy, Althusser (less so Colletti) had to re-read Marx's own texts as embodiments and explications of these epistemological principles. 'Symptomatic' readings of texts like the Introduction to the *Grundrisse* or of the theoretical structure of *Capital* revealed that Marx's 'immense theoretical revolution' was, essentially, a philosophical enterprise.[11] Marxist philosophy, in this account, assumes the status of the general theory of theoretical practice.

The consequences of Althusser's distinctive systematization of Marx's 'implicit' epistemology were significant. Marx's *substantive* ideas, including that of the limitations of pure abstraction, could be justified only by reference to Althusserian epistemological norms. Among other things, the latter implied the radical *internality* to sciences of criteria of validity and justification. This is not a conventionalist point about the practitioners of science coming to an agreement about method (Althusser is not a Kuhnian), but it is a conventionalism in the sense that scientific theories sustain their own logic of categories, methodologies, and means of verification. Experiment, on this view, becomes a theoretical product, not a means of independent assessment.

Althusser thus begins with the healthy—and characteristically Marxist—aim of ridding science and Marxism of metaphysical intrusions into the proper business of analysis. Notoriously, however, the Theory of Theoretical Practice enjoys a predominant position as the key to *and judge of* what counts as genuine knowledge. In Althusser's hands, an attempt to defend the generalizing function of philosophy once again becomes the stipulation of the credentials all thought (and not simply Marxist or historical propositions) must display. Given the dubious manner in which Marx is construed and the lengths to which Althusser's own views take him, it is not surprising that some critics have taken his work to be outside Marxism altogether.

Althusser's materialism, for all his pithy slogans, is rather gestural. He is certainly hard-pushed to explain why it should be that science and philosophy should themselves be explained by their material and social conditions. This has usually been enough to condemn Althusser. But it seems to me that caution is requisite here. To begin with, the charge that Althusser rejects a social analysis does not necessarily stick. There is no reason why the social determinations of thought should exhaust its epistemological characteristics, and in taking on the latter task of clarification, Althusser need not deny the former. Second, there are indeed philosophical objections to Althusser's account, but the objections are *Marxist* only if a Marxist philosophy clearly superior to Althusser's is available. The standard criticisms of his work usually assume—without being aware of it—that Marxism has a clear philosophical basis. This, however, may be doubted. In any case, it is insufficiently noted that the objections are mostly philosophical, and not just 'Marxist' or 'historical'.

If Althusser is to be rejected, it must be both on the grounds of philosophical self-awareness and because his operation does not in fact succeed. On both counts, the Theory of Theoretical Practice has *not* achieved its intention to do away with 'the philosophy of guarantees'.

I have said that Marx's concepts could be justified by the Althusserian norms alone in Althusser's account. In fact, they can be *formulated* only through a detour into 'scientificity'. Hence Althusser's cryptic claim that Marxist philosophy must be *applied* before it can stand as the object of investigation.[12] As it affects substantive issues in historical materialism, Althusser's project can be described as a 'rationalism'. His re-worked account of causality leads to an a priori relation between key Marxist concepts and the historical process. The main principle here is *structural causality*, and it refers to the mutual and logical interdependence of cause and effect. Althusser has made several attempts to formulate this idea, some of which have been productive. His intention is to escape from the mechanical implications of the base/superstructure model in historical materialism. In attempting this, he makes his concepts useful for historical analysis.

By proposing that society be regarded as a structure in which the economic base is 'overdetermined' by its multiple superstructures, Althusser tries to establish the 'relative autonomy' of the other social levels, and even the possibility of their dominance. This is clearly a historically flexible idea, paradigmatically for noting the place of religion in pre-capitalist societies. But it is another question whether this idea of structure-in-dominance is the same as the 'structural causality' advanced in *Reading Capital*. The former appears linked to the concept of a social formation, and without too much effort the reciprocal effect that the superstructures have on their economic base (a familiar enough Marxist notion) could be usefully re-thought in these terms. However, structural causality is the notion that a structure (not a 'base') is causally present only in and through its effects, and this may be ambiguous. It seems linked to the concept of mode of production rather social formation. 'Mode of production', in Althusser's scheme, is the conjoint structure of forces and relations of production. Indeed, there is more than a suggestion[13] that built into the mode of production conceived as a structure is the *necessary* presence of an economy's superstructural conditions of existence. In other words, structural causality is the conception of an *economy* as a 'global' mode of production, that is, in its larger *social* form rather than in its narrower sense of the mode of production of material wealth. And this view differs in key respects from the idea that an economic structure is dominant *within* a wider social formation. In the later version, the base/superstructure metaphor is strictly inapplicable, because structural causality is a whole-part relation and not one between parts. And, for Althusser, mode of production as a structured totality is a purely theoretical construct, since it does not exist as such. Rather, it is instantiated in concrete social formations. This conception is *not*, it seems to me, historically useful.

First, Althusser's account is not coherent. He slides between a restricted and a global concept of mode of production without attempting to clarify the relationship. If structural causality is the logically inseparable reciprocity of cause and effect, I cannot see how such a clarification could be made, for here Althusser has gone over to an 'internal relations' view of concepts and objects.

Second, therefore, the notion of a structural bond between cause and effect reflects a *conceptual* or logical view of the real connections between things. Modes of production are the social forms of the logical principle 'structural causality', but they too are theoretical objects, and conceptual templates. Real social structures may exist 'as before, outside the head'[14] but they are knowable only as and through the 'thought-object' specified by the theoretical system. Only with great difficulty can the principles be conceived as operating as real tendencies in socio-historical life. Althusser, like Colletti, ends up on the side of Kant, and shares the latter's dilemma:

if the real object is given only by the thought object, what grounds are there for believing in a real, ordered, independent world?

Finally, if Marxism is a theory of history, of the relations underlying social change, then for 'structural causality', history must be a theoretical sequence of modes of production. But actual change is very difficult to incorporate into this system. Structures are internally unified totalities, and human beings, for Althusser, are for the most part only the 'bearers' of structural relations. [15] History is thus conceived of as a series of large social slabs whose corners may bump, but they do not seem to grow into, or become transformed into, one another. Balibar posited a 'transitional' mode in an attempt to overcome this stasis, but that is feasible only if the strict structural logic is dropped. [16] In building up modes of production as a series of conceptual entailments (rationalism), and as structures well over and above human practices (structuralism), the extreme moments of Althusser's project display glaring examples of how philosophy can take on substantial form beyond its legitimate role in the explication of guiding principles. [17]

2. Realism

Realism is a philosophical position that encompasses many of the features of Marxist explanation. Its advantage over other views is its acknowledgement of the theoretical moment in science, together with an emphasis on the independence of empirical evidence. Before examining realism, however, it must be distinguished from empiricism, because some Marxists, in arguing for the one, have defended the other. Historians, in particular, tend to do this when confronted by what they see as an extraneous glut of Theory.

Marxists are never simply empiricists, because in its positivist forms, empiricism is the doctrine that all knowledge is reducible to atomic propositions that correspond to discrete impressions, sense data, and the like. Similarly, the positivist conception of scientific laws depends on the view that statements of empirical regularity constitute the logical basis of genuine explanation. Neither idea is compatible with the belief that there are systemic or 'hidden' causes of empirical phenomena—this being the basis of the Marxist claim, for example, to have revealed the true nature of exploitation. Even so, Marxists have often seemed to argue that the facts and reality declare themselves, whether in social experience or in the correspondence of thought or perception to reality. And Marxists are sometimes quick to deduce from any and every piece of empirical evidence that Marxist laws have been corroborated. Two examples can be briefly cited. Barry Hindess[18] has persuasively argued that Lenin's tome of statistical support for his thesis about *The Development of Capitalism in Russia* is the opposite of empiricism. But in *Materialism and Empirio-Criticism*, Lenin's account of knowledge (mixed as it certainly is) veers too close to simple empiricism. Part of that book is one kind of defence of the independence of objects, but Lenin sometimes argues (against 'fideism' and 'subjectivism'[19]) that the objects of knowledge are *directly* knowable, and that the material world alone causes our thoughts and perceptions to 'copy' reality. He virulently denounces Plekhanov's notion (reasonable, in my view) that ideas and sensations are 'hieroglyphics' rather than mirror images. Lenin's polemic thus trades on an equation between 'knowledge' and 'perception' and accords the latter a rather mechanical-materialist treatment. In effect, Lenin virtually rules out the possibility of real processes being opaque rather than transparent.

Ernest Mandel is a Marxist whose tendency to empiricism compromises the argument of his important *Late Capitalism*, which 'attempts to demonstrate that the "abstract" laws of motion of this mode of production remain operable and verifiable in and through the "concrete" history of contemporary capitalism.'[20] This statement is ambiguous as between a 'realist' and an 'empiricist' meaning. I would not wholly support Athar Hussain, who argues that Mandel simply interprets *all* evidence as confirmations of Marx's laws.[21] But Mandel's thesis is limited, because it is open to this kind of criticism. The empirical moment in research and proof may be indispensable, but the process of abstraction need not be pinned to the data point for point to be theoretically viable. Indeed, as Ben Fine and Laurence Harris point out,[22] Mandel takes 'laws'—especially that of the falling rate of profit—to apply to 'the secular development of capitalism'. In fact, Marx's laws concern only the cycle of production, and even in that domain movements in the rate of profit, etc., cannot be simply explained by the law.

A realist theory cannot be cognitively assessed primarily on empirical evidence, though realism must explain empirical phenomena. Realism is the philosophical view that knowledge is knowledge of objects or processes that exist independent of thought. In the terminology of one of its prominent spokesmen, Roy Bhaskar,[23] science discovers the 'generative mechanisms' that, when known, causally explain phenomena. Natural science works by creating artificially 'closed' conditions in which relatively decisive empirical tests of theories can be carried out. But the natural world itself is an 'open' system, a system that cannot be adequately grasped in terms of the constant conjunction of observed phenomena (the latter being the dominant empiricist criterion).

Society, too, for realism, is an open system, but social science, unlike natural science, cannot construct decisive evidence, because human beings can and do change their social practice in the light of knowledge and self-consciousness. Agency and thought are thus constitutive of the object of study. As a consequence, social theory is necessarily historical, because the relations of social structure to knowledge and practice are always relations over time.

Realism, stated in this way, retains many of the central interests associated with hermeneutic and humanist traditions. The latter, embracing many Marxist 'dialecticians', have resisted the very concept of social science, its apparent aping of natural science, and its abstraction from concrete historical reality. Bhaskar, for example, agrees, for the above reasons, that social science must be incomplete, critical rather than definitive, and intimately bound up with social practice. But the irrationalism or subjectivism that so often accompanies beliefs of the humanistic and neo-Kantian kind is given no encouragement by Bhaskar and others. Important arguments on this point would be that, for example, theoretical abstraction is as inescapable and necessary in social as in natural investigation; that theoretical explanations in social inquiry must be systematic and coherent at a number of levels; and that while empirical controls are crucial and indispensable, concrete phenomena are explained by causal and other sets of propositions: they do not themselves have any privileged status.

For the new realists, historical materialism, as a major component of the social scientific enterprise, follows these criteria. By means of theoretical abstraction, Marxism postulates generative mechanisms at the level of the mode of production, which help to explain the nature and development of historical and empirical problems or phenomena. Social forms, conjunctures, and strategies are to be understood in terms of theoretically expressed tendencies that have a real, structural status but are not empirically transparent.

The development of such tenets is conducted by the new realists with novel cogency and care. The preface to one major collection, *Issues in Marxist Philosophy*, proudly (if a bit pretentiously) announces its kinship with British analytical philosophy, at least in its attention to clarity of argument. The arguments are indeed competent and persuasive: they read like a short list of what one always assumed Marxist thought should deliver. But the careful (to some, no doubt, pedantic) tone of the British

academy should warn us against any easy identification of these ideas as
Marx's.

The labour of precise philosophical statement was (rightly) not Marx's
priority. The whole fracas about 'symptomatic readings' of Marx arises
because his general protocols are implicit rather than explicit. Accordingly,
while one may agree that Marx's presuppositions were realist in character,
and can be elaborated as such, it is important to be aware that they form a
cluster of recommendations and prohibitions, and not a philosophical
theory.

Realism, for all its intuitive appeal, is such a theory. It is a philosophical
position—a metaphysic, even—that does not begin with Marx and goes
well beyond him. And its contemporary formulations are cultural products
very different from Marx's classic texts. So although realism may be preferable to rationalist or empiricist constructs of the 'essential' Marx, it must
also *abstract from parts* of his work, must make a case about the spirit, rather
than the letter, of Marx's endeavour.

The point is belaboured here because there is a danger that realism, for
all its clarity, might perpetuate current squabbles rather than materially
advance discussion. We have seen, for example, that Derek Sayer advocates
Marxism-as-method. He constructs this view of Marx along realist lines.
(This is somewhat inconsistent: realism must substantially wed method to
doctrine, but the point is a small one.) But in his haste to extirpate the
Althusserian heresy, he overplays his hand. First, he exaggerates the extent
to which Althusser's Marx is sheer invention, rather than one (perhaps
extreme) rationalization. Second, Sayer argues that Marx—*contra* Althusser,
irony of ironies—was the empiricist *par excellence*.[24] A more self-critical
presentation of realist tenets and less concern to appear as the representative
of the real Marx would be more helpful here. As it is, substantial points are
clouded by the kind of terminological sophistry that is supposed to be the
trade mark of the tradition Sayer opposes. In general, however, the debate
is indicative: those who object to philosophy in Marxism can find no solace
in realism.

As a philosophical position, there are a number of problems with realism. First, it may be doubted whether it is *a* position. There are clear
divergences even amongst the Marxist realists. Bhaskar, for example, is
committed to the view that generative mechanisms, powers, and agents are
the things that make up the basic structure of the world. Such an ontology
and the necessary features of its appropriate science, for Bhaskar, can be
established by philosophical argument alone.[25] These claims are contested
by another realist, David-Hillel Ruben.[26] In his neo-realist account of

Marx, Derek Sayer relies heavily on the work of the American philosopher of science, N. R. Hanson. But as (yet other realists) Russell Keat and John Urry suggest,[27] Hanson is in some respects a 'constructivist': he doesn't allow that objects, even those of everyday perception, are theory-independent. And it does seem that from a realist position that view is untenable. Finally, Ted Benton (perhaps wisely) states realism in a more general way, and even draws upon Althusser to express it, without committing himself much to ontology.[28] This stance may well be excessively general, and in parts it is problematic *just because* it is not elaborate, but it is a view with which I sympathize.

The second important problem is that realism need not be a *materialist* philosophy. Benton, Bhaskar, and Ruben[29] all rightly say that 'material' should not be construed as simply meaning 'physical', but in that case materialism becomes subsumed under realism rather than the opposite. Yet there seems no reason in principle to rule out a possibly *idealist* conception of 'the real'. Of course, the latter has a long pedigree in philosophy, and in Ruben's important book *Marxism and Materialism*, he cannot withhold the label from thinkers such as Berkeley and Hume: no materialists.

The third and over-arching difficulty with realism is whether transcendental arguments are essential to it. By 'transcendental' is meant a priori: arguments about the conditions of all knowledge, and thus arguments not dependent on any particular body of knowledge. Bhaskar says yes, they are necessary and important.

Indeed, Bhaskar's ontology and view of science depend on them. He argues that science is possible only if the world is structured in a certain way and if certain objects endure. Ruben, on the other hand, shares Bhaskar's *belief* in structured objects, but maintains that this is impossible to prove. Therefore, transcendental realism cannot be the only possible explanation of science or the world, even if we think it is right. Ruben grounds this objection to Bhaskar in the view (correct, in my opinion) that transcendental arguments are in some way or other circular: they state what they presuppose. And Ruben emphasizes the common Marxist and materialist belief that science, not philosophy, tells us what exists and in what way. Similarly, Marxist knowledge is itself about particular societies, not about the social *per se*.

An important juncture is reached here. Ruben has argued that transcendental arguments, being circular, are not essential to realism: science gives us at best good inductive reasons for the belief in structured enduring things and processes. However, this conclusion is unorthodox for a realist, for is it not the case that realisms are ontological accounts of what exists independently of knowledge? And does not ontology, in its foundational sense, *require* transcendental argument? Bhaskar, with typical rigour, accepts this commitment. More hesitant realists, such as Ruben, seem content with the justified belief in real objects and their essential structure. However, realism on this view is more a question of a realist interpretation of *theories* rather than an a priori argument about the things to which those theories must conform.

The point made above may be developed by suggesting that, as an argument made by Ruben himself indicates, realist interpretation can be seen to differ significantly from the realist ontological standpoint in its hard sense. But the elaboration requires that Ruben's case against Kant and Colletti be judged misleading.

In *Marxism and Materialism* Ruben tries to elucidate what is distinctive about Marxist materialism. Following Lenin, he argues that a 'reflection theory of knowledge' is crucial. Despite the militant labels, however, Ruben fails to show that 'materialism' is any different from realism, broadly conceived. Nor does he, in my view, establish that 'reflection' is the only, or the best, way of conceiving the relation of knowledge (including historical knowledge) to being. He clearly does not intend it in an empiricist way, so it must mean something like a 'correspondence' theory. The belief in correspondence with reality is indeed a basic and defensible account of knowledge. But it is compatible with a fairly generous view of theory-formation, and criteria of adequacy.[30]

Ruben's important discussion of 'epistemological inconsistency' provides another opportunity to explore the apparent tension in his position. In accordance with his reluctance to accept that a realist ontology can be transcendentally deduced, Ruben develops the following argument[31] about the notion of epistemological (rather than logical) inconsistency. He maintains that Kant (and also Colletti) are epistemologically inconsistent when they combine the following propositions.

1. Claims to knowledge necessarily presuppose the activity of interpretative thought.

2. There are objects essentially independent of interpretation.

Ruben maintains that Kant is inconsistent when he posits a mind-independent realm of 'noumena'. In fact, Kant is thought to be doubly inconsistent because he makes a further distinction, within the 'phenomenal' world, between thought-dependent objects, which are knowable, and mind-dependent ones, which are not thought-dependent. Kant's inconsistency is alleged to lie in the fact that no possible evidence can be given for the existence of *any* object (phenomenal or noumenal) independent of interpretative thought.

This argument is, in my view, unconvincing. To begin with, Kant's concept of noumena is defined by the fact that no evidence could possibly be given for their existence; and the latter is a matter of faith for Kant. So it is strange for Ruben to assert that Kant holds that some *phenomenal* objects are essentially thought-independent, and therefore unknowable, since they would be, just on that score, noumena. But since the issue is not wholly about what Kant meant, my defence of the traditional reading is secondary.

More fundamentally, it is Ruben's description of *what* is inconsistent in Kant (or anyone else) that is puzzling. For claim 1, as set out, need not entail that there is no evidence for 2. 1 seems to be the idea that 'claims to knowledge' are necessarily dependent on interpretative thought. 'Any known object is *essentially* related to thought.'[32] This is doubly ambiguous, because there is obviously a sense in which a *claim* to knowledge is the product of someone's thinking that something is the case. The second quoted implication is not about the claim, but about the known *object*. This is still ambiguous because the fact of an object's being known is 'essentially' related to the interpretation of it. And if the argument is rather that the object of which we have knowledge is *essentially* dependent on thought, then there is no inconsistency at all, because 1 and 2 are the same! Or rather, 2, the claim about the independence of the object, is not being asserted. To assert only 1 is idealism, but Ruben knows that there is no *logical* inconsistency there.

This has been a complicated but necessary detour. It suggests that Ruben's notion of epistemological inconsistency is not tenable if it is intended to take on some of the weight of logical inconsistency without being such. The relevance of the discussion to Marxism is this. Ruben calls the 'independence' claim *realism*. He allows that, logically, realism is not identical to materialism (because idealists can embrace it). However, for Marx, 'there can be no distinction between realism and materialism'.[33] If it could be shown that epistemological inconsistency is a tenable and evaluative criterion, and non-materialists like Kant are epistemologically inconsistent, then a strong (if not a logical) reason will have been provided for Marx's distinctive version of the general philosophical view. Ruben's attempt to eschew a priori philosophical Marxism in favour of a non-transcendental but strong Marxist case as realism is important and laudable.

For the reasons given, however, I do not think Ruben's solution quite works. The Marxist outlook is realist and 'materialist': this much must be correct. But it is not necessarily true that realism as such is specifically Marxist or materialist. Materialists and Marxists can hold justified beliefs about independent objects, and they can argue that the realism of a Kant or a Hume is phoney or wrong. But scientific realism cannot be *proved* by philosophical argument either on deductive grounds or on those of 'epistemological inconsistency'.

If this argument is partly right, realism's advance over Colletti and Althusser is less profound than first appears. On the one hand, the distinction between being and thought made by Althusser and Colletti, and the consequent emphasis on *abstraction*, was intended largely to establish with precision the 'independence of the real object' (Althusser) and the 'positivity of the empirical sensible, or material element'.[34] These ideas have, however, been taken by Ruben to support a 'Kantian' agnosticism rather than realism. On the other hand, that some of these issues may be unresolved within realism itself is indicated not only by the disagreement between Bhaskar and Ruben, but also by Bhaskar's somewhat puzzling argument for epistemological relativism.

Bhaskar's adherence to the relativity of knowledge is not, in one sense, surprising, for he rightly holds that claims about the world are inescapably bound to pre-existing historical and scientific conditions. Yet epistemological relativism is usually taken to mean something stronger, namely that the truth of a claim (however formed) cannot be established 'objectively', owing to the relative character of all conceptions of objectivity. In fact, it is unlikely that Bhaskar does hold to relativism in this strong sense, for he insists only upon 'the impossibility of knowing objects except under particular descriptions'.[35] The above statement is held not to entail *judgemental* relativism, but to refute the correspondence theory of truth, and it is this further step that is puzzling. Judgemental relativism is the view that all beliefs are equally valid.[36] This is not entailed by Bhaskar's epistemic relativity principle, because, presumably, some particular descriptions will be supported by better theoretical and empirical grounds than others. But it does not seem to follow from this, or from the fact that science is socially conditioned, that 'propositions cannot be compared with states of affairs'.[37] Of course, the term 'compared' is ambiguous, but 'correspondence' is not, after all, synonymous with reflection, nor does it mean that thoughts and real processes must be existentially similar. The historically conditioned belief that capitalism is in terminal crisis is, perhaps, more rationally supported than the idea that it will persist indefinitely. But a third view is possible: capitalism is in crisis but not in its death-throes. If this view is more acceptable than the others, it is partly because capitalist societies *can* be 'compared' to it, in a broad sense. And if we do accept the third claim, we will probably hold that it is true *because* it corresponds better to reality. So whilst beliefs are formed in specific and changing circumstances, and whilst their expression is inevitably a matter of particular (theoretical) descriptions, their truth depends on whether the states of affairs posited by the beliefs obtain. Actually, Bhaskar retains something of the kind: 'A proposition is true if and only if the state of affairs that it expresses (describes) is real.'[38] But Bhaskar has not, to my mind, shown how this differs from the view that a proposition is true if and only if its descriptions correspond to real states of affairs. Unless something like this correspondence principle is adopted in realism, the existence of a world of real structured processes might be deemed, ultimately, a matter of faith rather than reason. That principle would not allow any strong epistemological relativism, but it does not contradict a weak or historical relativism.

3. Marx and Philosophy

Interpretations of Marx, especially of his philosophy, are inevitably influenced by and conducted through the assessment of other readings of Marx. There is therefore a kernel of truth to Althusser's insistence that readings are always 'symptomatic' and that the patient himself—Marx—is a product of the diagnosis as much as the source of its success. If realism is adopted, however, there must be something in Marx's writings themselves that supports particular interpretations. Having conducted my discussion in terms of the Marxist tradition and current issues, I ought now to indicate how my approach squares with Marx's own work.

To what extent does Marx's work suggest or supply a philosophy or epistemology? Another, perhaps more useful, way to put the question: what is Marx's conception of philosophy? There is no simple answer, because there is no single set of positions in Marx's work 'as a whole'. We might say that Marx always had a 'feel' for the dialectic, such as can be traced back to the defence of Epicurus in Marx's doctoral dissertation.[39] But I hope it can by now be agreed that *the* dialectic is something of a shibboleth and that much hangs on its substantive implications. I do not fully understand Marx's opposition to Democritus on behalf of Epicurus, but if it was partly to do with the latter's use of an essence/appearance stratification of reality, then it was also linked to the assertion of a universal self-consciousness. That, of course, is a Hegelian notion, and the dominance of Hegel's dialectic in Marx's early work cannot be brushed aside or abstracted as a 'method' only. Marx himself may have encouraged that view of methodological abstraction in metaphors of rational kernels and standing the dialectic on its head (or feet). But we should remember that these are metaphors used with grand hindsight.[40]

The *locus classicus* of humanist and dialectical readings of Marx is the 1844 *Philosophical Manuscripts*. These texts have been hailed as Marx's important 'inversion' of Hegel, and the emergence of a Marxian dialectic. It is with the *Manuscripts* that Ollman thinks the philosophy of 'internal relations' is developed, and where, according to Mészáros, Marx exercises his ontology of mediation, though the ontology is humanist, not materialist in the strict sense. But those who champion the 'early Marx' of 1844 can be questioned on two counts. First, the idea that historical epochs 'represent' the trans-historical loss and recovery of man's self-consciousness is, however progressive, a philosophical view compatible with many theories of history. And the idea that there is an 'identity' of humanized nature and naturalized humanity, if it is an internal, dialectical identity, is not merely a rejection of metaphysical materialism—it must undermine any materialism.

Second, the 'alienation plus dialectic' view of Marxist philosophy, while it grasps Marx's 'coquetry' with Hegel, must play down Marx's basic attitude to philosophy. That attitude suffers overkill in the hands of Althusser when he postulates a clean break between the philosophical and the scientific Marx (post-1845). In fact, it can be traced in Marx's earlier Hegelian dialectic. I refer to the idea that philosophy, *as* trans-historical interpretation, is to be ruthlessly eliminated from serious concrete analysis. If that is indeed one of Marx's basic attitudes, then it is possible to see in the *Philosophical Manuscripts* an important attack on Hegel's philosophical substantivism—but one that remains incomplete, because Marx himself tends, in the early work, to retain the trans-historical nuances of the dialectic.

For present purposes, all Marx's work can be regarded as the struggle between a critique of the illicit interference of philosophy into substantive theory, and those dialectical strands in his own thinking that encourage sweeping philosophical generalizations. Overall, it is the former that dominates the major texts. Actually, it works in part by severe 'logical' analysis. For example, in the early *Critique of Hegel's Doctrine of the State*,[41] Marx demonstrates that it is impossible to derive the *political* (state) organism from the general concept of an organism, as Hegel attempts. A similar and well-known point is made in *The Holy Family* (despite the weaknesses of that text). There Marx takes Hegel to task for striving to *explain* the particularity of fruits by reference to their 'participation' in the *general* category 'fruit'.[42] Marx prefers the honesty of a Proudhon to the guile of Hegel and his epigones.[43]

The most celebrated example of this sort of trenchant criticism of Marx's is in *The Poverty of Philosophy*, directed against Proudhon himself. Proudhon's book, *The Philosophy of Poverty*, is not strictly a philosophical work. What Marx dislikes about it is its attempt to employ Hegelian-style categories *as if* they constituted productive empirical analysis. So Marx's critique is, again, directed against the unmerited aspirations of philosophy. The ringing condemnation and its content is a warning to us, perhaps today more than ever: 'A noisy, self-glorifying, boastful tone, and especially the twaddle about "science" and the sham display of it.'[44] From *The German Ideology* on, Marx is more concerned with producing science than with criticizing sham displays of it. But the earlier writings are not unrelated to the substantive alternative to philosophy. To see this, we might postulate Marx's method as having two parts or moments. First, theories are subjected to internal criticism, and those philosophies that claim to be empirically significant are shown to involve circularity, fallacies, and self-aggrandizement. For Marx, however, such 'negative' analysis is of fundamental importance only in so far as it is allied to a constructive alternative. And it is historical materialism that comes to stand as that solution: the pretensions of pure abstraction and the fallacies of theologies can be explained by their own material and historical conditions of existence.

Marx may never have achieved a full elaboration of historical materialism, but his work does develop into a multi-layered theory. Consequently, the second moment, that of construction—the 'scientific' part— is necessarily much less developed in the early work of Marx. It is there: the critique of religion, for example, is also the critique of that 'vale of tears' in which religion is 'the opium of the people'.[45] Intellectual critique, in other words, is connected both to an alternative *account* of the world and to an alternative *world*. (This is the main emphasis of Roy Edgley's argument on dialectical thinking.) In the *Manuscripts*, the critique of capitalism is developed in relation to the philosophical errors of the Hegelians. In the *German Ideology*, the first major statement of the alternative to philosophy is given. In the *Grundrisse* and *Capital*, it is specified in detail, and so on.

We can also say, however, that the alternative is developed in the early writings in a *philosophical* way, just to register the fact that Marx's alternatives themselves emerged from the Hegelian context of 'substantivism'. Such a judgement, in my view, enables us to see the limitations of the young Marx. There is no need to read into Marx's work at any stage either a teleology of necessary complementarity or sharp discontinuities.

It follows from this account that Marx's main concern is to attack, and expose in dominant historical or economic theory, the false claims of philosophy regarded as constructive concepts. Moreover, the practical grounds for those illusions must be established, and the practical implications of the alternative made plain. This is compatible with two senses of philosophy in relation to Marx's work. First, the 'negative' part of his 'method' consists in the demonstration that arguments are good or bad, that premisses and conclusions are right or wrong, related or arbitrary. This is a 'logical' or philosophical task, and Marx depends on its validity as a theoretical form: there is nothing especially dialectical about it. However, philosophy is perhaps dialectically *related* to the exposition and defence of Marx's positive theses. Here philosophy puts itself in the service of 'science' by generalizing from, and drawing out connections between, substantive theories and concepts. This is the view of philosophy advanced in *The German Ideology*.[46] Marx's critique of philosophy, then, is not so thoroughgoing as might appear. The eleventh thesis on Feuerbach[47] is a criticism of philosophers who *only* interpret the world. It does not follow that the world can be changed without preliminary interpretation. And philosophy has a role to play in that process.

The second sense of philosophy compatible with Marx's ideas is the sense in which philosophical conceptions, rather than being usurpers of the role of science, are first approximations to science, which can be progressively firmed up. This conception of 'proto-scientific' analysis best grasps the significance of the early Marx himself. It can, without undue complication, be seen as the reason why the theory of alienation, for example, is *both* philosophical and anti-philosophical, Hegelian yet Marxian. *The German Ideology*, similarly, can be thought of as an argument about what kind of theory the alternative to the German ideology must be. Philosophy thus can formulate the preconditions and results of substantive knowledge—for example, that the world exists, that it can be deciphered, that material production is the presupposition of human life, that ideologies are practically formed, and so on. It is nicely (or dangerously) poised between a philosophy of history and a theory of history. It usefully reminds us, too, that the more general a theory is, the more important philosophical arguments are to its exposition.

None of this requires us to regard Marx's later work as free from philosophical 'influence' in the more dubious sense. There are Hegelianisms in *Capital*, for example, perhaps of damaging consequence.[48] What my argument suggests is that Marx did not subscribe to the idea that philosophical elaboration is automatically illegitimate. One text in particular seems to flesh out that rather skeletal conclusion: the '1857 Introduction' to the *Grundrisse*. Nowadays, the Introduction has become a compulsory reference-point for discussions of Marx's 'method', rather in the way that the '1859 Preface' to the *Contribution to the Critique of Political Economy* was for earlier generations of Marxologists. But there are reasons why we must not make too much of the 1857 Introduction. For one thing, Marx himself declined to publish it. Second, rather different sorts of Marxists appear to get considerable mileage out of the text for their own purposes. Thus Althusser concludes on the basis of his reading that 'it is perfectly legitimate to say that the production of knowledge which is peculiar to theoretical practice constitutes a process that takes place *entirely in thought*'.[49] Specifically against this interpretation, Derek Sayer has pitted the view that Marx's concepts are 'emphatically a posteriori constructs',[50] and Stuart Hall has argued for the 'historical epistemology' of the Introduction.[51] Another good example of how allegiances are declared on the battleground of this text is Andrew Collier's statement: 'There is here, then, a sketch for an epistemology which has broken with both rationalism and empiricism, and which is thoroughly realist in its ontological assumptions and experimental in its method—in short, which is scientific and materialist.'[52] How convenient that a mere 'sketch' delivers everything that today's Marxist philosophers have been waiting for!

In view of these claims and disputes, it may seem that there is little hope of coming to any firm conclusions about the 1857 Introduction. In fact, I do not think that it takes us *substantially* beyond what I have noted in Marx's other work. Nevertheless, it is possible to summarize and affirm what has been suggested, even through the clash of readings of the Introduction.

None of the commentators actually hold that Marx's piece *does* fully deliver the results that suit them best. Ted Benton rightly says that 'this text is a paradox',[53] and Hall calls it 'compressed and "illegible"'.[54] Sayer, for his part, is cautious about the Introduction, because it appears to outline only 'the form of exposition proper to a scientific analysis',[55] whereas Sayer develops an interesting case that the form of scientific *inquiry* is crucially different from that of presentation in Marx. We should, in addition, be fair to Althusser, for while he makes too much of the autonomy of scientific 'thought', he does state (reasonably, in my view) that, in the Introduction, 'This thought is the historically constituted system of an *apparatus of thought*, founded on and articulated to natural and social reality.'[56]

These convergences, beneath the polemical exaggerations, serve as a salutary reminder that it is difficult to ascribe a developed philosophical outlook to Marx. What we do find, however, are a number of indispensable guidelines or 'premisses',[57] which indicate Marx's philosophical orientation. Simplifying, there are two aspects of the knowledge process that Marx is keen to stress. The first is the necessity of abstraction: 'It seems to be correct to begin with the real and the concrete, with the real precondition, thus to begin, in economics, with e.g. the population, which is the foundation and the subject of the entire social act of production. However, on closer examination this proves false.'[58] It proves false because some ideas of what the 'real and concrete' is might form no more than a 'chaotic conception of the whole'. In contrast to this, Marx argues that 'the scientifically correct method' is to develop, by abstraction, a series of relatively simple theoretical determinations, and thence to return to the concrete as a rich 'concentration of many determinations'. These reflections may be taken as a rejection by Marx of an empiricist conception of knowledge. Scientific theory operates by the transformation of 'chaotic' concrete abstractions into 'the method of rising from the abstract to the concrete'.[59]

Marx's second emphasis may be termed materialist. He insists on the foundational role, and the independent ontological status, of the real object. Whilst, through abstraction, the concrete appears as 'the product of the thinking head, which appropriates the world in the only way it can', nevertheless 'the real subject retains its autonomous existence outside the head just as before'.[60] 'Hence, in the theoretical method, too, the subject, society, must always be kept in mind as the presupposition.[61]

In so far as realism is the philosophical view that currently best grasps both the theoretical character of science and the real existence of its objects and conditions, Marx is a realist in these lines. One important notion that emerges from his discussion is the idea that concepts differ with respect to their historical range and theoretical individuation. They operate, that is, at different 'levels of abstraction'.[62] For example, 'production in general' is, on its proper (trans-historical) level of abstraction, a 'rational' and necessary concept. But it will be quite misleading if held to be explanatory, without being supplemented, at a lower level (say, that of the capitalist mode of production). Similarly, 'value' alone will not suffice to analyse social formations or historical periods 'below' the level of the capitalist mode in general.

The last example is not Marx's, but it seems a fair extrapolation from his comment that after 'general, abstract determinations' should come 'the categories which make up the inner structure of bourgeois society'.[63] This level, in turn, is followed by a series of topics that Marx offers in note-form as further degrees of specificity: classes, circulation, credit, the form of the state, etc. 'Levels of abstraction' is therefore a useful criterion to dig out of Marx, for while it squares with the realist conception of a structured but complex world uncovered by science, there is no simple sense that concepts 'correspond to reality'. It reminds us too that Marx does not say *how* we can tell if concepts and claims are pitched at the appropriate level of abstraction. Marx was not a philosopher in the sense of someone who lays down criteria of a 'universal' sort by means of which to assess any epistemological stance. Even in the 1857 Introduction, his comments are tied to 'the method of political economy'. 'Levels of abstraction' will not, therefore, stand in for epistemology in its full meaning. Nor can it be assumed that, invoking the possibility of different levels of abstraction in a theoretical position, one's concepts *are* at the appropriate levels. That said, 'levels of abstraction' is a fruitful means of assessing the strengths and depth of theoretical assumptions without exercising a bulky epistemological apparatus.

We can conclude that Marx's 'method' requires, at some level, theoretical labour of a 'philosophical' kind; that is, to do with conceptual presuppositions, construction, and consistency. But Marx remains as ever opposed to 'speculative' philosophy. Even in the 'scientifically correct method', the 'reproduction of the concrete by way of thought'[64] harbours the inherent possibility of 'illusion'. In sum, from Marx's work can be drawn some important philosophical 'premisses', but he offers no detailed epistemology —not even a realist one.

3

Explanation and the 'Basic Concepts' of Historical Materialism

The scope and character of Marxist explanation are not given in any detail, in the view that it depends on a realist conception of knowledge. As I have interpreted it, realism is the claim that scientific knowledge illuminates the relationship between generative mechanisms and empirical phenomena. But realism embraces different types of explanation. Take the strange arm-actions of a bookmaker on a racecourse. They might be explained by the fact that he is a conveyor of odds, and collector of bets, in the horse-racing system. But they could also be explained by an account of how it is that signs of that kind have come to be taken up, rather than, say, the relay of bets to off-course bookies by pigeon; or no bets at all. Indeed, we might want to know why the cultural phenomenon of racing arose in the first place. The appropriate explanations to all three kinds of questions will tell us something about how real processes 'generate' phenomena. The second and third explanations would be causal in the sense that we could find out how specific signs or systems as a whole happened to come about. The first, however, is a matter of the function of the tick-tack man. It concerns not the details of those particular signs, but the role of, or need for, some kind of sign-convention, given the horse-racing system. The third question would also be 'functional' if it was to do with the *kind* of cultural role racing fulfilled.

This analogy can be generalized for social science and history. In particular, it can be asked whether historical materialism is a causal or functional theory, or whether it can be both. The question is important in its own right, since there remains a good deal of puzzlement about what the 'basic' concepts' of Marxism are, and how they fit together as a historical theory. But it is also related to arguments about the degree to which Marxism, and thus historical materialism, exhibits an explanatory structure in accordance with realist tenets. David-Hillel Ruben, on what appear to be realist grounds, has dissented from the idea that Marxism *is* a general theory of history. This conclusion is, I think, mistaken, but an argument to that effect first requires careful consideration of the controversies about the sorts of propositions historical materialism embraces.

1. Forces and Relations of Production

In the first chapter I sought to convey how varieties of historical materialism related to a range of philosophical options (and vice versa). The 'basic concepts' of Marxism receive correspondingly varied interpretations in the tradition. There seem to be three main options: that which emphasizes the primacy of the productive forces, that which asserts the dominance of the relations of production, and those offering a 'mixed' conception. Generally speaking, materialist Marxisms tend to favour the first position. In some cases, the humanity-nature connection was almost reduced to a technological and even geographical determinism (Plekhanov, for example). In the dialectical tradition, which adopts the second, nature itself is socialized, often to the point that productive forces are asserted to *be* social relations, which in turn could be defined as any human interaction at all. This common view is implied by Lukács, rendered a virtue by the 'dialecticians', and widely held amongst Marxists of a 'Maoist' inclination.[1] There have also been several attempts to avoid this polarity, such as in the versions of 'structuralist' Marxism. Althusser and Balibar, Nicos Poulantzas, and Hindess and Hirst have produced a variety of formulations aiming to secure an even-handed 'articulation' of forces and relations, and in so doing attempt to fight clear of both Soviet diamat and the 'humanist' reaction to it.

Current wrangles along these lines are very much tied to political questions of the day: the growth of Eurocommunism, for example, or the decline of independent working-class politics, or the involvement of radical intellectuals in various aspects of the state. But there is evidence in Marx and Engels to suggest that a statement of historical materialism has never been unambiguously presented, thus allowing for perpetual argument as to what is or is not a 'genuine' Marxist stance. Marx's clearest statement occurs in the 1859 Preface to the *Critique of Political Economy*. There the forces are held to determine relations of production, which (as the economic base) in turn govern the politico-legal superstructure of society. As we shall see, it is an issue as to whether other parts of the Preface and other of Marx's texts complicate this story. Engels, for one, found it difficult to stick to these principles. His epistolary caveats about determination by the economy 'in the last instance' are oft-quoted as either a problem for or the salvation of classical Marxism. In what is perhaps *the* Marxist text-book, *Anti-Dühring*, Engels maintains that insufficiency of production was the historical justification of class divisions, and that the productive forces under *capitalism* will 'burst asunder the bonds imposed on them' by the latter.[2] But Engels (unlike Marx in the Preface) seems to equate the mode of production with the economic base.[3] And whilst the forces are separate from the base, 'rebelling' against it, it is the failure of capitalism to recognize the intrinsically *social* character of the forces that Engels considers the central feature of the 'contradiction'.[4]

Despite the frequency with which the criticism is levelled that the assertion that the forces of production are paramount constitutes technological determinism, it is not wholly clear what this charge means. The idea that machines control their human operators may make good science fiction, but it is not, on reflection, a tenable theory of history. On the other hand, Marxists who subscribe to the primacy of the forces of production do not always do enough to dispel that asssociation. A major flaw in the most accomplished recent version of the 'forces' argument, G. A. Cohen's,[5] is the assumption that forces of production have autonomous *needs* in virtue of which relations of production emerge or disappear. This seems mistaken, for capacities or powers or forces do not have needs in themselves. Rather, they are developed or curtailed according to social or human needs (though these need not be wholly conscious).

In fact, theories of the primacy of productive power need not be associated uniquely with Marxism. It is well known that Fabian theory shared with Second International Marxism a 'functionalist' belief in economic evolution as an organic natural process.[6] Socialism, on this view, is the highest stage of the rational and efficient deployment of productive resources. And a conservative, W. W. Rostow, has constructed a celebrated 'non-Communist Manifesto', which sees modern history as a series of stages of growth in productive power, culminating in abundance.[7] Why, then, does the 'forces' theory have such staying power amongst Marxists? This simple question has no easy answer, and part of any answer must be historical. For example, the founder Marxists adhered in some part to the progressivist and positivist notion of the liberating curve plotted by nineteenth-century science and technology. Soviet Marxists, for their part, adjusted their doctrines to the mainly industrial goals their policies set, making sure at the same time that the theoretical credentials of the socialist opposition to Stalinism were downgraded. And in recent years, when 'Western Marxism' has appeared to reject the connection between Marxism and 'progress', or has seemed to sustain a spurious 'objectivity', a restatement of fundamentals is attractive again. This is especially so when capitalist crisis has supplanted the social stability in which questions of ideology and theory undoubtedly flourish.

G. A. Cohen has shown that a clearly expressed fundamentalism is a good deal less than 'vulgar'. But before considering his arguments in detail, the nature of the 'structuralist' alternatives to 'reductionist' materialism should be indicated. This is additionally important since in spite of the faults of the theoretical systems constructed by Althusser *et al.*, their concerns will be found pertinent to the reservations that can be lodged against Cohen-style Marxism.

The kind of orthodoxy to which structuralist Marxism objected is exemplified in this statement by the British Communist philosopher Maurice Cornforth. 'The historical sequence of social-economic formations is a natural history or evolutionary process in this sense—that production relations are always adapted to given forces of production, so that those that arise in adaptation to more advanced forces of production represent a higher stage of development of the economic formation of society than those adapted to less advanced forces of production. The stage of development that a given society has attained is objectively decided by the level of the forces of production and by how far its economic structure permits people to extract the maximum powers from those forces of production.'[8]

For Althusser and his followers, this perspective is no more than a series of uncritical assumptions, endorsing the Soviet political system and the narrow mould into which dialectical materialism tends to cram natural and social phenomena. It is the sort of Marxism, in short, that fuels bourgeois accusations of social determinism and philosophical naïveté. In consequence, the structuralists mount a critique of the teleological framework of the forces argument, and criticize its readiness to find in history convenient 'confirmations' of the basic thesis. In both these respects, 'vulgar' Marxism has been held to share a good deal with 'bourgeois' empiricism. Structuralists therefore attempt to construct a new Marxist 'science' of history, highlighting real complexity and theoretical sophistication. The efforts of Althusser *et al.* are aimed at a new theoretical comprehensiveness based on a structural account of social causality, as against what they allege to be alien teleological and simple-materialist philosophies within Marxism.

The major innovation here is the prominence given to the concept of 'mode of production', comprising forces and relations of production, at the expense of the 'base-and-superstructure' model. Production is conceived as a totality in which technical productive forces are necessarily bounded by social relations. Indeed, in Poulantzas's version, the 'global' mode of production comes to include superstructures and ideology too.[9] The basis for this move is to be found in Balibar's proposition that 'productive forces' is an umbrella term for a range of connections of 'real appropriation' between producers and nature. It should therefore properly *include* material relations of production and *entail* the entire wider social division of labour. These basic concepts better convey 'the radical anti-evolutionist character'[10] of the Marxist theory of history by disallowing any independence or primacy to the purely technical aspect of the forces.

There are two major problems with the account in which Balibar's concepts play a key role. First, the extended or 'matrix' role of the mode of production makes the notion of an economic base difficult to sustain. For example, in Poulantzas's earlier formulations, the economic instance is no longer strictly separable at all from the political, ideological, and even theoretical 'levels': each is structurally combined in the 'matrix' of social relations. And this view, whatever it gains in complexity, loses the directness and force of the classical Marxist model, perhaps even compromising any definite conception of fundamental factors.

Second, the structuralist conception of mode of production posits a logical or conceptual correspondence between forces and relations of production. But it is hard to see how historical change occurs if each mode is a totality of mutually supporting relations forming a discontinuous sequence. In order to avoid such a static view of history and society, Balibar was driven to argue that a *transitional* mode of production had to be conceived. It would be characterized by the non-correspondence of forces and relations. However, this solution is also an abdication of the structuralist tenets. To posit at the heart of history a 'law of necessary correspondence or non-correspondence'[11] is merely truistic, and such a law manifestly overturns the distinctive features of the notion 'mode of production' as painstakingly developed by Balibar.

Barry Hindess and Paul Hirst deliver such criticisms throughout their book *Pre-capitalist Modes of Production*. Their own contribution to this debate vehemently extends the campaign against teleology and inconsistency to cover *Reading Capital* itself. No general theory of modes of production is possible, they claim. What is possible, on this account, is the rigorous deployment of concepts of modes of production which nevertheless respect the 'material causality' of the class struggle and historical transition. Hindess and Hirst proceed to construct the logical features and possible variants of the major modes of production. However, the twofold character of their enterprise is in essence contradictory. They wish to maintain a pristine Marxist science at the level of the concepts: 'Marxism, as a theoretical and a political practice, gains nothing from its association with historical writing and historical research.'[12] But Hindess and Hirst also insist that the reproduction of the modes, their variants, and the transitions between them are strictly subject to specific class struggles. Otherwise the rationalism and teleology of Balibar's efforts would certainly ensue.

In fact, the solutions of *Pre-capitalist Modes of Production* have exacerbated the contradictions within *Reading Capital*, in the following ways. On pain of empiricism, modes of production are held to be rigorously *conceptual* totalities, 'articulated combinations' in which sets of productive forces are logically deducible from the dominant economic forms. However, on pain of rationalism, the question of how these theoretical or Platonic forms are instantiated in real social formations is left unanswered. Finally, on pain of teleology, theoretical accounts of specific historical transitions—especially when couched in the terms of forces-relations discord—must be resisted. But as we have seen, particular investigations having no theoretical premisses amount, in Hindess and Hirst's catalogue of sins, to mindless empiricism. Thus a series of sharp but ruthless criticisms sustains only a theoretical vacuum, which comes to be disposed of in a 'self-criticism'. The means by which Hindess and Hirst overcome the dilemmas of their earlier book is to attribute to the concept of mode of production an inherent dependence on the 'metaphysical' division between 'spurious' counterparts: knowledge and reality. This manoeuvre is, of course, convenient, but as I suggested earlier, it is unworkable.

In the light of the failure of rationalist Marxist elaborations of the basic concepts, two options seem open. One is to jettison the forces-relations combination altogether. This perspective has been adopted by Derek Sayer and his associates. Sayer is hostile to both technological determinism and to Althusserianism, which he thinks simply reverses the forces-relations connection. Sayer holds that forces *are* relations and argues that the analysis of these (broad) social relations is always and necessarily specific. In spite of the frequently expressed claims that they represent authentic Marxism, these ideas seriously misrepresent Marx's own views.[13] More importantly, they seem unable to provide a determinate theory of society or history in its overall outlines. That is a high price to pay for sidestepping what is thought to be 'determinism'.

2. Productive Forces Again

The other option is to reformulate and defend the productive-forces argument. In a timely and impressive work, G. A. Cohen does just that. Cohen reasserts the explanatory cogency of 'old-fashioned' Marxism at a time when traditional views are almost intuitively thought to be wrong-headed. Accordingly, he defends a technological thesis in terms of the validity of teleological or functional explanation. Briefly, Cohen's theses are as follows. Historical materialism explains phenomena because it provides a functional account of their existence. Superstructures are explained when their functional requirement by productive relations can be displayed. Relations, in turn, come to be and are what they are because they are necessary and suitable for the development of the forces of production. Forces are those things, capacities, and resources that, when utilized, produce material use-values. Relations of production are the powers exercised by, and rights conferred on, human agents in virtue of their control over the means of production (or lack of such control). Marxism is a theory of history because the development of the forces across and through sets of relations is the foundation of our understanding of social forms and social change.

In Cohen's view, there is no problem here of determinism, if by determinism is meant that the dependent variable is 'reducible' to, or has no effect on, the independent factor. Rather, it is just *because* the relations causally affect the development of the forces that they (the relations) come into being when they do. So the causality is reciprocal, and the relations (and superstructure) retain their distinctive features. But this is not to challenge the principal direction of dependence: those relations exist as they do because of their functional necessity for the growth of the forces. Another familiar objection is easily discounted: the theory does not contradict Marx's idea that, in reality, forces and relations are indissoluble. We cannot deduce relations from forces, and forces do not exist on their own. But it is important to establish the conceptual independence of the elements, for we can *infer* effects and attribute primacy all the same—there being many examples of this kind of causality in science. Thus: 'the "technological" reading to be favoured in this work is that the productive forces strongly determine the character of the economic structure, while forming no part of it.'[14]

Three related discussions are necessary to fully come to terms with the nature of Cohen's tightly-wrought arguments. The first concerns his basic concepts and the theses in which they figure. The second has to do with their faithfulness to Marx and to history. Cohen's own sense of 'complications' in both these areas is helpful in this assessment. The tenor of my argument is that, in some ways, it is Cohen's abandonment of 'mode of production' that renders his position skeletal rather than definitive. Cohen's account of functional explanation is important here, and is the focus of the third discussion, in which problems of a realist sort will be found relevant to the conclusions of the chapter as a whole.

First, then, we may doubt whether Cohen has adequately sustained his distinction between forces and relations, and between base and superstructure. For example, he includes subsistence and clothing in the forces, items that are subject to considerable cultural conditioning, and are determined by class struggle. Cohen's insistence, in the face of this objection, that only those amounts of food and kinds of apparel *necessary* to material production count among the forces, seems artificial and very difficult to demonstrate practically. Furthermore, productive forces operate, as we have noted, in accordance with (some) human needs, but they have none of their own. And Cohen's theory looks misleadingly *described* as 'technological' when we remember that he places knowledge and labour power at the centre of the forces. The basis of Cohen's exclusion of the forces from the economic base is that productive powers, not being properties, cannot be relations in the strict sense. But this also seems too strict. Some properties are more relational than others, and Cohen himself makes good use of that distinction elsewhere in his book.[15] Power or force is itself a good example of a relational property.

A similar problem is that the general distinction Cohen makes between material and social properties in order to support the narrower forces/relations case, fails to do so conclusively. His more general proposition is that we can always logically detach the material substratum or naturerelation from its social existence. Indeed, nature can count as 'the matter or content of society whose form is the social form'.[16] This formulation is not co-terminous with the primacy thesis, because the 'material' properties Cohen refers to include 'work relations'. Work relations are the forms of physical interaction, of co-operation, of task orientation, and the (technical) division of labour. Cohen maintains that they do not immediately reveal the social relations within which they operate, and so must be *excluded* from the economic base. But since work relations are still *relations*, they do not belong in the forces either.[17]

The idea that material relations of production are non-economic is surely strange. We need not obliterate the distinction between forces and relations to admit that these are abstractions from an opaque and complex process—the labour process—that exhibits a variety of 'natural' and 'social' connections. Here, a more natural approach would be to introduce the concept of mode of production. Since this would not especially promote the primacy of the forces, Cohen has to develop an account of work relations that holds that they are relational but not economic, and material but not technological. In another rather formalist argument, Cohen attempts further to discredit the 'modal' perspective.

According to Cohen, a mode of production is a manner of producing, and so cannot be a set of relations.[18] Nevertheless, he identifies a 'social' meaning and a 'mixed' conception of mode of production, which escape his instrumentalist strictures, since they are discussed in terms of forms of exploitation.[19] Having alluded to these modes, Cohen says virtually nothing more about them; yet to some extent they undercut his preferred forces/relations and base/superstructure hierarchies.

Cohen's account of the superstructure may also be questioned if we consider his discussion of the place of science. Cohen maintains that productively relevant science belongs in the productive forces. Indeed, 'the development of knowledge is . . . the centre of the development of the productive forces'.[20] The forces being external to the economic base, it follows that productive science is not basic. The rest of science is neither basic nor superstructural, since, for Cohen, the superstructure comprises *institutions*, and knowledge is not an institution. Finally, science *qua* knowledge is not ideology either, though ideology itself is not superstructural. Cohen's purpose in these classifications is to affirm materialism against 'Kuhnian' views of science, and to maintain the idea that dynamic forces of production are quite separate from the economic base, which in turn is uncomplicated by its superstructural effects. In the process, Cohen has assembled a model of society which has, in the words of one reviewer of his book, 'four separate compartments: two bases, a superstructure, and an area lying outside'.[21]

It is a model that seems to leave a good deal of what Marxists have found interesting free of the reach of its basic concepts. Marx's reference, in the Preface, to an 'immense' superstructure has not been taken literally by Cohen, though he insisted on the closest textual case when identifying forces and relations. There also arises the question of how satisfactorily to demarcate the 'productively relevant' aspects of science and the rest. Third, Cohen's insistence that the superstructure be 'institutional' is less than wholly clear. If it is to refer to anything more than a set of buildings, then science, like law or politics, *is* institutional. Thus, even parts of its productively relevant aspects will be 'superstructurally' produced. However, this tangle suggests that Cohen's definition of the superstructure is also excessively restrictive. The term 'institutional' does not appear in the Preface, which *does* mention definite forms of social consciousness that 'correspond' to the legal and political superstructures, and of Marx's more general statements, the idea that social being determines consciousness seems one that he thought particularly useful. In the absence of precise guidance from Marx, it is reasonable to include ideational forms and practices in the superstructure. This would allow us to rank part of science in the forces, but accommodate those 'ideological elements' that Cohen acknowledges, together with its institutional setting, in the superstructure. This rather better move is inhibited by Cohen's assertion that science cannot be ideology. Of course, only if this is a rigidly exclusive dichotomy will it contradict Cohen's underdeveloped suggestion that ideology and superstructural phenomena 'influence' science, and therefore the productive forces. But the onus is on Cohen more fully to resolve some of the tensions between his model and his considered opinions.

We can now turn to how these problems of definition affect Cohen's thesis that the forces of production develop throughout history, and that the level of their development determines the relations of production. And it is also relevant to consider here whether Marx's views, especially on historical formations, are as supportive of Cohen's theses as he claims. One of the impressive features of Cohen's book is that a great deal of Marx is cited as evidence for the primacy thesis defended by Cohen. As a result, Cohen has a clinical answer to those who posit Marx's hesitation over the allocation of primacy: 'Keat and Urry . . . say that Marx "occasionally" includes forces as well as relations in the base, but they cite no evidence, and in fact there is none.'[22] However, if the point is rather that Marx's conception of productive forces is not always clearly separated from relations, and if the direction of causality is not always clear, then Cohen may still be right, but his spare elaboration of Marx's theory would be less convincing. There is some evidence that Marx's views are rather messier than Cohen's. Throughout the *Grundrisse*, Marx speaks interchangeably of the 'social forces of production' and 'productive social forces'. This is not enough to sustain the idea that powers *are* relations, but it does suggest that the *content* of productive forces can be determined only in connection with specific social forms. Marx speaks of 'the general productive force arising from social combination in total production'.[23] Phrases like 'arise from' are opaque, but that does not mean that Marx means something simpler. And when *labour* is postulated as the key productive force, the nature of such a force is intimately connected to the manner in which social labour is organized.[24]

'It must be kept in mind that the new forces of production and relations of production do not develop out of nothing, nor drop from the sky, nor from the womb of the self-positing Idea; but from within and in antithesis to the existing development of production and the inherited, traditional forms of property.'[25] This sort of quotation does give encouragement to those who prefer to speak of a mode of production in which forces and relations 'combine'. In the case of capitalism: 'The production process, considered as the unity of the labour process of creating value, is the process of production of commodities; considered as the unity of the labour process and the process of valorization, it is the capitalist process of production or the capitalist form of the production of commodities.'[26] Here is a formulation that compresses (without obliteration) the notion of a 'natural' labour process, a (general) social relation, and a historically specific form. But they are held to make up a 'unity'.

In view of the priority given to the forces in Cohen's account, and the dominance of material or physical qualities over those that are essentially social, it comes as some surprise when Cohen declines to classify historical eras according to levels of productivity or abundance.[27] This refusal is astonishing because the productive forces are the independent variable, and the relations conform to their growth. Indeed, Cohen presents a table and a discussion that contributes to such a classification.[28]

Form of Economic Structure	Level of Productive Development
1. Pre-Class Society	No surplus
2. Pre-Capitalist Class Society	Some surplus, but less than
3. Capitalist Society	Moderately high surplus, but less than
4. Post-Class Society	Massive surplus

Moreover, Cohen assumes a 'perennial tendency to productive progress' such that the 'forces *select* structures according to their capacity to promote development'.[29]

One reason why Cohen might hesitate to offer a full forces-based classification is that it is the nature and logic of the *social* forms rather than the material 'content' that has traditionally been of concern to Marxists. Cohen has an answer to Ernest Gellner, who also put that question when accusing Marx himself of inconsistency: 'The question is misguided. It is often appropriate to classify entities by their form not their content, and formal classification is correct in the present case, for individuation by productive forces would not yield *social* types.'[30]One is entitled to feel that this too-brief response amounts to a concession to, and not rebuttal of, criticisms.

Cohen certainly accepts that his main theses are 'complicated' in various ways. For example, the theory of a rational human nature developing optimal productive power, which lies at the back of his defence of Marx, is 'seriously incomplete', because 'it is not evident that societies are disposed to bring about what rationality would lead men to choose'.[31] Cohen thus appeals to 'the record of history', arguing that societies rarely replace a set of forces by an inferior one.[32] In view of the *conceptual* strength of Cohen's model, this appeal to cases may be more damaging than he would like.

A second, and related, complication is that the *rate* of productive growth and the path it follows in specific circumstances are heavily influenced by the prevailing relations of production. This is a major qualification, because it allows the development of the forces of production to be retarded, and even reversed. It is also borne out by stretches of history, such as the period after the fall of Rome, which Cohen perfunctorily describes as an 'abnormality' with which his theory cannot be expected to deal.[33] The point, however, is that abnormalities form part of a spectrum of cases in which the role of the relations is by no means clearly derivative.

The status of pre-capitalist societies is interesting in this context, for Cohen allows that Marx's opinion that these modes are essentially conservative might be thought to 'embarrass' Cohen's theses.[34] His solution is to argue that pre-capitalist societies (in contrast to capitalism) do not *directly* stimulate productivity, but do provide a 'framework' within which the forces can and do develop. But this adjustment makes a difference, for the strong primacy thesis is that forces select relations. To accommodate without embarrassment the considerable military, political, and even super-structural constraints on production noted by a constellation of Marxist writers, Cohen's thesis would have to be flexible indeed. But it might be more accurate to say that when necessary Cohen withdraws from his more stringent formulations. That this is indeed the case is suggested by the less rigid generalization that follows his enumeration of the complications: 'The productive forces on the whole dominate the production relations.'[35] It is thus possible that the forces could be dominant in just one historical stage. Anthony Giddens has argued that the forces/relations connection is particularly apt only in relation to capitalist societies. His terms may not be the most appropriate, but he does make a substantial point. In early civilization, 'authority had primacy over allocation' in the sense that 'neither technical advance in the tools of production, nor control of property, were of primary importance in this . . . authoritarian division of labour'.[36]

Cohen's views seem to fit the case of the transition to capitalism rather better. Most Marxists (following Marx) accept that capitalism revolutionizes the productive forces. But because Cohen has excluded work relations from the forces, he cannot yield to the temptation that attracts other Marxists: to see the transition to capitalism as in central ways a question of changes in the forms of co-operation of labour. Others still, such as John Plamenatz, regard the appearance of new capitalist relations of production before 'modern industry' as a refutation of Marxism itself. Cohen responds to this challenge by arguing that relations may not only fetter existing forces, but can also prevent the formation of new forces.[37] The formation of forces suitable for capitalism is thus facilitated by the prior removal of the old relations. Cohen's response here is ingenious; it works, but it seems a little contrived, too.

How do we identify the pressures exerted by 'potential' forces? What of the real effects of commerce (noted by Marx) in the process of manufacture? Above all, how does class struggle come into this picture? In the 'sixth chapter' of *Capital*, Marx provides a dialectical formulation rather than an endorsement of the unidirectional primacy of the forces: 'On the one hand, *capitalist production* now establishes itself as a mode of production sui generis and brings into being a new mode of material production. On the other hand, the latter itself forms the basis for the development of capitalist relations whose adequate form, therefore, presupposes a definite stage in the evolution of the productive forces of labour.'[38]

Cohen's view of socialism would face similar sorts of questions, for he takes the general line that successful class struggles emerge only when they march in step with the growth of the productive forces.[39] In both cases, Cohen has established that material preconditions are crucial for revolutionary change, but he has not demonstrated, yet sometimes implies, that they are also sufficient conditions.

Undue emphasis on the couplet productive forces/functional explanation can encourage Marxists to regard crucial causal processes in history as *no more than* the forms through which the forces of production assert themselves. Albert Soboul, whose work will be discussed in a later chapter, is an example of a historian for whom this emphasis poses serious dilemmas. Cohen may not intend it so, but 'lazy Marxism' often results from an overly fundamentalist focus on the forces of production. He does not demonstrate convincingly that this consequence is unrelated to the theory as such. He writes: 'Relations which obtain at a given time are the relations most suitable for the forces' development at that time, given the level reached by that time.'[40] The strict ruling hardly supports the view that relations can retard forces, unless retardation is itself only a necessary function of the forces' inexorable progress. And the latter assumption approaches *functionalism*: whatever exists and however, it is there because it functions for the forces. Either this is true by definition (and no counter-example would be possible), or something like 'long-term' functionality is being invoked, and that is compatible with long stretches of history (the 'Dark Ages', for example) that Cohen has excused from immediate implication. If the former gloss is Cohen's, then his is as much a 'reading' of history as it is an informative theory of it. The second gloss—supported by Cohen's 'qualifications'—entails a theory of history, but one for which particular phases may be of more interest than the overall pattern, and therefore one in which the primacy of the forces of production cannot be taken for granted.

3. Functional Explanation and Marxist 'Laws'

Cohen's Marxism relies heavily on functional explanation, and he gives a thorough and interesting account of that procedure, as against Carl G. Hempel's standard explication. Yet Hempel's account can be faulted without accepting everything Cohen says. Functional analyses are often held to be illegitimate because they are dubbed 'teleological': they explain a thing by its purpose or its ultimate 'effects'. This seems to expose science to occult entities and animistic explanations. The importance of Hempel's article on the question is that it argues that functional explanation can be rid of these undesirable implications and can afford us sound inferences. He maintains, however, that functional propositions must be weakened so as not to claim that a factor z is the *only* one that could stand in a given functional relation to state y. Hempel then allows functional explanations into the select club of *bona fide* accounts. But not quite as fully fledged members: 'even for a properly relativized version of functional analysis . . . its explanatory force is rather limited'.[41] One of the reasons for this is that functional analysis is unable to sustain predictions and counterfactual conditions; another is the mixed record of many functional theories. Hempel's hesitation here, however, is connected to his neo-positivist conception of proper explanation. According to this view, scientific laws are statements of empirical regularity, from which states of affairs can be logically deduced provided a suitable statement of initial conditions obtains. This model favours prediction over retrodiction, and universality over tendential laws. Functional theories, which do not lend themselves to deduction in this way, must therefore appear flawed.

Realist-inclined philosophers have challenged Hempelian norms in detail. For Roy Bhaskar, real mechanisms rarely produce empirical regularities outside the artificial constructions of scientific experiment. In addition, while *some* relation to a nomic law would seem to distinguish theoretical propositions from 'accidental' empirical generalizations (such as 'all the cars in this street are pink'), it need not be the relation of deducibility. Cohen, for his part, abstains from further pronouncement on the nature of nomic generality, but a realist account is one main candidate. Causal and functional laws do not differ with respect to deducibility, their relation to nomic generalization, or the fact that future conditions may fail to sustain theories. Hempel's doubt is therefore unfounded. Another logical empiricist, Ernest Nagel, is less troubled. For him, the difference between functional and causal explanation is simply 'one of emphasis and perspective in formulation'.[42]

Functional explanation, then, is legitimate, and Cohen has given a valuable account of its mode of operation. A functional explanation makes reference to the effect or purpose of something, and is thus a species of 'consequence' explanation. But causes and effects are not simply reversed here, because causes are not explained *by* their effects. 'Rather, and very differently, it is the fact that *were an event of a certain type to occur, it would have a certain effect*, which explains the occurrence of an event of the stated type.'[43] It is not the appearance of the effect, but the disposition in virtue of which that outcome is effected that furnishes a functional explanation.

In one sense, Cohen's defence of functional explanation is misleading, namely his suggestion that we can devise sound functional explanations without knowing the mechanisms through which functional facts obtain. To give an account of these mechanisms is, in Cohen's terminology, to provide elaborations, and he identifies two main sorts: purposive and 'Darwinian'. Cohen, however, contends that whilst elaborations are preferable, functional claims can be valid without them. Here, reservations of the kind raised by Hempel can be suggested without endorsing logical empiricism. As one philosopher who admires Cohen and is sympathetic to Marxism has put it: 'I am simply at a loss to see why functional explanation should be of interest over and above the particular mechanisms that may justify it in a given case.'[44] In other words, functional explanations *without* elaborations of any sort give rise to pseudo-explanations. In social science, Jon Elster rightly detects elements of improper functionalism in the 'capital-logic school'. He therefore finds a contradiction in Cohen's argument over functionalism, and a false sense of antithesis between causal and functional explanation.

In fact, Cohen gives a misleading impression of his position. First, he maintains that functional explanations are a species of, not a threat to, causal explanations.[45] Second, besides deeming elaborations *desirable*, he states that the justified grounding of unelaborated functional claims must consist in precise sorts of correlations, and not in general assertions of 'eufunctionality' between factors.[46] In my view, such a criterion *already* amounts to a proto-elaboration or research programme. Cohen is insisting that functional ideas may not be fully confirmed, not that they can be justified when wholly lacking elaboration. For Elster to insist that mechanisms be fully displayed would be unrealistic in the light of how science develops, as Cohen's later discussion of pre-Darwinian biology makes clear.[47]

However, one of his hypothetical illustrations of justified belief in a functional fact is unconvincing. Early entrepreneurs judged without detailed knowledge that expanded scale yields economies, and production was therefore expanded. Their (correct) belief in the functional fact is explained by the fact itself. Yet something else is surely required. Early industrialists may have believed in a god who bid them act as if increased scale would enhance his glory, and who would reward them for their service to him through the industrial process. The functional fact explains why the belief is correct only if it can be filled out in terms of the causal mechanisms that make it material processes, and not god's grace, that so bestows rewards. My inclination is to return to Nagel here: though . . . 'functional analyses are illuminating and valuable, they cannot be rightly regarded as illustrating a distinctive theoretical approach in the study of human affairs'.[48]

In the purposive elaboration of 'ideology', Cohen emphasizes the importance of a conspiracy theory involving ruling class motives. This is a welcome reminder that people, as well as structures, must be held responsible for an exploitative society. But the conscious propagation of ideology is well-founded only if certain ideas do indeed have the hoped-for effect, *because* they operate in definite ways through certain kinds of processes (education, the media, etc.). In other words, there is no contradiction with Cohen's assertion of the explanatory weight of functional facts. But Cohen has not made it clear enough that these are explanatory only when they can be linked to identifiable causal sequences. We can 'rationally hypothesize functional explanations even when we lack . . . elaborations'[49] only if those elaborations come to be given in due course, and if they satisfactorily specify the mechanisms that render the functional analyses meaningful. Otherwise the hypotheses are *not* rational.

Cohen would not necessarily dispute this. But his position is ambiguous, for two reasons. First, he does not advertise the casual mechanisms that substantiate functional relations in general, because he is reluctant to do so in the case of historical materialism. Cohen seems content to leave the details of class struggle and history to historians of many kinds, establishing only that: 'Functional explanation applies to the long-term *outcome* of class struggle.'[50] In the absence of elaborations, this view confirms the high level of abstraction at which Cohen's theses are pitched. To ask for details of how it is that relations of production function for the forces, or to require the specification of the interaction seems (at least for pre-capitalist cases) to be to question the ultimate usefulness of the theory, if not its truth.

Second, Cohen seems keen to avoid committing either himself or Marxism to a general epistemology or ontology. His tacit refusal to sever causal and functional explanation might suggest an inclination towards realism, for it is typically realists who posit those forms in combination. Rom Harré, for example, has recently reaffirmed the need for both efficient and formal causes in the generative specification of the being *and* properties of things.[51] And as a consequence of a post-Humean view of causality, Maurice Mandelbaum has argued that: 'One cannot maintain the distinction that has sometimes been drawn between "causal laws" and laws that serve to correlate two sets of properties.'[52] Finally, in Dudley Shapere's persuasive account of the features of a scientific 'domain', 'evolutionary' and 'compositional' theories are held to complement one another.[53]

On the other hand, it has been proposed that Cohen's account can be further modified in the direction of a realist framework. In general, causal and functional analysis must be wedded more closely than Cohen seems to allow. Substantively, a strict functional account produces a too-restrictive theory of the primacy of the productive forces. A critic of Marxism like G. C. Homans[54] is answered more appropriately with the modifications than without them. Homans maintains that the concept of 'base and superstructure' in Marxism does not qualify for theoretical status: no specific accounts can be given of *what* the changes in the superstructure might be. In this respect, according to Homans, Marxism resembles functionalism. This charge, however, confuses explanation with prediction: many good theories cannot supply the specifics of future changes. Moreover, it underestimates the extent to which functional explanation *is* explanatory. But it also underestimates the link in Marxism that binds functional explanation to the mechanisms of specific societies, eras, and conjunctures. Functionalism in the sense of reductionism is therefore not implicit in Marxism.

Some Marxist-realists, such as David-Hillel Ruben, have also denied that Marxism can be a general theory of history. The inadequacy of the latter is due to the laboured use of notions like 'production in general'. In his view, there cannot be general laws across modes of production. There are indeed good grounds for this sort of concern, and for the belief that 'for Marx, generality and explanatory force run in opposite directions'.[55] Yet several points count against Ruben's position. He writes that Marxism, conceived 'realistically', explains by means of laws of tendency relating to complex individuals. It does not involve generalizations from empirical cases. But this protest is *insufficiently* realist. History itself can be seen as a (complex) individual as much as a 'society'. Both angles require explanation in terms of fundamental tendencies, and not simply in terms of empirical appearances. 'Laws' are not confined to one level of generality beyond which lies pure speculation. For example, persons are complex individuals whose social combination can be expressed in law-like form without damage to their complex individuality. Societies too can be theoretically gathered into modes of production. It is quite arbitrary to draw the line at that: the different modes of production may display long-term tendencies, which can be expressed as historical laws. Moreover, Cohen has showed that functional explanation in general (not just Marxist) relates to nomic necessity in whatever way causal laws do.

Ruben's criticisms are thus invalid. But his concern is apposite. For though laws (or theories) are compatible and related at different levels of generality, the encroachment of one set on another's territory may be illegitimate 'reductionism' in some cases. And reductionism is indeed always a possibility in explications of Marxism that rely heavily on the functional side of its propositions. Thus the 'laws' of history relating to the social employment of productive power might (wrongly) be thought to exhaust the explanatory issues raised by each of its component individuals, the modes of production. There are enough instances of Marxists' conjuring difficulties away with the magic wand of 'development of the forces of production' to require that the possibility of reductionism be taken seriously.

But reductionism is not unique to historical materialism. Geographical explanation might (wrongly) reduce questions about *social* development. Social explanation might (wrongly) reduce *individual* behaviour. There is also reduction in an 'upward' direction ('expansionism' might be the typical fallacy here). For example, the laws and tendencies of individual behaviour or psychoanalytic processes might (wrongly) be thought to render unnecessary or impossible theories about the tendencies generated by the *social* interaction of people. The boundaries may be difficult to draw in certain cases (hence the 'debate' between Marxism and psychoanalysis), and precise theoretical and substantive work is always required. But that is not to deny that laws of different kinds *and* different levels express, at their own level, important relationships.

In an important statement of Marxism, Engels said that Marx's two fundamental contributions were the materialist conception of history and the theory of capitalist development.[56] If Ruben's argument were accepted, the first would dissolve into the second. In some versions of 'the productive forces' approach, the second is simply deducible from the first. G. A. Cohen presents a version of the first that bears on the second and avoids reductionism, but gives rise to reservations about its force. Engels is right to make a distinction between the two aspects of Marx's theoretical interests. Historical materialism might well apply even if the theory of value and surplus-value were wrong.[57] This violates no protocol of realism, or Marxism, because there may be rival explanations that are similar in formulation, have a common focus, and share ground in the principles of the higher theory, yet differ about the key mechanisms of capitalist production. In this sense, Cohen is correct to say that the theory of history functionally explains societies and 'modes of production' whilst leaving their mechanisms 'relatively autonomous'. But the modification, or change of emphasis, I have proposed here seems equally important: the general theory is acceptable only if, by reference to the mechanisms postulated by lower-level theories, it can be seen to operate tendentially. Here Cohen's silence on the question of an epistemology suitable for Marxism limits the productiveness of this contention: a realist outlook is essential for historical materialists.

My footnote on value and the separation of historical materialism from the theory of capitalism might be thought to undermine the centrality of socialist politics for Marxists. But this is not quite so. The separation is relative in the sense that *some* formulations of capitalist mechanisms (or those of other modes) must be entailed by the general formulas. And since Marxism deals with developmental tendencies, capitalism can be seen as being in certain respects 'more important' than, say, primitive communism. However, it is also true that the indisputably crucial moral and political reasons for which Marxists analyse capitalism are not directly entailed by historical materialism. The view that socialist politics need not be endorsed by the proponent of historical materialism should not be seen as a Hilferding-style 'bourgeois' outrage. Belief in the need for and desirability of socialism can be justified by theoretical and moral considerations. But socialism cannot be shown to be necessary, nor can Marxism be adopted as a theoretical framework, *just* because it seems to support socialist politics. Only in reductionist theory and dogmatic politics could the connection between history and socialism be considered theoretically guaranteed.

Given this relative separation, historical materialism might be too general to have a *decisive* bearing on theories of particular modes, because the workings of the particular mechanisms will show whether and to what extent the general 'laws' of history hold. In the light of this claim, the principles of historical materialism are not those of history as against modes of production, or of modes of production as against history. They are historical only insofar as they can be causally elaborated for specific epochs, and such elaborations are *of* more general relationships, which can be expressed as functions.

From this standpoint, the most important principle is: 'The mode of production of material life determines the general character of the social, political, and spiritual processes of life.'[58] Mode of production is taken here as the socially structured utilization of nature, technique, and scientific knowledge. In other words, forces and relations are 'combined'. The attractiveness of the principle lies in that very combination, together with the determinate, but not determinist, character of the historical correlations it entails. This double-sided conception of historical materialism is crucial if the latter is not to founder on the reefs of empiricism or reductionism. Empiricism allows only particularity and contingency in history, and reductionism occurs when phenomena are ascribed a logical essence that all but eliminates their other attributes. This essence is expressed either positivistically in terms of universal laws that cases then 'confirm', or in terms of functional relationships upheld without reference to empirical complications.

In fact, reductionism is a danger in historical materialism rather than in a species of it. To guard against it we may adopt the realist principle that the different levels and modalities of being are accommodated in science at different levels of abstraction.[59] We saw earlier how this principle was implicit in some statements of Marx, and its importance for historiography lies in its recognition that long-term outcomes must square with more particular mechanisms. These lower-level phenomena (class struggle, politics, historical 'accidents', individual careers) have conditions of existence that mediate the broader processes expressed at a higher level of abstraction.

The notion of the 'relative autonomy' of superstructures can thus be endorsed: the base strongly limits,[60] or determines, the superstructure, but the latter causally affects its material conditions, according to variations generally compatible with structural constraints. In cases of large-scale social transformations, long-term structural dislocations coincide with more immediate causal and purposive conditions of social change.[61] Hence the impact of non-basic factors is relatively more autonomous in some sets of conditions than in others. Historical materialism will thus appear more or less convincing according to *both* its theoretical power when compared to rival accounts, and its resourcefulness in the face of particular empirical circumstances. The proverbial idea that historical materialism is a 'guide to study', or a research programme, rather than 'some universally compulsory philosophical scheme of history' (Lenin) is therefore also correct.

Yet it is not *just* a guide, in the sense of a content-less methodology, model, or heuristic. True, the Marxist theory is often associated with particular models, especially 'base-and-superstructure'. That model is sometimes damagingly restrictive, and whilst it does capture something important (functional dependence), it encourages little imagination in particular analysis. But while models are necessary to theory-formation and argument, the realist perspective enables us to say that the principles of a theory, in its 'mature' expression, can be stated in terms independent of even the most closely associated model. The theory itself indicates the limitations, as well as the advantages of particular models. So historical materialism *is* a guide to study, but it guides according to substantive theoretical propositions, not 'methodologically'.

4

Realism and Philosophy
of History

The first three chapters have argued that historical materialism, broadly
conceived, relies on no specifically Marxist philosophy for its justification.
But this does not mean, as some Marxists have supposed, that epistemological issues are irrelevant. It may also be that there is no single definitive
'realist' epistemology, and that Marxism has little bearing on the detailed
ontological issues over which realist philosphers contend. But the explanatory structure of historical materialism requires that functional and causal
explanation support each other, and that the combination be epistemologically legitimate. A (scientific) realist conception of theory seems to provide
criteria of validation appropriate to Marxist theories (amongst others).
There is, therefore, a firm connection between Marxist historiography and
realism.

Philosophy of history is the field that typically deals in connections
between epistemologies and historiographical practice. My general case is
that philosophers of history are insufficiently realist in orientation. Were
they to become more realistically inclined, they would have to engage, as
part of their calling, in more substantive debate. And Marxism, as historical theory with realist premises, would have to be revaluated in spite of
the almost institutionalized doubts about it that affect even fair-minded
analytic philosophers.

It is, however, neither easy nor desirable to make this case in an over-
simple way, for example, by accusing philosophers of science and history
of being irrevocably 'bourgeois' and 'empiricst'. Philosophy of history is
an interesting and heterogeneous field, and various positions within it
require close attention if the pertinence of Marxism is to be made plain.
Presentation is further complicated by the claim that the dominant ideas in
philosophy of history 'lag' behind those in philosophy of science. A systematic realism is only now coming onto the agenda in historiographical
thinking. In philosophy of science, by contrast, various quite developed

post-empiricisms contend. Although realism has emerged from the ruins of the positivist-relativist debate, it is useful to consider some of the key moments of those earlier controversies, for their equivalents in philosophy of *history* remain important. I will argue, for example, that the 'new idealism' in the latter domain, best represented by Hayden White, is 'Feyerabendian' in character, and can be admired and criticized in much the same way as Feyerabend's stance in philosophy of science.

At the same time, differences between the two areas should be appreciated. 'Narrativist' philosophers, for instance, have been popular amongst practising historians, partly because they try to avoid 'scientist' analogies. In my view, narrativism signally fails to avoid general philosophical commitment, but it does illustrate how respect for the particularity of historical analysis engenders a number of relatively independent issues. One reason why Marxists should beware of excessively schematic critiques of orthodox philosophy is that (as Bhaskar has pointed out[1]) debates *within* Marxism have traditionally, if oddly, corresponded to the polarity between positivism and 'humanism' that has marked Western culture as a whole, and philosophy in particular.

1. Positivism and Anti-Positivism in Philosophy of History

That polarity, as it affects history, can be presented roughly as follows. The standard positivistic argument is that genuinely scientific knowledge consists in being able to explain and predict phenomena by bringing them under universal laws. This is achieved when, given a true statement that appropriate empirical conditions obtain, the phenomena is logically deducible from the law. For example, if all projectiles of a certain constitution and velocity collide at time t with stationary objects s, and if my delivery is a case in point, then it follows with logical necessity that the stumps will be spreadeagled. Unless, that is, the batsman's timing is good. But here the law doesn't apply, since part of what is meant by appropriate conditions is that other things remain equal (the 'ceteris paribus' clause). If historical explanation is to be scientific, on this view, its explanations must have that logical shape.

However, even the neo-positivists, or logical empiricists, realized that this model did not quite fit historical explanation. For one thing, history seldom, if ever, exhibits cases in which such a confident general law can be invoked. Rather, at best, its typical arguments concern particular cases that resemble similar kinds of cases, but none quite the same as the others. Thus we can speak of Archduke Ferdinand's assassination in the light of what we know about other assassinations, and about human beings when confronted with pressures and responsibilities of some kind. But there are no strict laws here. Carl G. Hempel, the foremost proponent of the covering-law model, was aware that history did not quite square with the natural-science paradigm in this respect. He argued that history provided 'explanation sketches' rather than logically rounded explanations. This, he said, did not diminish history; it registered empirical complexity.[2]

W. H. Dray's work, especially, set out the 'reactionist' critique and alternative to covering-law models.[3] The main idea here is that if the covering-law model does not adequately apply to history, then the model and not historical explanation should be jettisoned. Certainly, Hempel's criteria, even with the best will in the world, seemed to render history a poor thinker's science. In key historical cases, Dray and others claim, there is simply no covering-law to invoke. In others, a law may be invoked (for example, 'power corrupts'), but may not help in accounting for *this* case (Hitler, for example), or may even have this case as its sole instance (for example, power corrupts in this modern German fascist leadership). Dray maintains that in such cases reference to 'laws' is downright misleading. The logic of historical explanation is neither causal in content nor deductive in form. Rather, for Dray, the investment of human meanings or reasons in particular actions alone enables us to understand the past. This may not constitute scientific explanation, but it is quite adequate for understanding history; indeed, history could not be grasped otherwise.

The debate between covering-law theorists and reactionists has dominated academic philosophy of history for some time. Now, while there have been some notable developments of the dialogue recently, as we shall see, the issues here posed remain fundamental. In fact, despite the logical competence that characterizes the two sides (especially Hempel's logical empiricism), the issues can be seen to form perennial dilemmas. Is history a science, or is it *sui generis*? Does it concern causal explanation or 'internal' understanding? These questions have divided thinkers since (at least) Descartes and Vico. They have stimulated debates in academic history (Bury v. Acton), sociology (Durkheim v. Weber), and philosophical consideration of the human sciences as a whole (positivists v. neo-Kantians). The arguments have been weak and strong on both sides, and militant or gentle within each camp. But there does seem to be a deep chasm, over which the contending sides swap definitions of 'science', 'history', and 'explanation'.

That scenario provides an apt description of the way problems of science and history are often treated. It does not seem to me, however, that the divide is unbridgeable. It is by now customary for realists to point out that the polarities between 'meaning' and 'cause', understanding and explanation, particular and general (or universal), seem tenable only because humanists tend to agree with the positivist account of *natural* science. But this realist criticism is nonetheless valuable, and its recent popularity is to be welcomed. In what follows, I shall take up the realist standpoint in general.

Three instances of humanists' retaining empiricist norms may be briefly noted.

1. Dray concludes from the debate with Hempel that history cannot be scientific since it is not amenable to covering-law treatment. Part of the reason for this is that Dray, in the empiricist tradition, links causality to temporal and regular events, whereas human action is logically connected to the reasons people can give for action. As we shall see, however, this is to confuse explanation with justification.

2. Wilhelm Windelband's famous distinction between nomothetic and ideographic science (natural and historical, respectively) registers the same conclusion. There is an interesting discussion of the neo-Kantians in R. G. Collingwood's *Idea of History*.[4] Collingwood explains how Heinrich Rickert regarded the sciences as a *spectrum* of abstraction (including history) rather than two different modes of reasoning. Science, as a whole, was counterposed to the particulars of reality. So 'two realities' could not be asserted. Collingwood notes, however, that this argument of Rickert's does no justice to the systematic character of natural science, and it retains a conception of history as disjointed facts extrinsic to the historical mind. 'Thus, in the long run, positivism has its revenge on Rickert'.[5]

3. A final example from a third philosophical 'school' (phenomenology) may reinforce the general point. Alfred Shutz argued that causal explanation (the key feature of natural science) is only a special case of meaning-adequacy (which characterizes human understanding as a whole). But his account of causality is, ironically, exactly what we might expect from a die-hard Humean: 'A sequence of events is causally adequate to the degree that experience teaches us it will probably happen again.'[6]

It can be seen—without directly invoking realism—that there is something strange in the oscillation between impasse and compromise that marks these debates. In 'The Historical Explanation of Actions Reconsidered', Dray allows that there is more than one sense of 'cause', and so there *can* be generalization in history. Moreover, he seems to have ceded Hempel's rejoinder that to invoke reasons as the key to understanding actions is to allow the need for 'laws' stipulating that people act rationally in appropriate situations. Hempel, for his part, clings to the neo-positivist norm while acknowledging that many examples current in science and history either fail to fit or demand modification of the model. In their more generous moments, Hempel and Dray *do* compromise: 'Explanation is not a logical term but a pragmatic one.'[7] And: 'Explanation is a relative or pragmatic term.'[8] Actually, it is not difficult to cite examples of frequent 'compromises' of this kind in the work of writers often held up as paradigms of one side or another. I would not claim to have understood everything Wilhelm Dilthey wrote, but part of his 'hermeneutic' method would seem to be the following. *Any* kind of human communication is understood in terms of the necessary interaction between whole and part, content and form, meaning and purpose. Science and history are thus distinct, yet are both part of a larger body of meanings that is constitutively *human*, not just natural. Now obviously this involves asserting the 'priority' of human understanding over science. But this need not, suitably elaborated, involve any difficulties. Scientists and philosophers (Einstein, Popper, Feyerabend) have often made such claims. Neither does it prevent Dilthey from regarding knowledge—'human' or 'scientific'—as processes of abstraction involving induction, 'objective' causality, or even the construction of empirical regularities.[9]

Otto Neurath was an idiosyncratic positivist, the Marxist of the Vienna Circle. But despite his part in the attempt of that group to construct a universal physicalist language for science,[10] Neurath held to a conception of explanation in history that was largely retrodictive and situational. Like Karl Popper, he did not feel that the necessary 'correction' of *verstehen* methods rules out the importance of either human agency in history, or the reliance on a certain cultural conventionalism in science.[11]

These examples may not be conclusive or elaborate enough to challenge the basis of the logical disagreements between positivists and humanists. However, they do suggest that the 'debate' becomes stilted when considered from the point of view of an empiricist account of science. If a realist position offers a more satisfactory overview of the issues concerning *historical* explanation, it does so at least in part because it presents an account of *science* different from that shared by many humanists and positivists. We may therefore attempt a reading of recent developments in philosophy of science. Indeed, philosophy of history has begun to shake off the constraints of positivist canon because philosophy of science itself has opened up very considerably.

2. Some Developments in Philosophy of Science

According to neo-positivism, science consists broadly of the following elements. Scientific laws are universal statements from which the occurrence of phenomena can be deduced, given appropriate circumstances. Scientific *theories* are formalized systems in which theoretical terms are assigned meaning (or 'interpreted') by being related to statements about empirical data. The data is itself irreducible: ultimately, it is explicable only in observational terms. Scientific explanation thus accounts for empirically perceptible events by producing a scientific law, or system of laws. However, the laws themselves are logical calculi or axioms derived from experienced empirical regularities.

This view of science concerns itself with the structure or logic of valid scientific explanation. Consequently, theories will accord with it only if they are 'mature' and well corroborated in the requisite sense. In other words, it is a philosophical account of the logic of science, and as such, prescribes what valid explanation should be, and not just (if at all) what science is. (We can therefore see why Hempel's thesis must inevitably regard historical explanation as somewhat inferior to physics.)

Frederick Suppe[12] has sketched the nature, and decline, of this 'Received View' in closer detail. His account, however, underemphasizes Popper's contribution to that decline. More than most philosophers of science, Popper took up questions of social and historical explanation as well, so it is appropriate to recall his critique.[13]

Popper dissented from positivism on two related counts. First, he disagreed with the implication of the Received View that scientific theories were confirmed by empirical data or evidence. If theories are logical deductions, then no amount of empirical confirmations can ever properly establish the validity of a theory. Rather, cases that *falsify* a theory are much more productive, since a falsification challenges our knowledge and demands to be accounted for by more adequate theories. But, second, this protest involves a critique of the positivist conception of the essence of science. Rather than press theories into a mould of *validation* and be concerned only with logical systematicity, Popper maintained that the business of science is *discovery*, since empirical falsifications demand superior accounts of what natural processes *are*. Consequently, the job of philosophy is to provide a logic of discovery within which the changing content of science can be expressed. And the positivist obsession with logical structure and validation tells us little about this.

Popper's theses, important as they are, can be seen to be part of a transitional phase in the philosophy of science. He broke with positivism because its rigid schemas accounted neither for the complexity of real processes in nature nor for real progress in science. But his own account retained faith in the relation between regularities and single empirical instances as the key to the logic of science. Consequently, he stuck to a 'naive realism', probably better described as 'complex empiricism'.[14]

T. S. Kuhn, Imre Lakatos, and Paul Feyerabend have pushed Popper's falsificationism to its logical conclusions, and in so doing have generated some additional problems about relativism. Since these debates are relatively well known,[15] it will suffice to enumerate the key questions posed by 'conventionalist' or '*Weltanshauung*' positions.[16] The latter are characterized by their insistence (following Popper) that science itself is a historical practice, conducted by groups of people in cultural and social circumstances. Positivism, in this context, fundamentally distorts science by undermining discovery, the gamble entailed in theoretical construction, and the penetration of ideology into 'pure' science.

From the myriad crucial points raised by this perspective—itself something of a 'gestalt switch' in philosophy—Popper's position appears no more than a temporary breathing space. For Popper, at least initially, one empirical falsification was enough to refute a theory. But this is still to rely on the integrity of isolated, sensory 'facts', and to continue to insist that science can be expressed in terms of their centrality. Who is to decide what is a decisive counter-instance? Could there even be one such instance whose significance fell outside the terms of the theory? Three versions of the challenge to positivism can be briefly resumed, in order to show how the critique carries consequences of a 'relativist' or even 'idealist' sort.

N. R. Hanson[17] argues that even perception is theory-laden, so that in key respects Kepler and Tycho Brahe, for instance, could not see the *same* thing (i.e. the sun) in the east at dawn. In addition, Hanson revives the notion that retrodiction, not prediction, is the key to scientific inference, and that this could be accomplished in a number of ways. Since no clear relation between 'data' and scientific theory can be established, Hanson asserts that science is simultaneously creative and closely inter-woven with 'background assumptions'. These enter scientific theory largely through the kinds of models employed. Positivism ignores the fundamental and indispensable character of models and analogies to the construction—and logic—of scientific theory.

We can agree with Hanson that 'all observation involves "seeing that"',[18] and this is a cognitive or interpretative process. But we need not conclude that 'seeing that' is in all respects a theory-relative affair. Indeed, Hanson's account of retrodiction begins with the supposition 'some surprising, astonishing phenomena P1, P2, P3 . . . are encountered'.[19] A theory—'a cluster of conclusions in search of a premiss'[20]—is then constructed retrodictively around those phenomena. But unless the phenomena display some interesting features that are not yet theory-laden—that is, that are considered to be *real* (the point does not entail sense-datum assumptions)—then why should we want to engage in theory-construction at all?

The importance of the background assumptions of scientists is crucial for Kuhn.[21] He proposes that significant changes in science are changes that mark not just one theory, but a whole 'paradigm', that is, the dominant assumptions, problems, and analogies implicit in science at any one time. Kuhn's radical intervention shows that science is intrinsically *discontinuous* according to his paradigm-change account. This view undermines one basis for Popper's and others' (e.g. Stephen Toulmin's) critique of positivism, namely that science is cumulative and 'objective' without being a strictly logical or observational process. In addition, Kuhn also seems to undermine *philosophy*; if the explanation of the decisions of scientists to ascribe a certain paradigmatic value to theories and experiments is not, after all, about theories in isolation, then the move from a 'logic of science' to socio-psychological *history* is itself a clean logical inference.

Imre Lakatos and others have shown that Kuhn's position relies on a prescriptive distinction between normal and revolutionary science. His claims have been challenged in turn by Feyerabend, who argues that key historical cases are not Kuhnian. In addition, Kuhn's own restatement of paradigm shifts in terms of exemplars and disciplinary matrices is less overtly ambiguous than the fruitful but vague 'paradigm'.[22] The more radically subjective and non-cumulative implications of Kuhn's earlier views have thus been considerably softened. Lakatos was particularly worried, from a philosophical point of view, about Kuhn's 'mob psychology'. Lakatos's own account of research programmes[23] is thus intended to be something of an umbrella for elements of rationalism, empiricism, and conventionalism. The real unit of science, for Lakatos, is not a single theory, but a research programme, the 'negative heuristic' of which is a core of assumptions that render it 'irrefutable'. The 'positive heuristic' is the elaboration of that core in a flexible empirical and theoretical manner. Thus the core is *agreed* to be irrefutable, but contains indispensable notions of empirical corroboration and theoretical power. It is in terms of this complex of factors that research programmes come to be adopted or replaced.

However sensible this option of Lakatos's may be—it is a gentlemen's agreement rather than mob psychology—it is open to the ruthless criticisms duly provided by Feyerabend. The hard core of the programme, for example, is the product of a mere decision, so the logical problem of theory incommensurability is not resolved. Moreover, 'crucial' facts are said to be established, in Lakatos's account, only 'with hindsight'.[24] Indeed, since the multiplicity of patterns of explanation and discovery has no necessary shape either, the choice of theory remains, logically, arbitrary.

Feyerabend, notoriously, opts for anarchy rather than Lakatos's amiable community of philosophers.[25] He stresses that, if anarchism ('anything goes') is adopted in science, the multiplicity, incommensurability, and arbitrariness of science—so damaging to the rationalist Popperian accounts—become its principal virtues. They demonstrate the creativity of science and the primacy of human imagination; and they direct attention to questions about the human purposes of science.[26]

Despite the value of Feyerabend's critique and alternative, it does not resolve some of the key problems. To begin with, his anarchism is epistemological, not literal. It is the *attitude* of 'anything goes' that is important in science, the plea for tolerance in matters epistemological. But a liberal permissiveness is not a claim that anything *does* go in science. And if anarchism is an epistemological doctrine, then it too ascribes an essential structure to the form of science: other accounts are ruled out according to the protocol of necessary anarchy or divergence. It is not clear, then, that Feyerabend does abolish criteria for the rational assessment of apparently incommensurable theories, though such criteria will not be 'pure'. That his strategy is that of a devil's advocate is indicated in his reply to a somewhat hamfisted Marxist critique[27] alleging that Feyerabend has sunk into radical subjectivism. His response is to point out that, knowing this full well, he intended only that empiricism be seen to have arrived at its proper destination: irrationalism.[28]

I have suggested some points at which *Weltanshauung* approaches may be faulted. The axis of a realist critique in this respect is that, as Dudley Shapere puts it, the relativist revolution was not so much to reject the positivist distinction between theory and observation as to invert its terms.[29] This inversion leads to the kind of subjectivism exemplified by Hanson's assertion that 'causes are connected with effects, but this is because our theories connected them, not because the world is held together by cosmic glue'.[30] The realist response to empiricism and conventionalism is that 'sticking together' appears artificial only to those who (absurdly) presume that the world consists of discrete bits that can be fused only by the superordinate powers of the human mind. The logical inseparability of observational and theoretical terms is not the same as their dissolution into the imagination. Both macro- and micro-entities (for example, tables and atoms) can be adequately attested to exist, and both can figure as theoretical terms in explanatory statements.

Realism asserts that the world consists of structured processes of different kinds, which manifest themselves as tendencies. Consequently, theory is indispensable if natural structures are to be inferred from empirical phenomena. But the relations posited by realism identify empirical effects and conditions. There is no question that the relations held to exist are constructed by science, and that the theories that identify them are only instrumental.

However, it may be that the new realists lack a common programme. After all, realism need be no more than the fairly modest view that 'idealism is unacceptable, that science is concerned with a common world'.[31] It is therefore worth citing some of the related problems within post-empiricism. First, is realism a purely philosophical doctrine? The frequent claim that realism cannot be proved, and so is metaphysical, is answered by Bhaskar. Given that science is possible, he argues, it must be so in virtue of the structured, enduring character of objects and relations. This, however, is less a 'proof' than an explication of the over-arching hypothesis that science provides good reasons for the truth of realism. Ruben has said that Bhaskar must take realism to be the *only possible* account of science in order to reach his transcendental conclusion, and this claim, says Ruben, is in important respects circular. Hilary Putnam, by contrast, allows that realism holds if the connectives in Alfred Tarski's famous definition of truth ('*x* is *y*' if and only if *x* is *y*) are realistically interpreted. So it must be *possible* to interpret them otherwise; but, Putnam reasonably asks, given our knowledge of science, 'how could we not interpret them realistically?'[32] In consequence, Putnam maintains that realism is an over-arching scientific hypothesis.[33]

Second, what is the nature of scientific theory? Shapere has said, 'There is today no completely—one is almost tempted to say remotely—satisfactory analysis of the notion of a scientific theory'.[34] His own fruitful proposal is that science is a domain in which both data and theory appear, successively, as series of problems, research programmes, and general frameworks. This respects the 'transitive' dimension of science, but maintains a realist notion of the intransitive.[35] But exactly how theories illuminate the world, and what form they must take, is an open question. Many writers now agree that the role of 'models' is central to theory but is not identical to it. And Marx W. Wartofsky, for one, has proposed, in the name of 'immodest' realism, a 'continuum among the meanest linguistic expressions and the grandest theoretical constructs of science'.[36]

Third, is realism ontological? Milton Fisk, for example, has elaborated a physical and 'essentialist' ontology,[37] whereas Mary Hesse believes that a realism based on an epistemology of models and matrices 'has negative implications for universal ontology and cosmology'.[38] Amongst realists, then, agreement has been reached to reject the 'evasion' of ontology, but the ontological 'postponement',[39] advocated most openly in this century by Rudolf Carnap, still has a following, even within realism. These lingering problems do not mean that the eternal opposition between idealism and materialism has not been substantially mitigated. But it has not been eliminated either.

3. Obstacles to Historical Realism

Philosophy of history is not yet in the happy position of disputing which version of historical realism is appropriate. But we can expect some of these problems to enter historical thinking as the obstacles to historical realism are gradually overcome. In my view, two main problems can be identified. First, what might be termed 'compromises' with empiricism exercise considerable influence. In the human sciences G. H. von Wright's views along these lines have been influential. Morton White's bringing together of positivist and 'reactionist' concerns has played a similar role in philosophy of history. Second, philosophers of history have tried to identify the *autonomy* of historical thinking in the narrative procedures that are held to delineate the historian's craft.

A compromise, of course, is often an advance, and White's and von Wright's contributions have significantly eased the rigid division between positivism and humanism. Von Wright reaffirms, against positivism, that lawfulness is a matter of *necessity* and not universality.[40] Laws do indeed apply to nature, but there are various mixtures of causal and teleological explanations. Also, von Wright maintains, the very notion of causal necessity arises from our ability to intervene in nature, to know how to produce an effect. Causes are not agencies in this sense, but our confidence in them springs from knowledge of our own capacities *as* agents.

On this basis, von Wright offers a solution to the vexed question of whether the relation between reasons and action is logical or causal. He argues that wants and desires have a causal effect on our behaviour, but that it does not follow that our reasons for action are causally related. Here the humanists (Dray, Peter Winch, A. I. Melden, *et al.*) would agree. But the conceptual link between premises and conclusion in a practical inference, von Wright argues, has not been properly conceived by those writers. He asserts that the logical connection between intention and behaviour lies in the intrinsic interdependence of the *verification* of the premises and the conclusion. The connection, however, is *not* one of logical deduction: action cannot be deduced from reasons or intention. Thus does von Wright establish his synthesis.

The import of von Wright's argument as applied to history is that understanding and explanation are not the same thing. In historical writing, causal and teleological modes intermingle. But causal analysis remains only *indirectly* relevant,[41] because it is significant only inasmuch as it shows the causes, or effects, of *human* action. So *typical* historical explanations are only 'quasi-causal': they do not require covering-laws, because they emerge through a series of practical reasonings (the teleological aspect).

There can be no denying the strength of von Wright's contribution. Yet it is not a genuine synthesis. At the general level, it does not seem to follow from the fact that we come to have *confidence* in causality as a result of human agency that our conception of causality depends on an analogy with human action. Von Wright's anthropomorphic account implies that it does. He transfers a fact about our *belief* in causality to the sphere of causality itself. He says, in turn, that causality operates outside the human sphere, but that we must think of it under the aspect of (possible) action. The force of the 'must' here is unclear. If it is a logical 'must', then objective causality is ruled out. If, on the other hand, it is psychological or epistemic, then anthropomorphism is not logically entailed. Similarly, von Wright says that no proof can be given as to whether action or causation is the more basic concept, yet he immediately votes for action, since it is, he thinks, contradictory to conceive of agency as wholly bound up in causal nets. As it stands, this flatly contradicts the claim that there is no proof of the primacy of causality or of agency. His own choice is therefore arbitrary, related to his strong (but unconvincing) aversion to determinism.[42]

The effect on history is that causal processes must be seen as separate from and logically secondary to matters of human agency. But it is only because von Wright has not broken decisively with the Humean view of causation that this is so. For those who cling to the latter, social structures tend to appear as merely 'external' determinants on the free decisions of individual agents. There is no need to take this view; von Wright's entire discussion is about whether the *Humean* conception of reasons-as-causes applies or not. Whatever his criticisms of idealism, von Wright places himself firmly in the humanist camp by answering this question without posing others.

Many of these questions were broached in White's *The Foundations of Historical Knowledge*.[43] There he argued, against Dray, that while reasons are not causally related to actions, the *historian* could provide a causal account of the relation between reasoning and historical activity. On a related question, White defends the idea that laws can account for historical *particulars* (for example, 'Whenever John eats spinach, he gets a rash'). Moreover, a *single* statement that is not itself a law can be properly explanatory if reasons for the *existence* of a generalization might be given (even though we do not *know* the generalization).

In historical thinking, then, causal analysis can be maintained. But since historical statements are usually about particular cases, and since reasons for action often do count as causes, there is considerable flexibility in White's notion of causal explanation. He goes on to characterize 'the cause' as 'that which makes a difference' to a situation. But the *relevant* difference, and therefore notions of *the* cause, is a matter relative to the kind of questions and values the historian has in mind. White's account thus welds together a law-like conception of causality, the importance of human reasons for action, and the idea that the historian is the interested constructor of significant narratives (the value angle providing a synthetic vantage point for a series of explanatory singular statements). White, like von Wright, extirpates the excesses of the reactionists while maintaining the view that historical, unlike scientific, explanation is essentially human and value-oriented. Some objections can be lodged against White's arguments. First, the notion of a generalization whose existence can be reasoned but which need not be adduced is problematical. Murray G. Murphey has urged that, because White does not accept probabilistic 'scale-downs' of covering-laws, the only way a reason for the existence of a law would count as a *good* one would be if the law was actually exhibited.[44] And until it is, observation will always disconfirm the alleged law. Leon Pompa has remarked that arguments are *adduced*; they do not, strictly, exist.[45] Yet White says that historians do *not* usually adduce that kind of generalization. In any case, if a law *can* be adduced, why is it not? White provides no clear way to refute these criticisms.

That White is only partially convinced that causality applies to history is confirmed by his comments on historians' values and their essentially narrative explanations. The existential gap between historians' grounds and the relevant causal laws finds a parallel when he argues that causal explanation is a product, largely, of what interests historians. In fact, here there is *no* conception of cause as 'what makes a difference', since the full clause must surely read: 'what makes a difference from a particular point of view or set of interests'. This contradiction in White's position arises from his desire to reconcile positivism with the fact that, as he sees it, historians select 'charter facts' according to their personal values. Other narrativists have maintained that the second belief undermines positivism entirely.

Narrativism has earned appreciation for philosophers amongst historians, because it seems to respect what historians actually do, rather than impose an alien conception of scientific adequacy on them. Thus Leonard Krieger has said that W. H. Dray is the 'historians' philosopher' because 'what he wants is precisely the particularity of the action'.[46] And recently Lawrence Stone has made out a defence of narrative close to (if less rigorous than) those of the narrativist philosphers in the 1960s.[47]

The concept of narrative intuitively appeals to historians for various reasons. It seems to capture the particular and factual qualities of history as against the universality and theoreticism of science. Being a story-telling form, narrative also emphasizes the essentially human character of history, its concern for central subjects and their reasons for action, rather than the apersonal forces that drive them on. Accurate portrayal of temporal sequences is necessary in history, and a penchant for 'timeless' generalizations is felt to be inappropriate. Finally, narrative allows room for literary style in a way prohibited by the arid propositions of sociology or physics.

Obviously, there are elements of caricature in this picture. Under pressure, narrativists would qualify some of these points. But this model of the working historian has impressed itself upon philosphers and historians alike. From W. G. Gallie to Lawrence Stone, the idea of the historian as a common-sensical story-teller fearful of analysis is remarkably potent.

It is, indeed, a highly prescriptive persona, one whose credibility depends upon the 'obviousness' of empiricist norms. But its propositions are not all obviously true. For example, stories may be sequential, but need pay no attention to *chronology*. Similarly, the particulars of a narrative can be of many kinds: people, certainly, but also institutions, towns, economies, ideas, and so forth. Finally, histories contain much more than narratives, and narratives themselves require 'thick description': the presentation of a story as of one kind rather than another. Narratives consequently involve explanation and require argument on a number of different levels if they are to be sustained against rival interpretations. The idea that concern for *types* of phenomena, as opposed to individuals, is inappropriate in history is simply dogma.

The 'factuality' and 'particularity' of narrative is therefore questionable. But the image of science propagated in narrativist common sense is equally misleading. Sequences, particular occurrences, and changes are as much the subject of the natural as of the human sciences. Indeed, empiricists play down the fact that many sciences are in essence *historical*, and in which significant narratives, anomalous particulars, stylistic originality, and theoretical laws can happily consort.[48] To say that science involves the subsumption of particulars under universally valid laws is to invoke the now-discredited 'covering-law' model. Also, the view that human intentions, reasons, and motives cannot be causes and so are unamenable to generalization is questionable. It presupposes the untenable Humean view that causes must be mechanical, logically separate, and temporally distinct from their effects, but that they must be constantly conjoined in empirical observation.

The narrativist platform, then, does not, as is sometimes claimed, avert general epistemological commitment. This can be illustrated by examining W. G. Gallie's version. Gallie's account of narrative in history is directed explicitly against the prominence philosphers have accorded causal explanation. Analysis may enter into narrative historiography, he supposes, but it is parasitic on the main business of story-telling. For Gallie, a story makes sense because it is a 'teleologically guided form of attention'.[49] Its elements are essentially contingent, but it is a *followable* contingency due to the purposes and motives of its individual human protagonists.

Gallie perceives a connection between his model and the general metaphysical choice between nominalism and realism. On the whole, he considers that the deification of abstractions, which he thinks is the characteristic of realism, is 'one of the last infirmities of the human mind'.[50] He thus opts for nominalism, which, while it has its own drawbacks (the idea that those general terms that are allowable pick out individuals), at least gets the nature of narrative right.

It is important to see that this argument is perfectly dogmatic. Gallie characterizes realism so that it cannot be concerned with particulars. And he has already defined 'successful' history as 'essentially' narration, and narration as essentially the stories of particular sentient agents. Methodological individualism is bound to be more appropriate, thus defined. But Gallie's position has the merit of exhibiting the uncomplicated logic behind even the more complicated narrativisms. That is, he holds to a positivistic conception of *natural* science, and a view of human affairs that disallows generalization. This bifurcation is a necessary concomitant of the assumption that the human and natural worlds consist in innumerable discrete events. In the case of science, these are observationally gathered into causal laws, while in social life they are attributed significance as they figure in human-interest stories.

These presuppositions are present, though muted, in the more nuanced stances of Arthur C. Danto, Morton White, or W. H. Dray. Danto and White take narratives to be meaningful and explanatory, since bare chronicle admits of no beginning or end. Historians must construct accounts by selecting 'charter' facts that serve as the basis of causal reasoning within the significant narrative.[51] But as Dray points out,[52] there is no compulsion to see narrative significance as mainly causal at all. Different degrees of plain narrative or chronicle are possible, and White admits that 'causal' attributions are in any case bound up with notions of 'memorability'.[53]

In the face of these loose ends, the long-standing anti-positivism of Dray or W. H. Walsh might seem impressive. In his *Introduction to the Philosophy of History* (1951) Walsh maintained that the historian's way of 'colligating' data into significant narratives always involves a value-laden perception of what constitutes particular historical 'wholes'. Dray, for his part, proposes a 'synthetic unity' principle that might identify an historical whole in terms of a range of criteria, perhaps including causal sequences.[54] But in the absence of any critical rejection of the claims of empiricist theories of science in general, these notions about organizing the data seem more or less arbitrary. At bottom, they share with neo-positivism the view that concepts and theories are heuristic instruments with which to unpack or lard the plain facts. As we saw, this was a component of the Received View, but it was also one of its principal weaknesses.

4. The New Idealism

In philosophy of history, as in philosophy of science, there has been a shift from empiricism to ideas that emphasize the historical and epistemic relativity of the historian's methods. But whilst there are elements of Kuhnian 'gestalt' principles in, say, Dray's synthetic unity model for narrative, that model remains tied to a fairly narrow conception of facts and values, and the verification conditions relevant to historiographical practice. It was only in the 1970s that the full armoury of *Weltanshauung* criteria entered the debates. Today, the notion that criteria of truth or theory-commensurability are difficult, if not impossible, to state in historical work has many adherents. It is true that this attitude encourages important criticisms of empiricism, but its consequences are 'idealist' in the sense that the reality of historical processes becomes shrouded in doubt. If a genuine synthesis in philosophy of history is to be achieved, then the challenge posed by the new idealism must be critically appraised.

According to Roy Bhaskar, the possibility of realism (or naturalism) rests on undercutting the arguments of both humanists and positivists. Science is the explanation and discovery of generative mechanisms in nature and society. Empirical regularities are but (some of) the manifestations of mechanisms that exist, due to the presence of *other* mechanisms, only in the form of *tendencies*. In this account, there can be no difference in principle between natural and social science. However, the *objects* of each science are distinct, because of the mechanisms appropriate to each. Correspondingly, the *methods* of analysis appropriate to one branch may not be suitable for use in another. Bhaskar thus advocates naturalism, but strongly repudiates its customary identification with Humean or positivist norms. The latter are plausible only if the open system of causal process in reality is confused with the artificial or closed systems distinctive of natural-scientific test conditions.

Bhaskar does not deny some of the humanists' claims. The peculiarities of the mechanisms of causality in history or society are indeed those of human agency in relation to 'structural' conditions that are in part created, sustained, and dismantled *as* structures by human action itself. In addition, the self-knowledge distinctive of the human species in social life makes prediction (in the strict sense) impossible, and reasoning about motives necessary. But this is only to say that social science is difficult, being subject to considerations that do not concern natural objects. There are no grounds here for undue scepticism, solipsism, or metaphysical celebrations of human freedom.

Many theorists have put points like these before,[55] which might best be thought of in terms of Marx's memorable dictum that men make history, but not in circumstances of their own choosing. But equations of realism and empiricism are still frequently encountered, or, alternatively, many critiques of empiricism fail to result in an epistemological commitment to realism.

The challenge of one idealist, Leon J. Goldstein,[56] is directed against narrativism, but he misleadingly refers to the empiricism of the narrativists as a species of 'historical realism'. Goldstein states that Gallie *et al.* continue to impose an artificial criterion of 'correspondence to reality' upon historians, without really appreciating the research methods that distinguish historical work. Those procedures, according to Goldstein, exhibit a 'constructionist' account of history: the past is constituted by the agreed principles by which historians illuminate present evidence. However, Goldstein underestimates the idealism already implicit in narrativist assumptions, and whilst he is right to sense a 'correspondence' criterion in narrativism, the correspondence is with the empirical 'facts' rather than with reality.[57]

Goldstein's wider case for constructionism is based on the equation of senses of 'the past' with 'past events', and 'reality' with 'the facts'. Consequently, he is driven to the idea that historical knowing is the very *constitution* of the past through making sense of present evidence. Goldstein blurs the issues here. He argues from the inadequacy of empiricism to the opinion that historical knowledge *qua* constitution is a licit way of knowing. *We* can say, holding no brief for empiricism, that history is licit because it does, like science, involve theoretical procedures that produce knowledge, but still maintain that the real processes of history are not those (simply) of the natural world. Constrained by his equation of realism with empiricism, Goldstein falsely reasons that because evidence is marshalled into theoretical constructs, the past itself is theoretically constructed. Because no body of *evidence* is naturally ordered,[58] Goldstein wrongly concludes that reality (historical or natural) cannot be ordered.

Goldstein shares with the narrativists the view that what counts in philosophy of history is the opinions of the practitioners. This seems misguided, for two reasons. First, it is possible that no simple count of heads, especially over time, could establish the preponderance of Gallian rather than Goldsteinian opinions. In any case, these two attitudes do not exhaust the field. E. J. Hobsbawm[59] has vigorously defended the historian's concern with analysis, and C. Behan McCullagh has shown that the historian's suspicion of neat stories or theories is a necessary part of his or her tendency to argue from incomplete evidence to real complexities.[60] However this may be, it is unnecessarily conservative, and inconsistent with the growth of knowledge as we know it, to rule a priori that the dominant opinions embody the truth. If the kind of practical empiricism sustained by Gallie happened to be the standard common sense amongst historians, it would be the more misleading just because of its orthodoxy.

An interesting case has been made by Louis O. Mink and, especially, by Hayden White that history texts should be treated as what they most manifestly are: literary artefacts. In this view, narrative becomes considerably widened as a category, to refer to the 'imaginative space'[61] that constitutes all historical accounts, even the most apparently factual.[62] Mink's argument is that events exist only under some description, and descriptions belong within rival narrative structures that are mutually exclusive. It is thus the fact or event that is held to be an abstraction from narrative explanations, and not vice versa. Mink concludes from this that truth-claims in history rest upon the pervasive but fallacious myth of 'universal history', that is, the idea that 'there is a determinate historical actuality, the complex referent for all our narratives of "what actually happened", the untold story to which narrative histories approximate'.[63] Mink's consolation that the past is not completely put at risk here, because 'individual statements of fact' are verifiable, seems perversely gestural, given his critique of facticity.

Hayden White offers a full and stimulating account of the modes of 'emplotment' in historical discourse. He identifies four major literary 'tropes' or forms of comprehension and expression that enable the construction of 'different strategies for constituting "reality" in thought'.[64] Each of the modes of emplotment is associated with specific forms of argument, which in turn connect to definite ideological implications. White sets out the most important of these inner connections as follows.[65]

Explanatory Strategies

	Argument		Emplotment		Ideological Implication
Modes of Articulation	Formism	....	Romance	....	Anarchism
	Organicism	....	Comedy	....	Conservatism
	Mechanism	....	Tragedy	....·	Radicalism
	Contextualism	....	Satire	....	Liberalism

The strategies are discursive in the most literal sense: they are 'prefigured' in an aesthetic or poetic preference for one of the tropes of metaphor, metonymy, synecdoche, and irony. Rarely does one historical writer exactly fit the posited literary sequences. For example, Marx, according to White, moves between comic and tragic emplotments, and between mechanistic and organic arguments (though his ideological stance is usually radical).[66]

White does not hold that this unusual and elaborate grid is a logic of history, since the essentially moral and aesthetic grounds by which a discursive framework is adopted is not open to straightforward rational assessment. Thus White's *Metahistory* reveals the discursive tendencies in the work of the nineteenth-century 'master historians', and sets out the sorts of factors in their work that might generate admiration in their readers. Our choice of historian will depend on our preference for one set of 'elective affinities' rather than another, and this is not governed by their truth-content, but is 'a response to the imperatives of the trope'.[67]

White's historiographic landscape completely upsets the norms of analytic philosophy of history. The customary distinction between history and 'philosophy of history' is annulled, and indeed the great speculators rather than the meticulous data-gatherers turn out, according to White, to perceive more clearly the essence of all history writing. This part of White's case is akin to the critique of the theoretical/observational distinction in philosophy of science. Similarly, the elements of contradiction have been shown to have been immanent in the empiricist presuppositions themselves (in this case, narrativism). Moreover, a comparison with Feyerabend suggests itself in the following features of White's account of historical paradigms (apart from the verve and panache with which these writers dismantle their respective orthodoxies).

a. The paradigms are incommensurable gestalts, and their truth or falsehood is not decidable 'on the evidence'.

b. The construction and choice of paradigm is determined by social, moral, and aesthetic considerations.

c. The imaginative core of 'objective' knowledge is laid bare.

d. The state of conceptual anarchy in historiography, which the position entails, is held to be both theoretically appropriate and intellectually emancipatory.[68]

One significant fact renders this analogy imperfect. White, like the narrativists, contrasts science with historiography. The former *is* held to be objective in a way that history can never be. Now this is, I think, a flaw in the metahistorians' account, for White has identified the narrative centre of specific scientific theories (such as Darwin's),[69] and since the critique of empiricist history is based upon considerations about representation in realist discourse generally, there seems no good reason to exclude science from 'fictive discourse'. Such a claim might, however, draw attention to the implausibilities in the metahistorians' view of *history* too.

Several other hesitations within White's argument can be adumbrated. For example, the reason why science is exempted in the constructionist framework of Mink and White is that their idealism is of a Kantian rather than an Absolute sort. That is, 'reality' is not so much non-existent as 'noumenal'—impossible to reveal in itself. Thus, our imagination and conceptual apparatus renders any connection with reality necessarily perspectival. The world is not so much constructed as unidentifiable outside of constructed *accounts*. This Kantian residue explains the life-line offered realism by Mink and White. White continues to hold that one element of 'good' history is its factual content, and that history is not reducible either to ideology or to poetry.[70]

However, these admissions, though common-sensical, are damaging to the more exciting metahistorical theses. For they prise open the logical space between the idea that historical writing takes place in discursive modes that can be interestingly examined as such, and the claim that discursivity is the *essence* of history, and that the question of its truth does not arise.

The hesitation in the metahistorical picture can be illustrated in another way. White has to allow that his abstention from judging historians in terms of truth or correctness is itself a form of the 'ironic' consciousness.[71] He acknowledges that if irony is only one of the possible prefigurative modes, then it may not be the most useful. Indeed, White's hankering after a return to historiography's 'Golden Age' in the nineteenth century is a *romantic* aspiration. The noble vision of a reunification of the scientific, philosophical, and literary elements in the master historians (which is the context of the proposed return) is quite inappropriate to irony, which systematically undermines such a positive world-view. And one cannot simply choose a non-ironic mode because it seems to *have* positive moral qualities, for that would be an exercise in bad faith, a typical trait of troubled ironic thinkers. To hold, as White does, that irony is not a necessary framework, it must be conceded that discursive frameworks might be commensurable in key respects after all, and that the choice between them can be decided on more than aesthetic grounds, at least in those respects. In other words, a modified realism is inescapable if the possibility of non-ironic modes is to be taken seriously. It must be *believed* that science, philosophy, and history, together, can tell us about the real world, and recommend courses of action, if White's aspiration is to have any meaning. The ironic mode will not stretch to that belief. Some of White's invariably perceptive discussions develop along these lines, but in so doing, the underlying framework of 'metahistory' is compromised. For example, he admires Foucault for the latter's discovery that the trope of irony is a characteristic feature of modern cultural history, not for the latter's irony in itself.[72] White also suggests that the rejection of realism so fundamental to much contemporary literary theory has reached the stage that the very point of departure of discourse theory is unrecognizable within it.[73] In order to escape the inward contortions of the ironic mode we would have to accept that a historical or theoretical perspective can be discursively interesting and critically incisive, yet be substantively wrong. Hayden White's metahistorical reflections are a case in point.

6. Marxism and the Analytic Philosophy of History

In the preceding critique, the possibility of historical realism was preserved despite the critical success of the new idealists against empiricism. It follows that anti-empiricists may not abstain from the realism/idealism debate either. Murray G. Murphey, for example, provides a lucid demolition of 'narrow' narrativism on the basis that history is not a matter of selecting charter facts from myriad particular events. Rather, history deals with the theoretical discovery of social relations and structural change. But Murphey thinks that the question of realism versus instrumentalism is not germane to his conclusions, because it is not susceptible of strict proof.[74] However, if this choice is arbitrary, then so is the question of whether the past is itself the product of historical discourse. This in turn leaves as a matter of convention the sense in which phenomena *merit* explanation and the significance of theoretical propositions about historical structures. Here, some back-pedalling would be required if criteria of value-relativity and linguistic preferences were to be kept out. Epistemological indifference is itself a proposition *within* the instrumentalist or idealist framework. In fact, Murphey does opt for realism, if only because 'it is more natural'. This is just as well, for Murphey's claims, especially that historical inquiry discovers and uncovers, require a realist framework if they are to be fully appreciated. Far from being an apology, the naturalness of the realist commitment, when developed, speaks in favour of it.

A related and also misleading view is that expressed by Harriet Gilliam.[75] She argues that realist and instrumentalist ideas are not as opposed as their advocates pretend, and that in detailed discussion, each side concedes the other's criticisms. There is some truth in this, because realism emphasizes the considerable theoretical scope of science, whilst idealists seldom go as far as to insist that reality is a figment of the imagination. But, again, the plausibility of epistemological indifference is vitiated by the subsumption of the realist/instrumentalist contrast under the dialectic of positivism and anti-positivism. Whilst (as I indicated earlier) positivism and humanism do indeed share common features, those features are precisely an instrumentalist conception of science and an empiricist notion of 'real' facts. Realist positions strive to go beyond that debate and cannot therefore be regarded accurately as accepting its terms of reference.

These comments are directly relevant to the defence of Marxist historiography against the criticisms levelled against it by the analytic philosophy of history. Marxists agree with metahistorians that the very distinction between analytic and 'speculative' philosophy of history is bogus. But Marxism is only tolerated in this refusal, not vindicated, since for metahistory its acceptance depends, like any other theory, on moral and aesthetic grounds alone. It is important therefore to give a Marxist-realist flavour to the critique of analytic philosophy. Indeed, it is due to the realist quality of Marxism when contrasted with the radical scepticism of metahistory that those who have 'demonstrated' the logical hiatus in historical or dialectical materialism feel obliged perennially to reconsider it. This is partly to do with a growing and impressive body of Marxist historiography, but it is also because Marxism urges a debate about general criteria for historical knowledge.

Karl Popper's critique is the standard refutation from the more 'positivistic' angle. Popper is forced to caricature Marxism (and 'historicism' at large), because his own precepts are closer to realism than other neopositivists. Of course, there *are* examples of Marxist writing that provide grist for his mill. But Popper's arguments are not, just on that ground, well founded. The propositions of Marxism, he argued, are unscientific and false, and this has something to do with the idea that laws are inapplicable to the unique process of history. However, the fact that history is irreversible means neither that it is a *single* process, nor that, even if it was a single process, laws would automatically be inapplicable. Moreover, if trends are conceived as law-like tendencies, then reasoned forecasts (if not strict predictions) are possible, though by no means primary. In short, Marxism expounded along these lines would require rather than reject verification procedures: but the falsity of forecasts does not necessarily entail the invalidity of Marxist explanation, which is retrodictive. Popper's notion of the centrality of unfalsifiable 'prophecy' to historical materialism is simply a pejoratively guided image: it is not a good argument. Peter Urbach has also shown that Popper's so-called 'logical refutation'—as opposed to his general criticisms—does not work.[76]

Recent philosophers of history continue to press Popper-like refutations. Morton White gives a trenchant account of how Marxists appeal to general philosophy (dialectical materialism, empirical realism) in order to make up for the unclear, partial applications of its historical laws. White finds this appeal unacceptable, though his points are reservations rather than refutations. This is because he recognizes that the move to justification of a *purely* metaphysical sort is not a necessary procedure for Marxists. Second, White's criticisms are inseparable from a defence of the covering-law model, in the light of which Marxism is revealed as ridden with 'fallacies'. A *tu quoque* argument is possible here, since we have noted how White's own explication of a historical law is extremely vague. But the main point is that his criticisms too make an appeal to general philosophy, namely, an empiricist account of historical facts. Moreover, I hope to have shown that it is one thing to say that a uniquely Marxist general philosophy is uncalled for, and quite another to find the realist critique of empiricism congenial to Marxism. White's most fundamental criticism is in fact more specific. He argues that the general statements of Marxism do not succeed in *logically* binding, say, 'class struggle' to 'history'. This may be right. But it does not follow (though White thinks it does) that Marxist generalizations are only summaries of some factual conjunctions. The empiricist notion that statements are either clearly 'analytic' or 'merely' contingent lies behind White's critique here. Realists and empiricists might agree that 'speculative' philosophy of history (and perhaps some versions of Marxism) comes away 'empty-handed after its appeal to general philosophy'.[77] However, if 'speculative' means any theory that defies empiricist 'analytical' norms, then it is only fair to say that the exclusion rests on the unfounded assumption that empiricism uniquely avoids the same kind of general appeal.

Yet the analytic/speculative distinction continues to play a central role in current expositions of the subject 'philosophy of history'. For example, R. F. Atkinson wastes no time in mobilizing the separation in order to discredit historical materialism. The analytic philosopher of history, he says, 'anxious to confine himself to considerations of the methods and intellectual apparatus of the practising historian, cannot avoid taking sides against or for Marxist substantive philosophy of history'.[78] This argument is disingenuous and unsatisfactory. Atkinson says that there can be interaction across the divide between analytic and substantive philosophers (the latter saying things about real historical development as well as historical method). So Marxism, for instance, 'cannot fail to have implications for the analysis of history'. This point is disingenuous (and there are others like it), because an impression is given that some things *are* important about substantive philosophy of history, that 'interaction' might be productive, and that Atkinson is being tolerant. Yet nothing could be further from the truth: it is just *because* substantive theories have 'implications' for historical method that Atkinson cannot accept them as *bona fide*, i.e. analytical, philosophy of history. In this context his claim that substantive philosophy can 'interact' with analytic, that it can 'challenge' the distinction (though the challenge fails), is downright misleading: interaction itself is such a challenge, and Atkinson simply wheels in his stipulation about the necessary form of philosophy of history to disembowel 'interaction'.

The argument is also a bad one. For one thing, it pays no attention to the significant body of practising Marxist historians. This is far more than an oversight, given Atkinson's claims about the implications of Marxism for historical method. Second, it posits that one can usefully abstract a 'neutral' historical method from historians of any kind, and Atkinson never considers that this might be problematic. Third, I hope to have shown that philosophy of science never simply 'analyses', but itself raises questions about ontological commitment, the social function of science, and the nature of explanation. If Bhaskar's point about the necessary component of action and human self-consciousness in socio-historical science is accepted, it is little short of outrageous to suggest that there could be a disembodied 'analysis' of history that did not raise those sorts of issues *as part of its subject matter*.

The analytical/substantive division confuses two distinct concerns. First, it rules out those 'readings' of history for which no empirical evidence could possibly make a difference. I have argued that Marxism, as a (realist) *theory*, is not a *reading* of history, and so could not be of this kind. But actually, very few examples of 'speculative' philosophy of history *would* fit this model. Spengler's *Decline of the West* (1922) probably, but surely not all of A. J. Toynbee's *A Study of History*, or even of Hegel.[79] It is more likely to be useful in pinpointing areas within theories where propositions are insufficiently substantiated. This *would* include some Marxist accounts, but it might include historians like G. M. Young, too. Second, the division between analytic and substantive rules out any logical connections between philosophical premisses, theories, and substantive accounts in historiography. The conflation of the first with the second effect seems to me both pernicious and wrong. As a matter of fact, historical work is about those very relations: empirical interest and procedures are partly the product of theoretical, moral, and ideological predilections. It is true that research would temper those predilections. But research is not just a matter of using the tools of empirical method and discovering factual nuggets (the content of which is irrelevant to philosophers). No one holds such a view in any rigid form. Empiricist premisses, however, including the analytic/substantive division, encourage it.

I do not mean to deny that there is a necessary *moment* of philosophical analysis, if by that is meant the analysis of the kinds of explanations offered in substantive work. But to stop there would be artificial. Not even philosophers can raise their questions outside of an interest in the comparison and *assessment* of historical explanations. To assess means to confer upon some explanations the philosophical seal of good argument, and this, in turn, ratifies—and should be seen to ratify—some accounts of the world as against others. So where the distinction between analytic and speculative modes drifts into a disjunction between 'neutral'-analytic and committed-substantive philosophical approaches, it is highly misleading. Analytical philosophers themselves ratify accounts in discussing methods. The distinction thus deprives philosophy of history of the relationship between theory and practice with which it should be centrally concerned.

In sum, I think philosophers of history should reject the distinction in its current debilitating form. There is some indication that it is at least coming under scrutiny. J. L. Gorman, for example,[80] rightly points out that there can be analytical or speculative approaches to analytic or speculative types of historical thinking. Apart from strengthening Marxism, rejection of the analytic/speculative distinction facilitates the revaluation of the main lines of *past* philosophy of history. For example, from the point of view of the necessary connection between theory and method, figures like Vico and Herder, Collingwood, or even Hegel, cannot simply be dubbed 'strange' or 'speculative'. Each of these thinkers, in my view, expressed important realist beliefs that tend to be suppressed in the dominant readings. But a further proposal is to insist upon a fuller cultural and historical appreciation of historians and philosophers alike. This investigation of intellectual production, of the transitive dimension of historiography, would highlight the properly double-sided task of substantive and theoretical analysis.

Part Two

Methodology

History constructed by excerpting
and combining the testimonies of
different authorities I call scissors-
and-paste history. I repeat that it
is not really history at all, because
it does not satisfy the necessary
conditions of science.

R. G. COLLINGWOOD

Historical Methodology

This and subsequent chapters will examine some important historiographical issues and developments from the perspective delineated in part one. This is not a matter of trying to solve methodological problems in history with epistemological guidelines alone: no relation of 'deduction' is intended to hold between the parts. Accordingly, the subjects of chapters 5 through 7 are more indicative of my own reading and interests in the historical field. Nevertheless, it can be said that questions of methodology have been discussed by historians in terms that reflect the debate between empiricists and relativists. And the tendency of radical and social history to reject the strictures of empiricism or 'specialist' historiography simultaneously raises the question of their connections to Marxism and to historical realism.

In the chapters on Marxism and philosophy, I cast suspicion on the idea that methodology provides a means of sidestepping the substantive commitments of historical materialism. That argument also stands as a proposition about historical reflection in general. Practising historians do not often explicitly broach philosophical questions about the objects and status of their 'craft'. One good reason for their reluctance to do so is that it involves much theoretical labour and must consequently deflect historians from the business of 'doing history'.[1] But the image of the historian as humble fact-seeker is not logically compelling. Neither is it altogether true of historiographical practice, and those historians who help foster the division between 'theory of history' and 'historiography' can take no credit for what is, in my view, an artificial separation of intellectual competences. Philosophers of history are bound to endorse certain kinds of substantive accounts. But historians also require, and sometimes provide, theoretical justifications for the conceptions of method and causality at work in their practice.

'Methodologies of history' is a convenient category under which to discuss these questions. It serves as a legitimate extension of real historiographical practice, yet seems to avoid unnecessary speculation. Historians, after all, have to be trained in the general skills of the 'craft', and methodological discussion, when spared metaphysical elaboration, can summarize the debates and perspectives within which those skills can be put to effect. It is consequently in history 'primers', guides to research, and inaugural lectures that questions of methodology are most often broached. But general points about 'methodology' *as* a category help to locate the historians' theoretical manifestos properly.

In fact, methodology of history is an inherently ambiguous notion. Does it refer to the forms of thought, or concepts, peculiar to historical work? Or, rather, is it the *techniques* that historians use, however they think? Merely to pose this question challenges the function 'methodology' is often taken to fulfil, namely that of specifying a relatively neutral set of objectives and 'tools' common to all historians. For *do* historians agree about the 'object' of history or about its discursive modes? Relevant to this question are debates about whether historians describe, narrate, or analyse, and whether their object is the past, humanity, societies, or events in time. And even if historians agreed about those things (which they do not), their practice might not square with their precepts. Most historians would agree that some technical features of historical research are indispensable. Since most 'primers' are largely taken up by these, there might be some initial plausibility in distinguishing, as the sociologist Talcott Parsons does,[2] between general and technical methodology. The former concerns the validation of particular modes of reasoning and forms of verification, the latter expounds research procedures and the *means* of verification. But even this is asking a lot of the historical community: *would* historians agree that the latter, without the former, constitutes the *essence* of their craft? More drastically, *does*, say, documentary or evidential criticism distinguish historians from others (for example, archaeologists, geographers, antiquarians, espionage intelligence agents). All the questions in this paragraph seem to warrant negative answers on both philosophical and empirical grounds. For the 'historian' himself ('he' is usually cast as a man) is not a metaphysical entity. *Within* historiography, Marxists vie with conservatives, relativists with empiricists, academics with 'amateurs', men with women, and so on. And they tend to disagree on just about all these questions. In short, methodology does not resolve any of the important issues. It is an umbrella that covers G. R. Elton's *Guide for Research Students Working on Historical Subjects*, as well as Marc Bloch's *The Historian's Craft*. But Jerzy Topolski's encyclopaedic neo-Marxist tome *Methodology of History*[3] can legitimately be squeezed in, too.

1. 'Empiricism' in the Historians' Methodological 'Manifestos'

In Britain, disagreement over the fundamentals of methodology has only quite recently become a notable feature of historians' discourse. Previous quietude, however, was not so much a rejection of philosophical underpinnings as a consensus around *empiricist*, or at any rate particularist, norms. Of course, it is characteristic of empiricism that theoretical reflection is systematically discouraged in the promotion of the primacy of observational facts or data. This philosophical statement of priorities emerges in the guise of a common-sense embargo on 'useless' speculation as a diversion from everyday practical consciousness (including that of the practical historian).

Thus historians of a particularist turn of mind, when they make statements of a general methodological kind, tend to assert the *sui generis* nature of history. The autonomy of the profession is acquired apparently only by withdrawing from theoretical and political considerations. For example, in 'The Future of the Past',[4] C. Vann Woodward, the American historian, expresses relief at the relatively uncontroversial work of the historian *qua* scholar, and reaffirms his lack of essential connections to social scientific or ideological issues. However, the exemplars he offers—Johann Huizinga and Friedrich Meinecke—are by no means free of philosophical assumptions and ideological preferences. Huizinga's advocacy of cultural history[5] has general implications for our very conception of history beyond its embodiment in, say, *The Waning of the Middle Ages*.[6] Meinecke's *Historism*,[7] too, is nothing less than a reconstruction of historiography in the grand manner, favouring a clearly idealist lineage (and Goethe, of all people, is Meinecke's exemplar).

I do not wish to exaggerate: some historians have been and are out of sympathy with empiricist norms. But it seems worth tracing in some detail the kinds of tenets to which empiricist historiography adheres, for they affect the very character of the opposition to them that emerges. As in philosophy, a realist methodological stance lodges significant reservations against relativist reactions to positivism. The general prohibition on theory in empiricist historiography itself encourages relativism or subjectivism as a natural response. Carl Becker's relativism, for example, denied the existence of historical facts, maintaining a 'constructionist' view of history.[8] Even in America, where historians seem generally to be more theory-conscious than in Britain, [9] Becker's standpoint was commonly regarded as an uncalled-for intrusion of philosophy (in this case, idealist philosophy) into historiography. One effect of this was to encourage the idea that the reflections of other historians, such as Charles Beard, were the same as

Becker's. In my view, this is mistaken, for the realist element in Beard (though it was only one element) was impressed into a relativist mould.[10] In other words, Beard and Becker—*historians*—become cast as spare-time philosophers. On the other hand, few voices in the empiricist tradition would be raised against the spare-time *historical* reflections of an economist and ideologue such as Ludwig von Mises, or F. A. von Hayek. Von Mises excludes history from the sciences by definition, asserts an ontology of brute atomic facts, and ridicules opponents by wild caricature. Such an argument as von Mises's *is* necessary if that kind of historical autonomy is what historians desire. But it is certainly not a position that historians alone can pronounce upon, nor is it in any sense a presuppositionless technical ruling.

Woodward and von Mises, perhaps for different reasons, share a certain psychological perturbation about philosophy. Von Mises, in a characteristically leading way, calls it 'a chimera of the Group Mind'.[11] Earlier historians had similar worries: 'History is an astringent, philosophy a dissolvent for the mind of the ordinary student . . . "that way madness lies".'[12] Oman's rather extreme views are given some support in many manifestos. Theorizing, if not always avoidable, must be imbibed in small doses.[13] The technical methodological requirements are mainly those of internal and external criticism of documentary evidence. External techniques are tests of the time, place, and authenticity of a piece of evidence. Internal criteria, which generally come later, assess the quality, reliability, and usefulness of witnesses' reports. The former require some purely scientific techniques: 'auxiliary' methods such as diplomatics, paleography, and numismatics.[14] But the acquisition of these skills is often accorded moral status. For Langlois and Seignobos, in the classic empiricist primer, the mastery of auxiliaries is seen as a 'serene' achievement. They set 'prudence, patience and accuracy' against 'dilettantism'.[15] In Barzun and Graff's modern equivalent, the personal virtues of the researcher are themselves part of the technical apprenticeship—again, they are love of order, patience, accuracy, and vicarious imagination.[16] V. H. Galbraith, too, puts 'humility and devotion at a high premium in history'.[17]

The model for the historian in these accounts is that of a serious under-labourer engaged in the external-critical examination of sources. It is surely one that can be questioned. First, it places 'auxiliaries' at the centre of the historian's activity, which is a contradiction in terms. Second, the very notion of 'auxiliary' aids is unclear. Does it mean *techniques*, or intellectual *disciplines*, or just anything a historian happens to find useful? Certainly, one could draw up a long list of them, especially today. The 'hard' scientific methods of computerization, dendrachronology, and carbon tests rub shoulders with the 'softer' but still sophisticated tools of anthropology and sociology. External criticism, in any case, is the precondition of history more than its principal task. But 'internal criticism' is even more a purely formal category. The reliability of a witness and the value of his or her testimony can be assessed only in the context of long (and 'theoretical') considerations about the relation between certain kinds of discourse and their place in the social formation. The conception of the historians' methodology as theoretically neutral, then, is untenable. Especially where external criticism is said to be the main task, this misconception can be termed 'the technicist fallacy', that is, the identification of a theoretical discipline with certain parts of its technical instrumentation. It is not a fallacy unique to empiricist historians: Gaston Bachelard and Alexander Koyré, for example, have been among those who think it rife in natural science.[18]

A major impediment to adequate reflection on historical method has been the association of scholarly techniques with claims on behalf of history's *scientific* status. Thus, those who argue that history *is* a science (Niebuhr, Fustel de Coulanges, J. B. Bury) by and large supported the technicist conception. Those who felt the pulse of history to lie outside the study of Dryasdust did not disagree that source-criticism was part of history. Rather, they relished the literary or moral freedom to which historians could aspire once the fact-checking was concluded. (Macaulay, Acton, and Trevelyan are prominent in this lineage.[19]) The idea that rational theoretical considerations are germane to the assessment of evidence and simultaneously preclude subjective indulgence would not be embraced by either camp. Figures such as H. T. Buckle, who in his own way attempted a sort of synthesis between fact and theory, were destined to remain shadowy, odd historians.[20]

That peculiar relationship between empiricism and humanism—at once of opposition and collusion—has structured debates in the methodology of history down to the present. The ethos of facticity is one in which the scholar and the enthusiast conflict and converge. Thus, preconceptions can be blotted out not simply for accuracy's sake, but for the phenomenological union with the past that accuracy enables. 'Historiography is but an extension . . . of the simple utterance "I was there; I saw it; let me tell you about it".'[21] 'Every student of history ought to know an event when he meets it.'[22] 'Once your subject has found you, your difficulty will be escaping from it.'[23]

The 'facts' of history thus appear double-sided. On the one hand, they are 'statements of fact' to be verified by clear-sighted and unadventurous souls. 'Every statement in a source must be factual, i.e. based on correct observation.'[24] 'Some are not cut out for the labour and minutiae of preparatory criticism.'[25] 'Truth and rhetoric are bad bedfellows.'[26] 'The prime function of the historian is to inquire and determine how things came to be, not to moralize or predict.'[27]

On the other hand, if, as Langlois and Seignobos also say, criticism works by 'reproducing the conditions under which authors wrote',[28] then the facts are themselves *states of affairs* to which the historian has unique access. A moral and empathetic window can thus be opened on the past: 'History is vicarious experience.'[29] T. R. Tholfsen terms this methodology 'historical *verstehen*',[30] and Louis Gottschalk prefers humanistic 'verisimilitude' to pseudo-objectivity.[31] As the illustrations indicate, relatively few writers fall unambiguously into one particular interpretation of the facts of history; and they would largely agree about source criticism. But clearly, the facts 'themselves' cannot long dominate metaphysical and moral preferences. Lord Acton was a classic exponent of the identity of truth and morality, but G. M. Young's distinctive literary conservatism provides more recent gems. His empathetic listening for the way an age speaks itself is not always as open as he pretends. 'History', he has written, 'is the conversation of the people who counted.'[32]

The more self-conscious historians relate values to theoretical accounts of humanity. Sir Lewis Namier, for example, sought the 'music of emotions' and 'universal human nature' that underlay historical, political action.[33] That aspiration too finds some support in the older 'primers'. For example: 'Every written document is a little scrap of human nature.'[34] Here the *particular*, so revered by some historians, is not annulled, but becomes the carrier of universal psychological traits. Namier is an exceptional case, since he eminently fulfils the scholarly requirements. A book like *The Structure of Politics*[35] seems to overcome the tensions that worry technical methodologists: it is admirably researched. But it endorses the intuition and self-seeking of its subjects—the Whig magnates—on the basis of universal generalizations about 'man'. And that is not merely *conservative* historiography; it seems to deny that specific historical changes *as such* are the key focus for historians. I do not subscribe to Namier's views, but glib rejoinders about the necessarily *specific* concern of historians are of little use. Namier at least demonstrates the crucial role played by non-source-based knowledge (to use Jerzy Topolski's useful term) in the historians' 'pragmatic' methodology.[36]

More recent manifestos are perhaps less archaic than the earlier empiricist handbooks, but they are not essentially different. Many historians unite in an offensive against those who would seek to systematize the discipline. But the tensions are only pragmatically resolved, not magically overcome. Barzun and Graff, for example, acknowledge the role of causal explanation in history, and that facts come 'dripping with ideas'. But the 'bare facts' remain the touchstone for generalization, and 'adequate enumeration' guards against speculation. In short, these authors do not really know what to say about the theory/history question. Someone who knows all too well what he thinks is J. H. Hexter. Langlois and Seignobos argued that abstractions should be shunned in favour of collective names, and Hexter carries on this nominalist tradition.

Historical terms are but names and descriptions.[37] Hexter's intention is to defend the autonomy of the historical understanding, but this is argument by *fiat*. If it means 'terms having an historical denotation', then, of course, they will be names and descriptions. However, the entities of *all* sciences can be named and described, too, so history is no different in that respect. It seems likelier that Hexter is saying that all *genuinely* historical terms are particulars, thus ruling out abstractions and differentiating history from science. Clearly, though, this is a definition, not an argument. If it were, it would be easily refuted, since all historians employ abstract terms with which to make sense of particulars. As a definition, it holds little rational weight. In general, Hexter reaffirms the notion of a core of 'basic data', but places a premium on the 'rhetoric' of history as its non-scientific, distinctive supplement. History's 'processive' explanation, according to Hexter, 'works by closely moulding itself to the actual contours of the past and to the appropriate rhetoric of history'.[38] Since almost every term here ('closely', 'moulding', 'actual', 'appropriate') begs questions, the 'rhetoric' of history is more aptly taken in the contemporary denotation of 'rhetoric' as licence to evade than in its hallowed academic sense of 'disquisition'. And its defence displays a common frame of mind rather than an original literary approach: 'The historian moulds his mind on the contour of the actual.'[39] With regard to teaching strategies, it should be noted that while these accounts raise intuition above conceptual clarity, history is not necessarily thereby rendered more accessible or popular. To their credit, Hexter and Hugh Trevor Roper[40] do say that it ought to be. But Langlois and Seignobos thought that history was of no use in life, and that historical forms more popular than the monograph, therefore risk 'great dangers'.[41] Naimer, too, expresses contempt here. For him, popularized history is 'a babble of blurred reminiscences and fanciful interpretations'.[42]

The elitism and empiricism of this kind of position is most elaborately set out in G. R. Elton's *The Practice of History*. Elton is not naïve: he is careful to distinguish between an event and its trace. But his anti-theoretical defence of the disinterested historical scholar is deep and entrenched. Elton's militant stance is at times deceptively easy-going. The historian's *raison d'être* is that 'it is a pleasant occupation';[43] and 'Professional history, however dull, contributes truth' is a jaded justification for time spent relishing minutiae.[44] But Elton's targets are real enough; his book is directed especially at E. H. Carr's influential *What is History*. Elton takes 'visionaries' in history to be a 'menace', and abstraction or morality are deemed dangerous luxuries. He defends instead the qualities of apprenticeship, professionalism, and the authority of the 'man' expertly trained in source-work. His work is above all the defence of the Oxbridge ethic. Yet even amongst scholars temperamentally close to Elton, such certitude is lacking.

George Kitson Clark, for example, agrees that the *career* of historian is one good reason for studying history, and he sympathizes with the aspiring specialist who 'resents' initial 'wider reading'.[45] Kitson Clark's own contribution to methodology (*The Critical Historian*) is not, however, wholly conducive to the Eltonian standpoint. For example, Kitson Clark has doubts about the distinction between uniqueness and generality, and rejects nominalism.[46] Indeed, the very problem with his standpoint is that it accepts 'generic categories' such as class and race, but shows little desire to define or discuss them carefully. Such reluctance is the *typical* perspective—if such there be—of historians on methodological issues. J. H. Plumb and Sir Herbert Butterfield, in different ways, illustrate these more liberal historiographical 'solutions' to these problems.

Both Plumb and Butterfield see the importance of the connections of history to politics and philosophy. Butterfield criticizes the *Whig Interpretation of History* and declares history morally neutral. However, he does not consider history neutral in the sense that it can offer objective criteria by which different moral interpretations can be judged. Rather, it is 'all things to all men', in the sense that the facts support a *variety* of interpretations.[47] It is clear from Butterfield's other reflections[48] that history is bound to 'see both sides' of a debate, partly because, in this vision, tragic antagonism is a part of the human condition. Butterfield's methodological liberalism is thus fully intelligible only with reference to a Christian-humanist metaphysic.

Butterfield draws his conclusions through a serious and somewhat pained consideration (and rejection) of Marxism.[49] J. H. Plumb's views emerge from a similar confrontation.[50] Plumb accepts something of a materialist conception of history, and the view that the function of historiography is to teach the nature of social change. But because of his human-ist *belief* in or hope for a common identity for mankind, and because that identity must, in his view, attribute to human rationality the power to overcome material constraints, Plumb wants to reject notions of class struggle. Here, in accordance with the general liberal world-view, a state-ment of moral belief grounds his conception of what historiography must be and do. But he offers no account of what 'social change' amounts to—indeed, no close account *could* be given, since it refers only to the arena of free human affairs, not to the mechanisms in terms of which those affairs might be explained.

2. Relevance, Relativism, Realism

I have tried to indicate how certain liberal or humanist accounts of histori-cal aims and methodologies differ from hardline empiricist historiography. But the contending tendencies within and between authors are, ultimately, less important than the underlying consensus: that facts be established, and that narration, rhetoric, morality, art or whatever be tolerated as possible superstructures arising from the technical basis of historiography. True, the humanist interpretation can come close to overturning the time-honoured *methodological* hierarchy of fact and interpretation, past and present. For example, Geoffrey Barraclough sees no reason to exclude con-temporary political problems from the historian's brief, nor does he seek to excuse the historian from commitments of some kind.[51] The demand that history be *relevant* to life has often been the source of trenchant criticism of established academic norms. In America James Harvey Robinson advocated a 'new' history for the (then) early twentieth century.[52] Recently, in Bri-tain, G. Connell-Smith and H. A. Lloyd have given an account of Elton's *England Under the Tudors* that nicely reveals the range of generalizations and dubious abstractions that mark the professor's own work.[53] But 'relevance' is a hazy notion, and like Robinson, Connell-Smith and Lloyd have little positive to offer. For all its polemical (and political) force, 'relevance' is a relative concept: it could mean simply 'all things to all men'. We would want to ask 'relevant to what, and for whom?' Moreover, unless we adopt the full relativist view, it does not seem obvious that monographs on feudal structure, for example, are 'irrelevant' to contemporary concerns. If theory does have an important function in historiography, it is by virtue of its *general* explanatory capacity, not simply its immediate object of analysis.

The most sustained critique of British empiricist historiography is perhaps E. H. Carr's *What is History?* Carr attacked the idea that theory and politics or value-judgements were extrinsic to historical thinking. Many of his points were along the lines I have followed in my critical overview of the manifestos. But Carr's arguments are not wholly convincing. His account is based on a distinction between the facts of history and historical facts. For Carr, only the latter constitute history proper, because historians invest them with theoretical and moral significance. The facts are thus not 'primary' with respect to interpretation. Rather, there is a reciprocal, mutually dependent, interaction. Since 'subject and object belong to the same category' in the human sciences, 'history is shot through with relativity'.[54]

These propositons seem unacceptable. Carr is getting at something vital, namely the *relational* character of the objects of investigation to their own social context, and to our own. Moreover, he raises the important matter of an adequate epistemology. His concepts do not, however, embody such an epistemology. 'Subject and object' are notoriously slippery: they do not fully grasp the determinate relations that hold between knowledge and the world. If subject and object *did* belong 'to the same category', they would be—as in idealism—conceptually *equivalent*. Here, Carr's terminology, and perhaps his meaning, can only suggest the intrinsic relativity of historical *knowledge*, as opposed to the relativity of the reasons we have for particular investigations.

These suspicions are confirmed when Carr discusses the role of causality in clarifying objectivity in history. He says, correctly, that history is the study of causes, and declares himself for determinism.[55] However, his reason for that belief, it seems, is that 'the total disintegration of the human personality' would follow were we not to assume causal ties. This formulation is at best ambiguous as between causality as objectively 'in the world' and causality as a necessary part of the human cognitive apparatus. That Carr tends to the latter view is suggested by his footnote given over to one J. Reuff's avowedly Kantian declaration that causality is indispensable, but that it is not imposed on us by the world.[56]

This view of Carr's is untenable if relativism is to be avoided and realism accepted. Here, Elton is right to proclaim that the historian's 'experiments' are not constructs, and that the objects of inquiry have a real, independent nature.[57]

Paradoxically, there are also relative advantages to Elton's view over Carr's on the question of historical facts. Elton regards all facts of history as historical facts. This, of course, allows him rigidly to split fact and value, and we need not follow him along that sidetrack. Carr, on the other hand, takes the question of the *significance* of some 'facts' over others to be a matter of our selection of facts according to a range of beliefs. In effect then, Carr, like Morton White and others, posits a shadowy, infinite world of background facts out of which *we* highlight some. Or, in his own metaphor, we choose facts like catching fish in a vast ocean, not just as from a fishmonger's slab. This seems unfortunate, because it entails the *arbitrariness* of our selection, and thus, ultimately, the impotence of theoretical history to explain the structured (objective) hierarchies of the real historical world, or to rationally justify some moral stances over others. A strategy preferable to Carr's is more firmly to reject the notion of discrete historical facts and so to avert the dichotomy of selecting some rather than others.

Some 'manifestos' attempt to surmount the empiricism/relativism dichotomy. If Marc Bloch's *The Historian's Craft* is the classic text of the genre, it is not because it gives solace to practising historians keen to avoid theory. M. M. Postan's slighter *Fact and Relevance in History* similarly conveys a realist conception of historical method. Both writers argue that the dissimilarities between physical experiment and historical research cannot exonerate the historian from the task of causal explanation. Accordingly, arbitrary definitions of the object of history cannot be sustained: for Bloch, 'the past' is an impossible criterion.[58] For Postan, the alleged uniqueness of its discrete parts is a fiction. Of the two, only Postan explicitly embraces 'realist philosophy',[59] but both rightly regard historical 'facts' as the product of abstraction.

What does this entail? The position taken up (by Bloch especially) breaks down some entrenched oppositions in historical thinking. First, his realist stance refuses both what he calls the 'pan-scientific ideal' of positivism and the sceptical, aesthetic, and anti-intellectual response which that ideal encourages.[60] It is an interesting historical fact that Bloch's realistic view of natural science and history was developed in the demise of Comptean positivism. Analogously, contemporary neo-realism has followed the demise of resurgent neo-positivism and the relativist responses to it, which together dominated the middle decades of this century in philosophy.

Second, history, like science, is rational explanation. This view at once opposes both empiricists and relativists. 'The very idea that the past as such can be the object of science is ridiculous.'[61] Third, for Bloch, the 'developmental fallacy', that is, the confusion between ancestry and explanation, is to be rejected: 'It would be a grievous error, indeed, to think that the order which historians adopt for their inquiries must necessarily correspond to the sequence of events.'[62] Bloch's thought here recalls Marx's pregnant aphorism in the *Grundrisse*: 'Their sequence (i.e. the economic categories) is precisely the opposite of that which seems to be their natural order or which corresponds to historical development.'[63]

Bloch is therefore anti-empiricist, but, like Marx, he has little time for the view that the past is simply the *product* of current concerns. He stresses that the usefulness of knowledge for action is due to its *intellectual*, and not just its pragmatic, legitimacy.[64] Among the more obviously realist claims that Bloch puts forward are that the objects of history are real, and are as real as those of the sciences. Moreover, Bloch holds that the distinction between direct and indirect observation is artificial. However, the objects of history do differ in kind from those of other investigations, and must be reconstructed from evidence. Consequently, abstractions 'cover' historical realities, but they need not 'exhaust' them.[65]

Thus Bloch argues, with due caution, that philosophical or theoretical reflection is crucial to historiography. It may be that history is a humanistic discipline, but 'it would be sheer folly to suppose that history, because it appeals to the emotions, is less capable of satisfying the intellect'. And the role of the intellect is to establish 'explanatory relations between phenomena'.[66] Two points follow from this. First, questions of method are relative to the explanatory capacity of history: they do not provide a way round talk of the latter.[67] Second, there is always an element of how the craft 'expects to improve itself' in methodological reflection.[68] Together, these propositions permit a decisive rejection of the historical common sense so strongly urged by most guides to historical method. Bloch says of the view that documents are collected and authenticated first, and used only afterwards: 'There is only one trouble with this idea: no historian has ever worked in such a way, even when, by some caprice, he fancied that he was doing so.'[69]

3. Specialist Aspirations

Economic History

My discussion of Bloch should have reinforced my argument that 'methodological' statements by practitioners are always philosophical, and often quite unconvincing. This contention receives support from the claims made on behalf of specialist histories, those that deal with particular kinds of historical facts or perspectives. In fact, it is here that the main battles over methodology and general historiography are often waged. Supporters of the 'documentary' conception, for example, sometimes invoke its Rankean ancestry. And the factual, documentary practice of the master (Ranke) was inseparably linked to his advocacy of diplomatic political history. However, 'the factual' in Ranke is more akin to 'the essential' than to 'the observed'. His own spiritual and ideological allegiances bear heavily on how the facts are transparently intuited as being of the essence of epochs or political states.[70] A brief examination of definitions of economic and cultural history should convince us that the kinds of argument employed by Ranke in defence of his specialisms are fairly widespread.[71]

Economic history is now a particularly important branch of the discipline. N. B. Harte's collection of essays by prominent practitioners of the subject reveals how the general issues I have been discussing lie at its heart. A key formulation of the problem was provided by Cunningham: 'Economic history is not so much the study of a special class of facts, as the study of all the facts from a special point of view.'[72] Three attitudes to this formula might be developed. First, it might be thought to go too far. W. J. Ashley, for example, preferred to see his subject as the 'provisional isolation of a particular group of facts and forces'.[73] T. S. Ashton, in a memorable lecture crammed with mixed metaphors parading as serious propositions, described economic classifications as a 'set of labels which we can attach, if we are so minded, to the files in which we assemble our facts'.[74] No better nugget of empiricist historiography could be found. But Ashton consciously avoids a second possible elaboration of Cunningham's proposition: that economic facts are important because they are *causally* primary. In other words, if the 'special point of view' is not to be entirely arbitrary, some commitment to an 'economic interpretation of history' is unavoidable. Both L. L. Price and J. H. Clapham (the dominant figure of the subject) attempted to retain pluralism, but had to allow that its force was limited. Price distinguished economic causes as more gradual, measurable, and profound than other historical factors.[75] Clapham, resisting Marxist implications, held the line at the idea that *methodologically*, economic history must be a 'measurer' above other histories.[76] Of course, unless those other branches admit of no measurable criteria whatsoever, it is surely difficult to maintain (as Clapham modestly claims) that economic history is *only* a 'help-study' or a linking expedient.

The spectre of Marxism, the most important 'economic interpretation', looms behind many of these accounts, as Clapham says, 'either by attraction or repulsion'. George Unwin—no orthodox 'bourgeois' historian—went as far as to avow a 'spiritual interpretation of history' in order not to be tainted by the brush of 'class analysis'.[77] Other economic historians, alongside Marxists, have been aware that Marxism provides a *social* rather than simply economic conception of history. The contributions of R. H. Tawney, Eileen Power, M. M. Postan, and Sidney Pollard, for example, clearly express disagreement with the view that any particular set of facts, even economic, could stand in for the 'structural analysis of society'.[78]

Key debates are as much about historiography and politics as about 'economic facts'. The long-standing argument about the standard of living in the early nineteenth century is one important instance.[79] Clapham and R. M. Hartwell, on the one side, are keen to establish data about material conditions only, while the Hammonds and E. P. Thompson dispute the validity of purely quantitative evidence. Typically, it is E. J. Hobsbawm who, with some success, strikes a balance of a theoretical kind, one that insists on the structural co-existence of quantitative and qualitative dimensions of social life.

This is a far cry from a third development of the 'special point of view', namely the economic interpretation *without* Marxist connotations. That view is evinced in W. K. Hancock's definition of economic history as the study of men as getters and spenders.[80] Another variant is the strong-minded view of G. N. Clark that 'it is a fundamental principle of the evolution of industry that a change of tools or machines brings with it a change of business organization and of the human relations which that dictates'. No doubt Clark was called to account for this suspiciously vulgar-Marxist proposition.[81] The general point should be clear enough: *however* Cunningham's dictum is interpreted, 'fundamental principles' are invoked. They correspond to substantive beliefs, and to methodological principles consonant with whatever general perspective is adopted. From our sample of practitioners, the 'discipline' of economic history seems a good deal less than an integrated specialism.

The meteoric rise of econometric history ('cliometrics') has been, in part, an attempt to ruthlessly weed out otiose philosophical preconceptions and sloppy qualitative evidence—or bad quantification. Lee Benson is a particularly strident representative of the 'new history', dedicated to exposing the impressionism he sees behind even the most apparently 'factual' economic histories.[82] In Benson's own work on the 1884 American elections, and in that of, for example, R. W. Fogel on railroads, or of Fogel and S. Engerman on slavery, the aim of these positivists 'armed with a computer'[83] is nothing short of a re-definition of historiography. Cliometrics, however, requires a metaphysic as much as other methodologies. For example, it is clear from Benson's critique of the (in his view) naïve and ideological Marxists—Eugene Genovese, Barrington Moore, Eric Foner—that his quantitative methods do not absolve *him* from theoretical and model choices. The production of data about investment potential in the antebellum South does not in itself resolve issues about a 'slave mode of production' or the quality of life. We need not espouse a cult of literary evidence to make that case. Fogel and Engerman's *Time on the Cross* is another site of the debate about 'hardware' in historical evidence. In my view, critiques like those of Herbert Gutman have established that a series of punch-cards are not methodologically autonomous;[84] they dance to the tune called by the historical questions posed, and by the theoretical problematic that frames those questions. Two essays by Fogel, one either side of the furor about *Time on the Cross*, affirm as much. In the first, Fogel declares that econometric history confirms the covering-law model of scientific explanation. He adopts an analysis of the American economy based on the counter-factual proposition that the commercial exploitation of new western lands would have continued had railroads not been developed. By treating cases as falling under deductive generalizations backed by statistical correlations, Fogel claims legitimation for his hard facts from pure logic.

But this is only to say that Fogel is a systematic empiricist (and therefore that the 'new history' is quite old). And the characteristic of these empiricist models is their failure to penetrate real historical causality owing to their allegiance to empirical regularities and statistical frequencies. Barry Hindess and Judith and David Willer have written detailed critiques of systematic empiricism and the official statistics it takes at face value.[85] Here it is sufficient to note Fogel's post-*Time on the Cross* reservations. The intrinsic possibility of different interpretations of the data, he now claims, will always render history a humanistic, qualitative discipline.[86] The note of resignation to be heard in this essay of Fogel's is itself of theoretical significance: it registers again the easy move from empiricism to pluralism.

Cultural History

Less bound to hard facts than economic history, 'cultural history' is open to many interpretations. With regard to *content*, it has been held to embrace— or even consist of—purely intellectual or spiritual expressions. But culture can be interpreted materialistically too, notable examples being Fernand Braudel's *Capitalism and Material Life* or Keith Thomas's *Religion and the Decline of Magic*. As with 'economic' history, those who favour a 'social' rather than narrow definition of what it is to which 'cultural' history refers, are unlikely to favour the view that it represents a *separate* form of analysis. Richard Johnson has pointed to some of the divergent treatments of 'culture' within the Marxist tradition,[87] but historical materialism in any of its variants would in principle refuse to acknowledge that cultural practices, particularly those of *popular* culture, represent 'a special set of facts'. A 'moderate' view of cultural history—in which the term refers to a heterogeneous series of historical areas that might usefully be analysed—is, of course, possible; methodologically, too, intellectual history can be conducted in a scholarly and informative way.[88] But the moderate position tends to abstain from the debate about the *concept* of cultural history; it represents only a pragmatic resolution of the issues. As soon as claims are made, or implied, about cultural history as a 'special point of view', that pragmatic view must, in practice, be abandoned.

Paul Conkin, for example, modestly claims for intellectual history a concern with 'ideational components'. But even to establish the credibility of viewing the history of ideas as a semi-autonomous developmental set of relations is to abstract from their social context and material conditions. Conkin thus maintains that if intellectual history is to be possible, ontological issues must be thought of as 'traps'.[89] However, to assert even this much is to admit that a certain kind of philosophical prerequisite is favoured, namely one that eschews materialism. Cultural history, then, as an autonomous inquiry, tends towards a cultural interpretation of history itself.

Methodologically, the aesthetic rather than the empirical mode is encouraged. J. R. Green, no oddity in his own day, provides an extreme example: 'I have a hatred, a sort of physical antipathy, to notes. There is something to me in the very *look* of a page'.[90]

Masters of cultural history—such as Jacob Burckhardt or Johann Huizinga—manage to avoid Green's idiosyncratic antipathies. Burckhardt, however, held to a philosophy of knowledge-as-intuition, much as he knew his sources and much as he despised (conceptual) philosophy. For Burckhardt, study was 'a loss of self in calm contemplation'. Substantively, his notion of history as a 'spiritual continuum' did not form a Hegelian evolution of the 'idea' (Burckhardt hated evolutionism, and Hegel). But deterministic and specific as Burckhardt the historian was, his conception of historical epochs was ineradicably idealist. The foci of history (the arts, states, religions) were 'spiritual totalities' in Burckhardt's schema. Social intercourse and technologies too were thought to be 'expressions of spiritual and moral life'.[91] Huizinga operated within a less exalted paradigm, which conferred value on the literary expression of epochs. In 'The Task of Cultural History', Huizinga raised this methodological preference to an all-embracing substantive account—a 'morphological understanding and description of the actual specific course of civilization'.

Without a culturalist content, of course, this formulation might fit any view of historical methodology.

Cultural history has thus acquired connotations of mystical or intuitive understanding. Emery Neff, for instance, designates the imaginative component in history as 'poetry' because that term 'seems the most adequate symbol for the quintessence of the human spirit'.[92] A recent exponent of the philosophical and psychological patterns that shape historical understanding is less cloudy, but the same suggestion emerges in some of Frank E. Manual's work: that the world is moulded in accordance with timeless human creativity.[93] E. H. Gombrich, a methodological individualist, defends cultural history without the kinds of holistic hypostatization that the genre seems to sponsor. Gombrich rightly charges Huizinga and Burckhardt, as well as Hegel, with an 'artistic expressivism'.[94] But Gombrich does not favour a more materialist conception of culture: this would be to yield to his other *bête noire*, the Marxist determinism that in his view is merely the inverse of Hegel.

However, Gombrich's argument too is no simple assertion of 'parity' for cultural history, for it requires the demotion of social history in favour of the individual. In turn, the individual's autonomous self-consciousness is to be taken as given. Values and cultural attributes thus stem from self-consciousness; they are not imposed on it. These propositions cast cultural analysis as separate from and above social history. For example, Gombrich prefers tracing the meanings of the word 'urbane' to investigating urban changes.

In fact, Gombrich's general views are not consistent. In *Art History and the Social Sciences* he claims to reject both empiricism *and* general concepts, though the entities he posits require both for their intelligibility. Empirical individuals are said to be everything, yet 'there is something universal in human psychic states'.[95] Gombrich's defence of culture is intended to be intellectually persuasive, and not a matter of subjective taste. Yet the 'insight and pleasure' derived from culture seem to depend on intuitive and aesthetic justification alone. Expressivism is taboo for Gombrich, yet 'overall values . . . are deeply embedded in the totality of our civilization'. Such values (as expressed in art history) are, for Gombrich, the preserve of 'the keepers of the canon', but somehow he manages to claim that 'this is not elitism'.[96] In sum, Gombrich's superficially plausible modern defence of a special cultural understanding in history is, like the rest of the genre, deeply contradictory where it is not simply an apology for idealist metaphysics.

6

Social History,
Socialist History

'Social history', Hobsbawm has written, 'can never be another specialization like economic or other hyphenated histories because its subject matter cannot be isolated.'[1] Hobsbawm's remark is true and important, and shows why 'social history' requires a separate discussion. Hobsbawm identifies a range of quite different approaches and methodologies within social history. The confidence of his declaration might thus conceal the serious difficulties posed in assuming 'social history' to be more than a catch-all category. This chapter will discuss labour, oral, and feminist history. These contemporary concerns raise—in very different ways—all the problems connected with the idea that *Marxist* historiography provides the most coherent elaboration of 'social history'. The chapter concludes with an analysis of the still uneasy relationship between Marxist theory and social history, examining some arguments by a prominent exponent of both traditions, E. P. Thompson.

Social history seems to aspire to a fuller understanding of the whole of social life: 'Social history *is* history, an approach to the entirety of the past. It is not a topic, like intellectual history, or even a set of topics (the Mulligan's stew syndrome).'[2] However, an 'approach' of this kind could still entail a loose, umbrella conception of history. Hobsbawm sets out several very different ways in which social history, or even 'the history of society' might be broached. He lists the study of demography, kinship, classes, mentalities, social protest movements, and social change as directions in which the subject has recently been developed. And yet, it is clear prima facie that there may be methodological and substantive disagreements within each of these approaches. Equally, some will necessarily intersect and even coalesce with others. Consequently, the use of the category of social history, even in Hobsbawm's 'objective' presentation,[3] seems to represent academic convenience more than intellectual coherence. According to the touchstone described in the last chapter, social history 'involves a social interpretation of history, not history from the social point of view'.[4] In other words, questions about *which* interpretative framework to adopt must be addressed. Methodologies are assessed with this larger question in the background. In this context, by 'methodologies' I do not mean just techniques, though those too are of great importance in substantive debates. For example, the 'new' econometric history has been attacked by social historians not simply because it is narrowly *economic* history. Rather, it is because new research techniques are exalted by econometricists in a pseudo-scientific way, then used as theoretical weapons against other interpretations. H. G. Gutman's critique of *Time on the Cross* best illustrates this reaction, though the general form of the debate goes back at least to the arguments between Tawney and economic history, narrowly defined, and to the brisker exchange between the Hammonds and Clapham. Gutman allows that *some* of Fogel and Engerman's data may be valid as economic abstractions, but he thinks the project is poor social history. He also demonstrates that *most* of the econometric argument has little to do with anything so appealingly simple as getting the sums right. Much of Fogel and Engerman's data, Gutman claims, is 'based on flawed assumptions about slave culture and slave society'.[5]

One particular argument—about the use of the slave owner Barrow's diaries in calculating the shipping of slaves—is an almost perfect instance of how fact, theory, and ideological position are closely interwoven, especially in social history. 'Methodology' is thus also a question of which approach to social history is adopted: the 'approach' that is deemed most appropriate for understanding the 'totality'. As I will indicate later, it is a weakness as well as the strength of the *Annales* school that it fosters a somewhat uncritical or eclectic sense of 'total history'. Indeed, in so far as 'totality' becomes a means of discounting particular theories just by the hallowed goal the term sets up, it is, ironically, no more than one partial, *limited* perspective. Theodore Zeldin, for example, invokes that term to advocate an anarchic pluralism in the place of cogent causal reasoning: 'Causation has been almost as merciless a tyrant to history as chronology.'[6] For Zeldin, total history incorporates 'everything', yet is, as he sees it, 'an emotional history of man'.

Two sets of debates must be distinguished at this point, though they will often be closely bound up in particular texts. The first is about whether 'social history' can be conceived according to what kind of substantive focus is considered most appropriate. For example, class-conflict approaches may be pitted against (only) demographic or geo-historical propositions. Eugene Genovese and Elizabeth Fox Genovese declare

Braudel a great anti-Marxist on just this basis.[7] Again, labour history may be thought to be social history in G. M. Trevelyan's sense—history with the politics left out.[8] On the other hand, labour history seems to encourage concentration on trade unions and work relations at the expense of those general aspects of popular culture (the family, leisure, popular 'thought') to which Trevelyan himself gave priority.

The second, over-arching question is general and methodological: how far and in what sense can or should social history be 'scientific'. For example, the neo-Marxist editorial of the first issue of *Past and Present* (1952) was keen to emphasize its credentials as a 'journal of scientific history', only to drop the term in later years without undue change of content. Similarly, the 'new social history' attributes its scientific status to a purely *methodological* concern with 'proper' quantification, whilst Gutman's critique is an appeal for a more sensitive humanist approach to history. But Gutman is not thereby vacating a 'scientific history'. Rather, his position is established by arguments showing Fogel and Engerman's 'science' to be nothing but positivistic misconception and liberal ideology.

Social history needs to be more explicitly aware of its own assumptions, and in particular to consider that 'scientific' history need not be set against theoretical and ideological choices. It is one of the strengths of oral history, labour history, and feminist history that these ideas are regarded as essential to a critical historiography. Here, the more overtly political aspects of commitment in historiography are stressed, and feminist and oral historians often forge a link between social history and *socialist* history.[9] They are, as I see it, intrinsically important as well as methodologically significant. I will argue, without intention of denigration, that 'history from below' is a problem shared by labour, oral, and feminist history. In addition, oral history confronts difficulties associated with its 'methodological' label. In feminism—perhaps because of rather than despite its fundamental importance—the entire gamut of questions about theory, method, and ideology in history is displayed, but those problems have not proved more tractable as a result. One concept continually highlighted in feminist and socialist historiography (and which has been stressed by E. P. Thompson in particular) is that of *experience*.

1. Labour History

Socialist and Marxist historians have commonly concentrated on the history of the labour and socialist movements. There should be no surprise about this: the modern working class and its forms of politics were either mythologized or ignored in historiography until fairly recent times. Labour history was thus an *intervention*. Organizationally, it grew out of the context of the workers' and adult education movements, and from socialist discussion and agitation. [10] Substantively, it represented the attempt of a social majority to reclaim and celebrate its own development.

However, 'labour' history is open to a number of objections that can no longer be avoided on political or theoretical grounds. One reason for this is that labour history can take on unnecessary teleological connotations: the history of the *rise* of labour, its progressive social prominence. There is nothing intrinsically socialist about these sweeping backcloths. Francis Williams's *The Magnificent Journey* (1954) is an obvious example of how labourist conceptions of legal unionism and 'participation' in the Social Democratic machinery of modern capitalism are deemed the goal and achievement of a genealogy of 'progress'. On the other hand, socialist accounts can also portray a somewhat poetic harmony of interests. Dona Torr's *Tom Mann and His Times* (1956), for example, traces the development of the labour *and socialist* movement, the apotheosis of which is Tom Mann—male, engineer, Communist, worker-intellectual. He is presented as the representative of 'the movement', its history, and its (communist) aspirations. Of course, teleological panoramas have political purposes, and historical rhetoric is itself a principal means of awakening a popular sense of the past. But there are surely dangers in this form, whether the content is 'progressive' or not; and even good labour history tends to remain a politically invested concentration on union struggles and male workers.

This leads to a second general question. As a rule, labour histories have not been histories of the working class as a whole, and may be criticized on that basis. Yet it is also difficult to see exactly what working-class history would amount to. An exemplary work such as E. P. Thompson's *The Making of the English Working Class* might be imitated for other periods, showing how politics and labour struggles have a wider basis in popular culture, for example. However, Thompson's work is controversial as well as brilliant, and books similar in scope to Thompson's that lack the style and bite (such as Cole and Postgate's *The Common People*) might not be thought to provide a model for a history of the class as a whole. Indeed, more thought needs to be invested in the concept of 'the class as a whole', for its meaning is not self-evident. It is certainly worth posing the problem of whether even 'class' history, and not just labour history, is limited by its very strength and identity as 'history from below'. The emphasis, quite naturally, tends to be placed on the achievements or potential of 'the labouring classes'. Working-class history, involving sympathy, is often celebratory or defensive. Important as this may be, it cannot serve as social history in Hobsbawm's sense of the history of society. If it is correct to include in the latter a conception of social theory, then a history of the working class is only one component of that larger project.

There would be losses as well as gains in such a project. It may be that the fire of a 'committed' class-history is dampened when a less focused, more analytical perspective is adopted. However, a mode in which elements of 'commitment' and 'detachment' are combined does not seem intrinsically contradictory, though it is undoubtedly extremely difficult to accomplish successfully. My point is rather to do with the object of attention. For a 'larger' project of the kind Hobsbawm has advocated, there would have to be important changes of emphasis from the aims characteristic of history from below. I have in mind here Thompson's concentration in *The Making of the English Working Class* on the *experiences* formed in, but going beyond, class subordination; this concentration is explicitly in opposition to a more 'objective' account of class relations in general. Since this issue has been widely discussed elsewhere,[11] I mention it only to illustrate the problem inherent in the task of producing a history of society.

Thompson's own pioneering work on the eighteenth century[12] shows that an analysis of class *relations* (and not just experiences) necessarily involves a wider perspective. And Perry Anderson has rightly said[13] that Marxist histories from *below* should be complemented by *Marxist* histories 'from above'. Some synthetic analytical work must find a bigger place in social history if the merger is to be more than mere juxtaposition. Such work has notable precedents, notably Maurice Dobb's *Studies in the Development of Capitalism*, though it is true that Dobb did not display the attention to political and cultural forms that writers like Thompson, Hill, and Hobsbawm have subsequently—and admirably—developed.[14] Still, the general point can serve to support the idea that particular perspectives do require a more extended theoretical elaboration.

Returning to labour history in its narrow sense, we may note that it need involve no theoretical or methodological innovation. It remains, in respects, perfectly orthodox historiography, as is evident from the most important of its rare 'manifestos', the Preface to Briggs and Saville's collection.[15]

2. Oral History

Oral history is a rapidly growing field. Its subject-matter is difficult to define, but it perhaps pays more attention to communities than to labour, and to consciousness than causation. In addition, its obvious methodological novelty embodies a challenge to academic histories of the right or the left. More directly than even Thompson's literary recovery of people excluded from historiographical memory, oral history gives a 'voice to the voiceless':[16] by means of tape recordings and working-class (though not only working-class) autobiography.

Oral history is community based, but it cannot be regarded as mere *local* history with a radical face.[17] Local history, in spite of its cinderella status in academic history, does not fundamentally challenge historiographical practice. There is little sense, for example, that 'the sources' in the locality need be handled differently from in the museum. Raphael Samuel mentions Professor Hoskins's deep distrust of oral sources, indicating the 'Leicester school's' professional fear of impressionism.[18] But the professionals in question have their own guiding image of the community they investigate: it is a pleasing picture of English consensus and of cultural harmony.

Paul Thompson, in *Oral History*, forwards these and other challenges that his method puts to academic history. Yet he is keen to argue for the legitimacy of oral history, reminding us that the documentary-political view of history and its sources is, historically, the exception rather than the rule. This criticism admits of a crucial dimension of historiography, one that is missing from many overviews (including this one): the power relations between, and class background of, the *practitioners* of history. For Thompson and Samuel, oral historians are as conscientious about their sources as anyone. They are also aware, as many historians are not, of the wider political and social implications of forms of historiographical debate and publication. Consequently, oral history does *not* treat 'social facts as things'.[19] Its subjects should be ordinary, (mainly) working-class *people* for whom a 'scientific' outlook is necessarily alienating, yet who are the subjects and makers of history. Although it is a humane enterprise, oral history is no less technical than its pseudo-scientific opponents. Its potential documentation is larger and its records more accurate than conventional sources, and its 'auxiliary' techniques involve a basic knowledge of modern equipment. The sources themselves (tapes, for example) still require the historians' apparatus of 'criticism' for their interpretation.

Important as oral history undoubtedly is, some (related) reservations can be made about it. First, oral history, literally, is a technique or a kind of source. In itself it is not a theoretical or political choice of a specific nature. It thus appears to refer to an unnecessarily methodological or technical definition of priorities in history. On the other hand, Thompson argues that all great historians—including Herotodus, Machiavelli, and Macaulay, as well as Mayhew—were oral historians of sorts: they *listened* to people. Yet *this* definition seems unduly broad, and misses what is radical about contemporary oral history's technical and political intervention.

Second, oral-history sources consist of the transmission of the historically equivalent experiences of various subjects to the historian-analyst. However sympathetic that historian may be, the subjects' reports are as transparent or opaque as documents, and which they are is also related to the framework employed by the analyst. So oral history does not at all dispose of *some* kind of 'objective' or 'external' relation in which the historian stands to the object of investigation. (Since degrees of 'alienation' are crucial, I am not suggesting that oral historians are *simply* professional historians; but they are that, too.) Also, the ability to listen to people, and to note down their authentic experience, does not strip the interviewer, transcriber, and analyst of theoretical presuppositions. Rather, it highlights them.

Third, there is no reason why the testimony of bankers, lawyers, lords, or clerks is any less valuable than that of miners or fisherwomen. Again, this point about the *content* of oral history undermines the notion that there is any *automatic* link between a methodological technique and a political objective. A more immediate political difficulty arises here, too. Oral history does tend to be celebratory: the people themselves, it must be hoped, express the sentiments of popular autonomy, and solidarity— perhaps even socialist aspirations. But a noticeable feature of some workers' autobiographical material, for example, is a lack of comment of a general social character.[20] Indeed, it is necessary, if painful, to speculate that what is progressive oral history on Clydeside or in Hackney might be reactionary in Birmingham or Bognor—and again, much depends on who is doing the interviewing. In short, oral history *as such* has no direct bearing on the question of 'objective' class relations or the problem of ideology. Paul Thompson's optimism on these critical issues for oral history is admirable, but it is a rationalization, and even a contradiction: 'If oral history reproduces the tension between (theory and fact), then that is its strength.'[21]

These reservations are substantiated by reference to two of the best works of oral history, Jerry White's *Rothschild Buildings* and Raphael Samuel's *East End Underworld: Chapters in the Life of Arthur Harding.*[22] The former is local history as recalled and experienced by the Jewish tenants of a London tenement block. However, the very gamut of experiences, perceptions, and politics requires strict organization by the historian and a substantial 'structural' contextualization. The latter book is one of the richest pieces of historical testimony likely to be unearthed, but the stylistic distinction of Harding's underworld narrative and the shrewd selectiveness of his memory only exacerbate the difficulties faced by the historian in deciphering oral sources. Here the paradoxes multiply, for the very 'authenticity' of Harding's account is at one with its questionable 'representativeness' in class and political terms. And the qualitative feel of the 'period' is conveyed through a peculiarly integrative set of personal representations. Not surprisingly, Raphael Samuel feels obliged to set to work on a companion volume on the political economy of crime in order to clarify some issues arising from Harding's opaque oral discourse.

3. Feminist History

Feminist history represents a profound critique and reorientation of social history. The latter's aspirations to be adequate to all areas of social experience and labour history's right to speak for history from below founder when the representation of women in history is considered. The motivation behind a critique of the history of 'mankind' that omits a good half of it is primarily, and rightly, political. Feminist history of necessity also raises theoretical problems about historiography, and 'technical' ones about research methodology. Even less than labour history is feminist history only one approach to the subject amongst others. And like oral history, part of the critique conducted by feminism has to do with the profession itself and its characteristic apparatuses, which are patriarchal both in personnel and in content.

It is a more open question whether the emphasis on conveying the experiential basis of women's oppression complements or precludes a more theoretical or analytical moment in feminist historiography. It is certainly a common view that the pseudo-objective manner of theoretical discussion (including Marxism) is a product of typically male modes of conduct, and is thus inappropriate to feminism. If this conclusion were generalized, then any attempt to develop a common programme of analysis for feminism and Marxism would inevitably seem fundamentally mistaken. However, without appealing in advance to a synthetic Marxist-feminist perspective, it can be suggested that the feminist critique of social history raises as a problem *within* feminist historiography the key relationship between theory and experience. And Marxist-feminism is one persuasive mode of addressing that question.

American feminist history, for example, has little to do with Marxism. The notion of a more adequate social history, however, remains fundamental. Berenice Carroll argues that writing women into history requires a new kind of *history*, a search for different categories.[23] In other words, feminism is not a matter of seeking out heroines or of restricting history to women only. It involves the critique and transformation of existing practices and concepts. For instance, in the collection *Liberating Women's History*, Linda Gordon *et al.* conduct an extensive theoretical exposé of a whole range of historical writings; A. D. Gordon *et al.* criticize standard notions of periodization; and Gerda Lerner questions the relevance and power of Marxist and structuralist.'alternatives' to the dominant models.

What problems arise when alternative feminist tasks and frameworks emerge from this engagement with orthodoxy? Should pioneers of women's (but not necessarily feminist) history—such as Mary Beard's *Women as a Force in History* (1947)—be recovered and proclaimed? Or should they be regarded with some detachment? More substantively, new concepts seem to be required in order grasp the nature of ideology and its historical representation. For example, it can be asked whether the representation of the Victorian mother has not been systematically moulded into a patriarchal notion of passivity and contentment. P. Branca and P. Scott-Smith have argued, in opposition to orthodoxy, that the concept of 'domestic feminism' facilitates a quite different historical representation.[24] Work of a similar kind in the Hartmann collection, to do with prostitution and voluntary motherhood, for example, aims to discover the essential *rationality* of allegedly deviant forms of resistance on women's part. This bears a marked resemblance to the Marxist work of Thompson and Hill in social history, in whose hands 'deviants', 'mobs', and 'eccentrics' become intelligible and intelligent agents in struggle. The feminist equivalent has a similarly revolutionary potential. However, it is salutary to remind ourselves that the method of 'empathy' entailed in those projects can easily be shared by very different theories and intentions—in this context, for example, *verstehen* sociology and radical deviancy theory, or most kinds of 'participant observation' studies. 'Appreciative' methods are not necessarily critical tools.

In Britain, feminist debates seem to be more closely bound up with the assessment of the value of Marxism. The more experiential element here has been questioned by Juliet Mitchell and Ann Oakley, who criticize the automatic assumption of 'sisterhood' and the general eclecticism they think ensues from its adoption as an analytical principle.[25] Anna Davin has highlighted the 'imaginative leap' required if feminist history is to reach into the experience of women in the past.[26] But concern has been expressed that such a recommendation continues to allot to women the role of only 'emotional' understanding. As a theoretical elaboration of one example of this latter argument, 'domestic feminism' could be criticized for the uncritical support it seems to lend to an *ideology* of domesticity, that is, one deeply related to the material and political exploitation of women.

There is thus a degree of tension between experiential empathy and ideological analysis, and the political effect of some feminist history need not, it seems, be radical in a *socialist* sense. This is especially true where women's history is not, methodologically speaking, feminist history. For example, Dorothy Thompson's interesting article on the role of women in Chartist agitation is content to register the sentiment that (some) women were there after all. Whether questions about the subordination of women within even radical or socialist movements get raised, depends a good deal on a further set of theoretical issues and political demands.

Some feminist historians adopt a recognizably Marxist theoretical framework. For example, Sally Alexander's work on female labour in Victorian London operates a Marxist conception of the changing forms of the labour process. [27] Her overview of the London trades (not dissimilar to Marx's in the historical sections of *Capital*) is combined with a critique of both Victorian records and Marxist predilections, both of which leave us very little information about working women. Such accounts are complemented by more narrowly theoretical considerations about women and the capitalist labour process. [28]

Sheila Rowbotham's work perhaps best exemplifies some of the issues and dilemmas of socialist-feminist history. Her histories are celebratory of the positive socialist goals and practices that feminists have adopted in the past. Those are held to stand in contrast, for example, to the sectarian and sexist tendencies within many left and Marxist groups. Rowbotham's work is therefore in part the recovery of key figures—Mary Wollstonecraft, Stella Browne, Anna Wheeler, Edward Carpenter—and her task is conceived as indissolubly about past and present alike.

Rowbotham's *Hidden From History* constructs a tradition of women in struggle which, in positing an essential unity of socialism and feminism, suggests the artificiality of 'Marxism' as a privileged theoretical account of society and of socialist politics. The same point is made, more autobiographically, in *Women's Consciousness, Man's World* and in her contribution to *Beyond the Fragments*. [29] But the condemnation of Marxism as theoretical is not as straightforward as it looks, for Rowbotham too expresses a contradictory attitude to the relation between the personal mode and more 'disembodied' ways of analysing political movements. This is particularly true of the different parts of *Women's Consciousness, Man's World*, where these two modes are juxtaposed rather than integrated. Assuming that such integration is possible and in some degree desirable, the problem is sometimes resolved by appeal to the notion that the personal is political, and this seems to avoid making a distinction and comparison between analytic and appreciative attitudes. There is certainly much to be said for this, but some feminists will be reluctant to cede too much to the appreciative side of the dialectic if it appears to sacrifice analysis. For one thing, they might, with reason, be wary of experiential identification or celebration alone. Second, the principle that history is largely dictated by present politics is not, in my view, a necessarily progressive one. For example, the 'long march' of labour, or Communism, or Social Democracy, might share these two aspects of celebration and progression. There is no great *long-term* value in a pragmatic approach to history. Another specific reason for objecting to the latter is that it is important to know that, say, liberal suffrage movements were stronger historical presences than socialist-feminism. In this context, it is legitimate to ask how far a slim biography like *Stella Browne* really illuminates historical analysis rather than laying claim to an easily-earned 'representativeness'.

These comments lead to a third consideration: that the 'experiential approach, however important, and on occasion revolutionary, is not (or should not be) thought of as opposed to analytical or theoretical argument. Rowbotham's work is certainly not untheoretical, and it is predicated upon a critique of 'factual' or 'neutral' historiography. But there is the feeling in her work that theory is a betrayal of the historical subject-matter, and that what counts in the end is 'understanding'—and in context that term means less than critical assessment. This view is part of the 'common sense' of historians of many political persuasions. Whether the 'theory' be thought of as feminist or Marxist-feminist, the problems illustrated in Rowbotham's methodology are ones that require more extended treatment. Until such time as a consensus is reached on the *role* of theory, and the sort of theory required in feminist work, feminist history—like labour and working-class history—will remain principally a descriptive category.[30] The *political* connotations of the term are very probably more important than the theoretical questions raised here, but that does not mean that the latter are of no consequence.

Current debates illustrate some of these issues. The concept of patriarchy, for example, has become something of a battleground of political and historical analysis.[31] Christine Delphy, for example, argues that it refers to the forms of material exploitation of women by men. In Delphy's view (and mine), this general proposition is compatible with historical materialism. That is, the theory and history of women's oppression also refers to material and economic forms as a key principle of analysis. This convergence does not necessarily vindicate Marxism, for it may be that Marxism, to its discredit (and in common with other theories predominantly practised by men), has not paid enough attention to some fundamental facts of material and social life. Nor is it wholly to support Delphy, for the *details* of her notions of modes of production are not necessarily convincing, or Marxist.[32]

On the other hand, feminist theory sometimes begins with a logical separation between itself and Marxism. The latter, it is held, does not speak of human subjects, and therefore cannot theorize the nature of female subjecthood. Similarly, since Marxism on this view is a theory of material determination, it cannot allow autonomous political and ideological formations to play a key role in the analysis of gender relations and sexual politics.

In so far as the latter arguments themselves lay no claim to material and economic analysis, then, we can agree that Marxism and feminism are irreconcilably opposed.[33] However, it is unlikely that feminist historians would be pleased with the prospect of analysing the *autonomous* political or ideological or even biological formation of female oppression. Further, the conception of Marxism touted in these 'feminist' arguments is distorted. An analysis of society on the basis of 'personification' rather than human subjects is the basis upon which real people can be thought of in a determinate way. It is just because Marxist categories are 'de-personalized' that they serve as the means by which forms of labour processes and material conditions can, in historical analysis, be seen to affect men and women *differentially*.

A related criticism is the standard complaint that Marxism has no place for determinations other than material. I hope I have said enough to avoid repetition: it is not so. That is, it is not *necessarily* so. The qualification is important, because if Marxism can be conceived as convergent with feminist interests, it is obvious that Marxists have been reluctant theoretically and historically to say so. Here a *real* difficulty arises, for the men/women contradiction does cut across social formations and modes of production, and thus appears to relegate the Marxist concern with *class* analysis. Without wishing to posit an easy resolution to this difficulty, I would say that historical materialism is capable of entertaining trans-historical concepts of various kinds, provided that the historical and material specificity of social relations is respected. It is unlikely that 'patriarchy' a priori need fail to meet that stipulation, or that Marxism is *inevitably* bound to questions exclusive to male workers. If there is a resolution to be advanced here, it must, I suggest, rest in part on the kind of considerations about theory and objectivity put forward by Marxist realists.[34]

4. Experience and Theory: Social History as a Domain

These surveys of some feminist, oral, and labour history give support to the idea that 'social history' is a *domain* rather than a perspective in its own right or a given set of interests. As a domain, social history's characteristics and problems are objects of contention among different theoretical frameworks. Bodies of evidence, methodologies, and political objectives are marshalled into accounts of *society*, which are assessed according to empirical and theoretical criteria. This conception allows for the primacy of the real object (societies), yet accepts the necessity of considerable theoretical and political dimensions in the construction and use of the accounts. To view social history as 'domain' therefore encourages wide-ranging, but not boundless, debate. On the other hand, certain accounts of social history that seem to respect the need for explanatory frameworks are incompatible with the above conception, at least as construed by Marxism. J. H. Hexter,[35] for example, agrees that social classes are of particular importance for social history, but he offers a 'new' framework to replace those that are either methodologically vacuous, or stultifyingly Marxist. Hexter challenges what he takes to be the Marxist idea that the rise of capitalism forms the exclusive 'subject' of the past seven or eight centuries. He argues instead that the landed aristocracy shows remarkable resilience and that an interest in the 'overmighty subject' can be fruitfully developed. This refers to the great individuals, one of whom, for Hexter, has dominated each of the last eight centuries in English history before capitalism proper. On this basis, Hexter argues, 'Many of us have got so preoccupied with analysis and argumentation that we are in danger of forgetting . . . that telling a story is the historian's real business after all.'[36]

Hexter's argument is of the 'Trojan horse' variety. He begins by accepting that social history must be about classes, and should not be theoretically flabby. On the basis of an over-schematic account of what Marxist history is, he then posits that individuals (not classes) are of most interest to historians. And since the individuals are associated with unrepresentative exploits, although they are formed by general social conditions, it follows that historians do not analyse history. Rather, they tell the story of unusual individuals. But this is tantamount to refusing to accept the premisses of a *social* history: Hexter's modest proposal is not for a new framework within the subject; it is for its replacement by the 'great man' theory of history.[37]

Within the Marxist tradition, too, there are substantial differences of opinion about the role of analysis and its relation to the concern of the historian to portray the experiences of historical individuals. So shorn of its ideological burden, Hexter's argument carries a deep-seated problem, one that is shared in different ways by the other historiographical approaches I have discussed. It therefore merits further comment.

One important feature of some oral and feminist history is that the notion of an 'objective' analysis at one remove from experience is itself thought to be part of the way in which historiography is controlled by, respectively, the professionals and men. Indeed, militancy has been vigorously defended by Jean Chesneaux as *the* feature of a socialist approach to history. Chesneaux argues that long-range theories, including some Marxist theories, remove history from 'the possession of the people'.[38] His own view is that Marxism emphasizes 'constant creation'[39] and the absolute dependence of the past upon present political interests. The justification of history, for Chesneaux, is that it nourishes social struggles with 'nostalgia plus wrath'.[40]

This standpoint has been found useful to the History Workshop Movement in their important efforts to create an 'alternative' discursive context for people's history. But there are dangers as well as strengths in militancy for its own sake. The sense in which 'the people' have possessed history is seldom made clear, and the historical apparatus does not 'control' the past, or function for capital in the simplistic way Chesneaux implies. In so far as Chesneaux's conception of Marxism is that of a *general political activism*, it is hardly persuasive. Marxism has never proposed that history only serves the present; or if it does, it does so because its historical theories *are* 'objective'. Chesneaux is not consistent, however. The cryptic view that historical accuracy and political intransigence are complementary may express a desirable goal, but it is difficult to formulate without obvious inconsistency. For example, he argues that 'historical facts' can be scientifically known, but that they are perceived differently, according to the distorting influence of 'different times and places, among different social classes and ideological currents'.[41]

A less inflated, and more persuasive, version of the primacy of social history over social theory is advocated by E. P. Thompson. Thompson requires little assistance in polemic, as can be seen from *The Poverty of Theory*. James Henretta[42] has recently adopted a similar stance, which exhibits both the strengths and the weakness of Thompson's distinctive mode of analysis. In ways akin to the perspective I adopt, Henretta explains some of the epistemological and substantive problems generated in social history as presented in *Annales*, Hexter, the 'new' history, and some versions of Marxism.[43] But Henretta's main concern is to develop a social history, and a critique of the other models, on the basis of the *lived experience* of those people whom social history takes as its subject matter.

Henretta's position has taken much from Thompson's own pronouncements—*for* class as agency and for the historical discipline of context; *against* 'positivism armed with a computer' and against 'structuralist' or static social theory. Henretta aptly describes Thompson's method—as in *The Making of the English Working Class*—as a 'pointillist' technique, building a 'coherent mosaic' from disparate materials. The substance of Thompson's history is the analysis of different modes of production 'at least partly in cultural terms' and so 'in the consciousness of the historical actors themselves'.[44] Henretta's own 'action model' for social history perhaps endorses theoretical explicitness more than Thompson does, but it is as much geared to history 'as it was actually lived'.[15]

Interestingly, the same keynote is struck in Thompson's defence of 'experience'. Richard Johnson's discussion of this and related questions has generated a widespread debate in the *History Workshop Journal*.[46] Johnson argues that Thompson's 'culturalism' lies in a tendency to reduce considerations of class formation and conflict to matters of the subjective consciousness of the agents. However, Thompson 'refuses' this idea, and he has now distinguished between 'experience 1' and 'experience 2'.[47] The first does indeed refer to history as *perceived* by participants. The second, by contrast, refers to what happens to subjects as they experience social life.

Henretta's idea of history 'as it was actually lived' is similarly in need of clarification. Does it mean, 'as people saw it', or 'as they had to live it'? Even to allow the distinction, however, is surely to undercut the extent to which 'experience' can be pitched against 'theory'. 'Experience 2' is clearly no more (and no less) related to people's consciousness than is 'social conditions' or even 'structural constraints'. Consequently, 'experience 2' requires a theoretical, not a *verstehen* approach. Of Thompson we are entitled to ask why the same term is used to cover an important distinction.[48] Of Henretta's recommendation that a rhetoric be found that can unite meaningful narrative, analysis, and quantification, we might approve, but its status as a goal rather than a detailed manifesto must be recognized.

The tensions in these accounts indicate that, suitably elaborated, there is or ought to be no serious objection to a social history requiring a theoretical

Marxist framework. However, it is obvious from the virulent responses to Johnson, and from Thompson's *Poverty of Theory*, that 'theory' is mistrusted in many quarters.[49] This is partly for good reason: when theory poses as the 'answer' to history, implying that hard empirical research can comfortably be ignored, Marxism has succumbed to idealism. As a mirror image to that kind of 'theoreticism', there are, unfortunately, those for whom Marxism or theory is little more than an illegitimate intruder into the historians' self-referential world. Thompson's position is not nearly as subjective as that. But in his account of the 'logic of process', which he takes to be distinctive of history, Thompson shows sympathy for some of those ideas. His own strong theoretical bent succeeds in countering these impulses. The price of the compromise is nevertheless a somewhat uneven, and unconvincing argument.[50] In his own inimitable way, Thompson represents the last outpost of the view that historical methodology is, *independently* of general theoretical issues, a licit way of knowing.

Since I have discussed these sections of *Poverty of Theory* elsewhere,[51] I will only summarize the main lines of the argument here. First, it can be said that Thompson defends a fairly traditional account of 'the historian's workshop'. 'The court of history', 'the historian's procedures'—such phrases ring throughout the text, and they refer rather narrowly to the conception of history as a technical discipline having the facts as its object. 'The facts are *there*, inscribed in the historical record.'[52] The context of the assertion is Thompson's attack on Althusser, who represents philosophy, abstraction, and static theory—all the things that seem to undermine Thompson's concern for the dynamic development of human consciousness and experience. Consequently, he is driven to defend an empiricist notion of the historian's unique object (the facts), and the non-generalizability of history's method as a separate discipline.

However, Thompson is well aware that this defence does not assume agreement amongst historical *practitioners* on matters of epistemology, method, and politics. When he is concerned to stress the facts against Althusser, Thompson adopts the general mantle of anti-philosopher: historical knowledge or logic is special, and is thus different from science, even social science. I have tried to argue that this is an indefensible position. In fact, Thompson says as much himself, and in his other work he has crossed swords with this theory-less empiricist ideology.[53] Here, he allows that 'some small part of what Althusser has to say about "empiricism" . . . is just',[54] and even that ' "History" had perhaps called down this revenge upon itself.'[55] According to *these* reflections in *The Poverty of Theory*, Thompson tends to argue (or at least imply) that an epistemological underpinning for historiography is inescapable. He offers the conception of a necessary 'dialogue' between hypothesis and fact. Like Popper's account, whose outlook it resembles, Thompson's emphasizes 'empirical controls', though perhaps still in the sense that 'hard' facts are held to disprove 'abstract' theories. This intermediate position begins to square with Thompson's recognition of the *different* meanings of 'experience' and the different modes of analysis relevant to them.

In yet other places, Thompson goes further. Once, he strays into a relativist position: 'For we are saying that these values, and not those other values, are the ones which make this history meaningful *to us*.'[56] This is the consequence, I imagine, of trying to have it all ways, and of the dual notion of experience. The statement is about the *facts* of experience, but the *experience* is logically tied to the value placed upon it by the subject whose experience it is. The third notion of experience, as the ensemble of lived conditions, allows Thompson to go further still, and to grant a good deal to theory. The court of historical appeal has, after all, two benches, the second of which is 'the coherence, adequacy, and consistency of the concepts'.[57] On the whole, it could be suggested that inconsistent and all-embracing as Thompson's always-shifting polemic is, it does have as one of its basic components a *realist* conception of history. 'The investigation of history as process . . . entails notions of causation, of contradiction, of mediation, and of systematic organization (sometimes structuring) of social, political, economic and intellectual life. These elaborate notions "belong" to historical theory.'[58] It is *this* conception that is most capable of developing social history as against social scientific abstractions. It also rightly questions forms of philosophical imperialism in which the abstractions are themselves insufficiently theorized or ill-equipped to analyse real social formations adequately. That does not entail, as Thompson so often implies, an end to philosophy of history, or the uniqueness of historical method, or the inappropriateness of Marxist theory. Notions of theory as 'expectation' or the proliferation of the connotations of 'experience' do not substantially aid Thompson's genuine insights in the work of formulating a more adequate realist 'logic of history'.

Braudel and the
Annales Paradigm

It is common today to speak of the *Annales* 'school' or even 'paradigm'. As we will see, there are dangers in using these terms, which ascribe a unity of some kind, to describe a French historical journal of fifty years' standing.[1] And yet, for all its heterogeneity, those mainly associated with *Annales* have indeed been concerned to raise questions about the relations between methodology and substantive work in an unusually sustained way. The first parts of this chapter will consider the sense in which it is misleading to ascribe a unified school or method to *Annales*, but will nevertheless show that some of the major figures (Fernand Braudel and Marc Bloch, in particular) have consistently pushed historiography in a more theoretical direction.

Discussion of these points will relate to problems of realism in history. In addition, Bloch and Braudel (especially his later work) raise substantive issues that increasingly join with a flexible Marxist historiography. It seems worth discussing some of the issues raised in such a dialogue. My conclusion is that, on balance, the relations are of convergence rather than unity or antagonism.

1. The Annales 'Paradigm'

In a book Fernand Braudel approved of in all but a few historical details, Traian Stoianovich claims the existence of an *Annales* 'paradigm'.[2] Drawing on T. S. Kuhn and G. H. Nadel,[3] Stoianovich distinguishes three historiographical paradigms, in order of succession. The first—the 'exemplary' paradigm—is characterized by the notion of history as a moral lesson. From the Greeks to Machiavelli, history is written about and centred on exemplary cases of public service and moral excellence. The sense that historians are distinguished from moral or social commentators by their belief that methodical source work is the ground of any opinion about the past is almost entirely lacking.

Narrative (Rankean) or 'developmental' historiography is Stoianovich's second paradigmatic category. It is marked by the establishment of particular historical sequences based on the critical examination of documentary sources. The structural-functional paradigm, the third, is held to eschew 'story-telling' in favour of problem-solving and systematic exposition. Here there is no preference for either moral norms or evolutionary sequences. Instead, the professional standards of the second paradigm, and the sense of *explanation* in history displayed by the first, are combined to form a qualitatively new history, one appropriate for the late twentieth century.

Stoianovich's account clearly offers a vantage point from which *Annales* and other historical perspectives can be usefully contrasted. But in introducing what amounts to a model for all historiography, he raises as many questions as he resolves. For example, I am not sure—nor, I think, is Stoianovich—whether the schema is itself meant to be descriptive or explanatory. Of course, this is one result of using the Kuhnian term 'paradigm', which is notoriously ambiguous in that respect. Stoianovich states his interest in an underlying logic for historiography.[4] But I wonder whether this amounts to any more than showing how the *Annales* school especially 'transformed the discipline of history generally . . . between 1946/49 and 1968/72'.[5] To be sure, these tasks are linked. But the latter only suggests a strong campaign by a group of historians for greater theoretical and inter-disciplinary work. The suggestion of a shared and coherent methodological standpoint is a more difficult proposition. Stoianovich further implies that the third paradigm is the most appropriate for adequate historical work as a whole.

Caught between these relatively distinct problems, Stoianovich satisfactorily answers none of them. His accounts of the paradigms are brief and correspondingly weak. As Stoianovich is aware,[6] 'narrative' history, especially in its German forms, is not lacking in attempted explanations or spiritual preferences. Moreover, he has admitted having trouble 'placing' a Hume or Stewart.[7] And *within* each paradigm, there are surely anomalies—are all Greeks on a par? Is Macaulay a 'narrative' historian? C. W. J. Parker[8] has offered similar objections, concentrating on the development of British historiography. However, all these points do raise a general caution. Kuhn has influenced many social scientists, and now, it seems, it is the turn of historians to warm to 'paradigms'.[9] This seems to me unfortunate, because too often virtues are made out of the very ambiguities of 'paradigms', or 'assumptions', 'ideologies', 'practitioners', and so on, when those in the human sciences uncritically apply Kuhn's natural scientific model.

Stoianovich exemplifies this uncritical borrowing. Here is his clearest statement of what mainly characterizes *Annales*. 'More than storytelling, the task of the historian of the third paradigm embraces problem-solving and puzzle-solving.'[10] Now, Kuhn describes the activity of 'normal science' (that is, science under an established paradigm) as a regular practice of puzzle-solving, *rather than* the fundamental questioning characteristic of revolutionary breaks before a new paradigm emerges. But Stoianovich seems to be arguing that puzzle-solving is the peculiar feature of the *Annales* paradigm, and that which makes it revolutionary. In other words, Stoianovich turns a general Kuhnian concept of the form any science takes into the *content* of just one paradigm. And this is, to say the least, confusing: we might have to regard the *Annales* paradigm as the 'paradigmatic paradigm'. So in particular and in general (why not just stick with 'approaches to history'?) Stoianovich's attempt to systematize historiography does not look promising. The example also indicates the need for serious original theoretical work in history and the social sciences: scientific terminology does not necessarily produce concepts adequate to their object.

2. Change and Continuity in Annales

Stoianovich does raise the problem of whether a genuinely unified approach to history is reflected in the work of those who have been most closely associated with *Annales*. At the outset, it is important to register the extent to which it is a heterogeneous tradition.

'Synthesis'—the term Henri Berr passed down to Bloch and Lucien Febvre, and one that comes to mind in discussions of *Annales*—resembles 'dialectic' in philosophy. It can mean different things to different people, but it functions as a term of approbation by suggesting that false boundaries are overcome. *Annales* stands for a 'synthetic' inter-disciplinary history, one that aspires to a comprehension more global or 'total' than traditional modes. But 'inter-disciplinary' history can be constructed in a number of ways, not all of which are complementary.

Febvre and Bloch, the founders, were influenced by a Durkheimian notion of collective psychology,[11] and a later *Annaliste*, C. Moraze, shows a preference for psychology to the point that this discipline acquires theoretical priority. Indeed, Moraze's article 'The Application of the Social Sciences to History'[12] gives such weight to that discipline (as well as linguistics) that we might wonder whether the founders had quite that specialist emphasis in mind. Similarly, J. Le Goff's appeal for a more structural *political* analysis in history is surely to be welcomed. But his concern to pay greater attention to vocabularies, rites, and symbols in political discourse, though indispensable, is no more than a call for fuller description.[13] *Annales* is also renowned for a concern with 'geo-history'. Febvre wrote a long critical text about the use and abuse of geography in history.[14] As we shall see, in Braudel's *Mediterranean*, geo-history plays a crucial role, some say a determining one. More recently, Emmanuel Le Roy Ladurie has urged the centrality of a scientific climatic and demographic dimension.[15] Whilst this is in keeping with a common interest in structural human geography, its relation to another hallmark of *Annales*—social history and culture— leaves open some grand questions about overall methodology. Each *Annales* representative certainly gives his preference a highly individual flavour. In short, the very vastness of reference of 'inter-disciplinary' history admits of strands that might turn out to be quite diverse (psychology, social history), in the absence of some coherent principles by which the interconnections are guided. Here general methodological agreement over the years may misleadingly suggest a common theoretical core.

There is also a wide diversity in the *objects* of study. Braudel's *Mediterranean* is ultimately a geographically-decided object. Bloch's comparative medieval studies focus on social organization (feudal society) or some distinctive cultural aspects (popular conceptions of kingship). Further, on a technical level, the methodology of *Annales* has become increasingly systematic as quantitative research. This does not necessarily undermine an approach based on 'problem-solving', but it does represent a shift from the more cultural and literary concerns of Febvre and Bloch. In general, there is no obvious consensus through *Annales*' lengthy lifetime about how societies are to be characterized. The interests expressed and the methods employed do not of themselves produce a conception of the substantive objects of history and social science. Provocatively: *Annales*' scrupulous techniques, combined with pluralism in direction and theory, are typical, rather than subversive, of the academic historians' ethical guidelines.

That generalization, of course, does little justice either to the anti-establishment impulse of the early *Annales* or to the value of some professional standards. But it does call into question the sense in which there is an obvious *Annales* paradigm. It is more important to look closely at the relation between methodology and substantive work in *Annales*' major figures. But provided the cautionary note has been struck, some general flavour of the *critical* character of the intervention of *Annales* as a whole can readily be given: it is justly famous (or notorious).

Drawing on 'synthetic' evolutionary philosophy, which Berr advocated, Lucien Febvre maintained an interest in scientific explanation: 'History can be a science only in the measure in which from being descriptive it becomes explanatory.'[16] Time and again in polemical essays, Febvre rails against 'the fetishism of facts' and the 'superficial and academic logical system of history'. One especially debilitating effect of the latter was the rigid scenario between 'Act 1 – establishing the facts' and 'Act 2 – apply them'.[17]

Bloch, less sensationalist than Febvre, was equally insistent on the necessity of *abstraction* in historical thinking. Braudel's motto, from Sombart, was 'no theory, no history',[18] and he supported it with arguments that have a constructive aspect and a more modern feel for issues in the philosophy of social science; Braudel considered narrative as a principle of historical reason as 'quite simply a philosophy of history like any other'.[19]

The *polemic* of Febvre and the philosophical confidence of Braudel have been transmitted to the third generation of *Annales*. François Furet has again demanded a transition 'from narrative history to history as a problem'. For Furet, *sources* (they are not 'facts') must not be merely interrogated, they might even be regarded as 'invented'.[20] A supporter of rigorous quantification, Furet nevertheless accepts that each stage in statistical procedure raises methodological problems.

Many of the problems raised about how to interpret *Annales* can be seen in Marc Bloch's work, though his own manner is serene rather than strident.[21] I argued earlier that *The Historian's Craft* embodied a 'realist' historiography. Braudel displays a rather cooler attitude to Bloch than to Febvre in his encyclopaedia entries,[22] but it seems to me that Bloch was as much concerned as they to develop an alternative to narrow-minded empiricism. The 'totality' that emerges from his classic works is more fully integrated, more *social*, than Febvre's. Febvre's histories tend to concentrate on the general cultural characteristics of a period, more than on specific interrelations of social levels or aspects. There is less the sense in Bloch that a cultural*ist* totality is being sought, though of course this does not mean that he was not extremely taxed by questions of cultural correspondences and mechanisms.

But it is also true that Bloch is open to very different appropriations. Many historians rank Bloch high in their discipline without making claims about his radical methodology. Moreover, it is common for Bloch to be cited as a Durkheimian, in view of his pursuit of 'collective mentalities' and the like. H. Stuart Hughes and R. Colbert Rhodes are sociologists who hold to such an interpretation. I firmly oppose that reading of Bloch, but it is easy to see how his interests encourage it. And if I have praised *The Historian's Craft*, it should be said that Alasdair MacIntyre has taken it to be a good defence of 'pluralism' (and so, by implication, not fully 'realist').[23] One might also refer to Bloch's essay gently advocating the comparative approach in history, for it hardly suggests a methodology motivated by a coherent alternative strategy for history.[24] These contrasting elements can be pursued through Bloch's major writings.

The *Royal Touch* is often thought of as Bloch's 'Durkheimian' book. There, popular religious belief in curative power is taken to be an index of 'social cohesion'.[25] Bloch expressed enthusiasm for Emile Durkheim and *L'Année Sociologique*, which contributed to his (Bloch's) views on the union of history and social sciences. Durkheim, like Bloch, challenged the positivism of historians such as Charles Seignobos. In this case, however, intellectual affinity need not be seen as theoretical identity. We should remember that in Durkheim terms such as 'division of labour', 'social cohesion', 'collective consciousness', 'organization' and so on are not the clearest concepts, nor is their scope very specific. Bloch's adoption of some of the *terms* is no real indication that he uses them in quite the same way. Similarly, Durkheim's 'social realism' is more firmly wedded to presuppositions distinguishing (in a positivistic way) between appearance and reality.[26] And 'social facts' in Bloch do not seem to be as detached as in Durkheim from their *particular* exemplifications.

Those who argue that Bloch employs Durkheim's *concepts* seem unaware of the critical distances outlined above. Rhodes treats Durkheim's theories quite uncritically, and simply assumes that Bloch embodies these norms. Thus Bloch's 'explanatory history' posits 'social solidarity as the basic reality'.[27] It is true that *The Royal Touch* can be seen as an essay on the rituals of social cohesion. The rites surrounding the healing of scrofula directed the popular mentality towards the central figure of the king, who 'personified' the whole society. However, unless one is looking in advance for a nice correlation, there is little to suggest that, for Bloch, 'the whole society' is *constituted by* the system of collective representations as it would be for Durkheim.[28]

When we turn to Bloch's two classics of 'total history', the comparison looks weak indeed. Stuart Hughes—quite unaccountably—thinks that, in *Feudal Society*, Bloch has some disinterested penchant for place-names, and that the 'spirit' of institutions is at the heart of the work.[29] Rhodes regards both *Feudal Society* and *French Rural History* as exhibiting a Durkheimian concern for the way in which 'social organization' is responsible for the growing imprecision of the *conscience collective*, corresponding to the rise of individualism and the division of labour. However, this account is surely not much more than the assertion that Bloch was interested in the social basis of ideas. Dealing as he does with the structure of feudalism and its disintegration, *of course* Bloch is concerned with the rise of individualism. But this is an impoverished gloss on what is being said in a text like *French Rural History*. It is no surprise that historians become irritated by interfering philosophers and sociologists. But the argument is not only naïve, but also wrong, because if the 'Durkheimian' label is to mean anything, it must mean more than 'a concern for the social basis of changing ideas'. That, after all, could summarize *any* sociologist's interests. Rather, the description must imply that Bloch's books illustrate that the fundamental realities of society are the developing systems of collective representations, and it is these that explain material developments. An example given by Rhodes is that the open field system (as in *French Rural History*) is, for Bloch, the 'material manifestation' and the 'outward expression' of underlying social realities.

I think the impression of Bloch that Rhodes and others give is mistaken, but there is no need to overstate the case. In the *Selected Essays* especially, and at times in *The Historian's Craft*, Bloch implies that historical facts are essentially psychological. My argument is that the substance and manner of Bloch's analysis do not support this view, and Bloch's assertion at the end of his methodological text is in no sense the logical conclusion of his account of causality, which is in principle materialist.[30] In the example before us, the nearest Bloch comes to Rhodes's summary is in *French Rural History*, where it is held that *enclosures*, like open fields, are the material manifestations of underlying social realities.[31] Bloch also speaks of the origin of rural customs residing in hardened and time-worn beliefs. But from neither statement can a causal relation of an idealist kind be derived. Nor is causality, one way or the other, exactly the point at issue. Rather, Bloch is explaining the likelihood of enclosure in those areas where there were sufficient amounts of uncultivated land available such that communal rights over small fractions of permanent arable land could safely be given up. Elsewhere, of course, fierce class struggle prevented such an easy transition.[32] So Bloch is in fact arguing against the interpretation that either feudal relations or their decline were only naturally conditioned. They are subject to adaption depending on the character of *social* relations. But it is quite apparent throughout the book that by the latter Bloch means primarily *class* relations and conflicting economic objectives. A dominant

theme in both *French Rural History* and *Feudal Society* is the refutation of
'legal' definitions of feudalism. Legal definitions tend to 'rationalize' and
naturalize the existing hierarchical structures. Instead, Bloch places the
social basis of law in class structures of exploitation and the resistance to
them.[33] His discussion (at least to my mind) is more akin to the Marxist
theory of ideology than to Durkheim's *conscience collective*.

But Rhodes's argument that Bloch was a functionalist is not wholly
dispelled, since it may be argued that Marxism is itself a kind of functionalist theory. It is true that Bloch is interested in the legacies of 'organic'
social structures and naturally-based customs, but there is no evidence for a
standard functionalist model of organic—modern or natural—market society in Bloch.[34] Marxism is not a functionalism, but if it were, Bloch would
still not be a functionalist, because there is a wealth of evidence against the
existence of 'reductive' attitudes in his work. He is at pains to show the
different variants of feudalism; its incomplete disintegration; the internal
divisions of classes; forms of kinship relations; cultural life; and conceptions
of rationality; all with an insight free of any 'functionalist' traces. Yet his
enterprise is remarkably integrated.

In sum, Bloch's work is a rich mine for prospectors of many persuasions.
It does not receive a full enough elaboration, independent of the studies, to
justify any clear attribution of his general theoretical allegiances. Nevertheless, it can be said that the combination of social theory and history, source
work and methodological clarity, does distinguish Bloch as a *realist* thinker. And it is not too much to say that his substantive guiding principles are
materialist, not idealist. They are closer to Marx than to Durkheim.

3. Braudel: Methodology and Social History

In 'History',[35] Berr and Febvre set out three categories of causality in
history: contingency, necessity, and logic. In principle, these levels were to
be complementary and interactive; they were not seen as competing for the
historian's attention. Fernand Braudel's key methodological passages take
up this same tripartite division, but he sheds some of their philosophical
burden, discussing the differences between them in terms of historical
scope.

'Contingency' in Braudel's treatment becomes 'L'histoire événementiel-
le', 'that is, the history of events: surface disturbances, crests of foam that
the tides of history carry on their strong backs'.[36] 'Necessity' in Berr and
Febvre becomes Braudel's second category of 'social history, the history of

groups and groupings'.[37] This embraces 'collective destinies and general trends', combining 'structure and conjuncture, the slow-moving and the fast'.[38] The third, 'logical', concept that Braudel expounds is the 'imperceptible' history of 'man in his relationship to the environment', a history almost of 'constant repetition'.[39]

Braudel is thus more firmly historical than Berr and Febvre, but he does accept that each concept's analysis and application involves a philosophy of history. Each of the (corresponding) parts of *The Mediterranean* is an 'essay in general explanation'.[40] There are, then, grounds for agreement with R. Forster's view that if there is an *Annales* paradigm, it is that of Braudel's *Mediterranean*.[41]

Massively important though those volumes are, they generate problems within Braudel's procedures. We must bear in mind that the second edition is better illustrated and substantially more 'socially' oriented than the first.[42] And given the physical division of the work into three parts, and the strong emphasis on the first (long-term) part, it is easy to see why reviews of the first edition expressed concern about 'geo-history'. We need not agree with Deleginski's charge of 'vulgar biological materialism' or (from a different ideological point of view) with B. Bailyn's or J. H. Elliot's over-humanistic concerns about determinism to see that these reviewers have a general case.[43] J. H. Hexter's critique—the toughest and most rigorous—sets out the objections at length.[44] The book, he says, is full of deceptive but inconclusive quantification,[45] and projects personifications of seas, centuries, and towns, thus metaphorically expressing a teleology of the structural model itself at the expense of human agency. The three parts do not fit well together, and each is too long. Hexter, of course, relishes exposing 'source-mining' and 'lumping', and so fails Braudel's script much in the same way as he rejects those of Marxists.[46] But in also revealing Braudel's own uneasiness about his model, Hexter has done a service, because the inadequacies of the model (the three-tiered structure is not integrated in principle) reflect *The Mediterranean*'s substantive dislocations. So what is at fault may not be Braudel's *application* of the model, nor the desire for theoretical guidance, so much as the conception of the model itself. By limiting theory to 'models', one concedes from the outset that real history will fault it. But actually, the fault often lies in the inadequate theoretical specifications. 'Models' always leave a gap between abstract and concrete, whereas—at least in principle—a *theory*, if elaborate enough and consistent, can explain history in such a way that our conception of reality cannot be other than 'confirmed' in and through the theory.

My own feeling is that Braudel has precluded integration, and thus totality, because of the way his object has been set up, and the way the production of the book occurred. It is no accident that the third part of the work, dealing with political history and events, sits oddly with the rest, particularly the geo-history. The racy history of Lepanto etc. must appear rather arbitrary, since it was written in the war-time years, before Braudel's full conversion to total history. This has the paradoxical effect of highlighting the dominant, glacial movement of long-term structural changes, whilst rendering the light crests of politics relatively self-sufficient. We can thus concur with the proposition common to Marxist and non-Marxist commentators, that the structures and times of *The Mediterranean* are insufficiently dialectical.

In 'History and the Social Sciences: the Long-Term', Braudel develops a more consistent realist programme. It is not, as many assume, the theoretical counterpart to *The Mediterranean*, but a re-working of its assumptions and aspirations. Braudel maintains his critique of histories of the short-term, implicitly placing narrowly 'documentary' historiography somewhere between the interest in the 'long-term' shown by eighteenth- and nineteenth-century historians and recent analysts of 'structure' (for example, E. Labrousse). However, Braudel's long-term is considerably less a matter of geography than in *The Mediterranean*, since he refers (though cryptically) to long-term structures other than geography. The *status* of the long-term, too, is less that of a determining than of a foundational structure. This is crucial for a realist position, because a foundation both enables and constrains. The extent of Braudel's shift in emphasis here should not be exaggerated; it remains less than explicit in the text.

As to the *logic* of history, Braudel argues in favour of *reconstruction*, not 'observation'.[47] In this respect, history is no different from the social sciences. And the false conception of history as a record of events is entirely applicable to parts of the social sciences. Braudel thus advocates the unity of the two branches of science: history, becoming more scientific, can be the explanation of social reality in its entirety, of the present and the past. His claim about history here is consonant with the kind of realism I have been suggesting, but Braudel's conception of *social science* might be less fitting, since he seems to set great store in its *quantitative* character. This is not at all to underestimate quantification—indeed, it is fundamental. Rather, it is to recall that those who make a fetish of that side of the scientific apparatus of the humanities often appear to have abolished critical thinking.

Braudel is fascinated by *time*, and that intrinsic character of being— sometimes elusive to social scientists—is not lost in his new conception of unity in social studies. Time is a force external to humanity, and the historian is closer to its pulse than is the philosopher.[48] Braudel would thus disagree with Althusser, who proposes the relativity of *all* historical time. Althusser rightly says that the *model* of 'a continuous and homogeneous time . . . can no longer be regarded as the time of history'.[49] But it does not follow that time 'has to be *constructed* out of the peculiar structures of production'.[50] Here I would support Braudel, for he retains the crucial 'nature-relation' without which historical materialism would appear, ultimately, in a relativist guise. (In fact there is indication that Althusser himself is aware of this.[51]) Of course, the retention of the 'external' relation is a problem as well, since it entails the possibility of reductionism. But it is preferable to the view that all sense of time as such is an empiricist aberration.

The last important feature of 'History and the Social Sciences' is Braudel's awareness that models are not theories. Aids and analogies they may be, but a model will always have elements dissimilar to the object. This insight allows Braudel both to advance upon the methodology of *The Mediterranean* and to continue to express reservations about the Marxist model of base and superstructure, and the 'laws' that appear to follow from its rigid application. This is paradoxical, because where he gets the logic of models right, including that of base and superstructure, Braudel gets Marxism wrong, failing to see that a theory is not identical even to its dominant model.

In *Capitalism and Material Life*, the three-tiered structure differs in scope and emphasis from that which organizes *The Mediterranean*. As we might expect, climate and geography are rightly still important, but Braudel's perspective is more *socially* defined. In this respect, the later work picks up and develops the themes of Book II of *The Mediterranean*. Book II was a discussion of the social structure and cultural formations of the Mediterranean. One might speculate that it could have profitably been expanded to include aspects of Books I and III—the patterns of transhumance and nomadism, or the nature of the Turco-Spanish conflict, for example. The discrepancy between levels of analysis might then have been overcome.

The subject of *Capitalism and Material Life* is the pre-history, development, and contradictions of the penetration of the world by the capitalist economy. It is therefore about the transition from feudalism to capitalism, but Braudel is wary of overt Marxist teleology: he concentrates on the *slow* transformation of material existence for the mass of peoples. The book predates 'History and the Social Sciences: the Long-Term', but it is, I think, theoretically significant in several distinct respects. Braudel emphasizes the two necessary sides of historical dialectic. The humanity-nature relation conditions social structures; and material practices set limits to the kinds of 'civilization' and culture that are possible. But the material and cultural practices themselves are not in any sense the straightforward product of a 'mode of production' or economic organization *simpliciter*. Indeed, Braudel's general concepts here are interesting in their own right.

Material life is said to include 'repeated actions, empirical processes, old methods', but it also refers to the changes in 'processes employed by blacksmiths, weavers and, still more, by miners and shipbuilders'.[52] It is therefore an exceptionally broad—if not unclear—category. But material life is distinct from economic life. The latter 'is born of trade, transport, and the differential market situations and of contact . . . between rich and poor, creditors and borrowers, monetary and premonetary economies.'[53] Capitalism is a more specific and sophisticated system of rules and calculations. It encroaches on all forms of life, though it does not cover the whole of even economic life.[54]

There are difficulties in this schema. Is each sphere of life empirically distinct? Or do they form a living whole, the distinct aspects of which are perhaps characterized by *degrees* of conscious economic strategy? Material life, though not uneconomic, is the aggregate of everyday practices *within which* economic activity takes place, and where economic rewards are enjoyed. Capitalism refers more to the operations of a smaller group of people who direct (and absorb) the economic life of the masses. So the schema seems to refer to different 'levels of abstraction' under which aspects and areas of material life can be analysed: no general *causal* processes are being asserted.

However, there is also the idea that the European countries—in virtue of material factors—develop into more specialist and capitalist societies. And here, while it is clear that Braudel does not, for example, employ a 'classical' Marxist notion of a capitalist mode of production, some principle of historical causality distinguishing *real* differences between aspects of life is employed. Braudel emphasizes the causal importance of technical means of production, though as a general historical formula, 'perhaps the solution is not primarily technical'.[55]

His account of 'capitalism' would appear to tie it only to a form of financial or commercial calculative practice. On the other hand, Braudel is quite aware that it begins to form a system that responds to the constrictions of material life by transforming those routines, customs, and accumulated knowledges. It is this general dialectic that Braudel refers to as the forms of *civilization*. Unlike many who have been attracted by this term,

Braudel's approach is a form of cultural materialism. Ideas and costume alike count as 'fashion'; cultural forms are said to be a decipherable social grammar—as important as demography or prices to the analysis of social structure.[56] Here Braudel adopts a view of social structure and cultural content based on the recognition of class division (though it must be said that as a rule Braudel does not go out of his way to emphasize class struggles).

4. Braudel, 'Annales', and Historical Materialism

I hope to have indicated the impressive combination of methodological and substantive analysis in Braudel's work. As with Bloch, it is reasonable to conclude that Braudel's 'synthetic' success is largely tied to his realist tenets of explanation. In the course of this argument, the relation of Braudel's realism to Marxism has appeared as a significant question. A discussion along these lines is also demanded by the nature of Braudel's later work, such as *Afterthoughts on Material Civilization and Capitalism*.

In general, the relation of *Annales* to Marxism has been mixed, often turbulent. Peter Burke holds that *Annalistes* have not subscribed to a 'determinist' theory of history, so they cannot be Marxist.[57] On the other hand, R. Mousnier and R. Pillorget argue that *Annales* is dangerously 'orientated in a direction conformable with the dogmas of historical materialism'.[58] This is also a debate about the *kind* of work *Annales* represents. Stuart Hughes sees only cultural or spiritual curiosities in a work such as *Feudal Society*,[59] while a more straightforward academic historian states outright that it is about the connection between feudal ideology and economic structure.[60]

Marxists have been equally divided. J. Blot criticized Braudel for his 'fetishism of exchange' (in contrast to the Marxist stress on production). Traian Stoianovich has traced the debates in France in the post-war years, showing Blot, Althusser, and Albert Soboul hostile to *Annales*, whereas Lucien Goldmann, Pierre Vilar, and J. J. Goblot have been more receptive.[61] M. Harsgor cites a Soviet criticism to the effect that *Annales* favours 'vulgar biological determinism', and someone as well informed as Jerzy Topolski expresses similar reservations.[62] On the other hand, Withold Kula, Topolksi's 'Poznan school' colleague, has become almost a member of the Braudellian company.[63] In Britain, Gareth Stedman Jones has accorded *Annales* high praise. But Rodney Hilton thinks this assessment is misleading: Stedman Jones 'somewhat overestimates the revolutionary character of the *Annales* school, which, however innovative, is by no means Marxist'.[64]

Given this background of controversy, it appears that any attempt to come to a view 'on balance' will be contested. The problem is exacerbated when we consider that Braudel has recently remarked that his views on the development of capitalism are 'basically identical' to those of Immanuel Wallerstein,[65] and Wallerstein has been heavily criticized by Marxists as being 'neo-Smithian'. The debates on the transition from feudalism to capitalism, of which these latter disputes form a part, are indeed highly relevant to our eventual assessment of Braudel. But since they are complicated in their own right, they are best discussed in an appendix. In any case, it seems important to discuss the ways in which there can be a fruitful dialogue between Braudel and Marxism that does not resolve itself into excessive fundamentalism.[66] Pronouncements about how Braudel, or Wallerstein, fail to be Marxist in the fullest sense can develop into unproductive intellectual self-satisfaction.

It is, of course, desirable to state important differences where they exist. I mentioned earlier that Braudel clearly recognizes class differences, but he does not employ the category in any central way. Further, the notion of class *struggle* finds no place in Braudel's long-term structural perspective. And it *is* true that Braudel is fascinated by the development of exchange-relations, to the point that he seems to consider capitalism no more than one of its subdivisions. Finally, we may note that Braudel sometimes speaks of Marx, but he shows little detailed acquaintance with Marx's work.[67] He has insisted more than once that Marx never used the term 'capitalism',[68] and will not subscribe to the idea that there are Marxist 'laws'.[69]

This is a weighty catalogue of sins for those anxious to defend historical materialism from the infiltration of 'bourgeois' ideas. But Braudel often does utilize conceptions consonant with a broadly Marxist perspective. And where his own distinctive formulations about capitalism are in evidence, Marxists can still learn from them. It is thus not absurd to posit an affinity between Braudel and historical materialism.

I have already alluded to Braudel's methodological importance. There are substantive affinities, too, as regards both his general conception of society and his understanding of capitalism. Here is an example of the former: 'Any highly developed society can be broken down into several "ensembles": the economy, politics, culture and the social hierarchy. The economy can only be understood in terms of the other ensembles, for it spreads itself about and opens its doors to its neighbours. There is action and interaction.'[70] One of the hallmarks of Braudel's thought is that he fuses material life and civilization. Whilst he is interested in the way in which *cultural* phenomena inter-relate (having much respect for Michel Foucault), Braudel never loses sight of material life, the nondiscursive: 'Civilizations—strange collections of commodities, symbols, illusions, phantasies, and intellectual models—work in this way. An order becomes established which operates down to the very depths of material life. It is inevitably self-complicating, being influenced by the propensities, the unconscious pressures, and all that is implicit in economies, societies, and civilizations.'[71] It is capitalist economic organization above all that permeates the whole of material and cultural life. Braudel's conception is not, as such, that of a capitalist mode of *production*. Rather, it is the idea that economic organization entails a whole range of complementary cultural phenomena: a civilization. Of course, Braudel does not plumb the precise location of determination or the notion of 'entailment' as Marx did. But the notion of a determinate social totality is present, and that is one crucial aspect of 'mode of production' in the Marxist sense—one that alone makes interesting historical analysis possible.

The accusation of 'fetishism of exchange' levelled against Braudel is exaggerated. Braudel needs no reminding that his writings deal principally with *merchant* capitalism. It is true that his use of the term 'capitalism' continues to apply mainly to interest-bearing capital, trade systems, and the echelons of high finance. But Braudel knows that merchant capital does not of itself form a 'mode of production'.[72] The slightly unorthodox terminology should not be taken as a sign of the absence of a concept. 'Capital goods', he writes, 'deserve that name if they are part of the renewed process of production; the money in an unused treasury is no longer capital, nor is an unworked forest.'[73]

Braudel's 'civilizations', unlike Febvre's, are not cultural or structure-less totalities: he prefers 'socio-economies' to 'society' as a guiding concept, and respects its source: 'By laying emphasis on socio-economic systems, I believe I refer to the most durable achievements of Marxist thought.'[74]

Genovese and Fox Genovese are mistaken to think Braudel a great anti-Marxist. His greatness is not borrowed from anyone else, but it is of a kind akin to Marx's, for he has made a contribution to historical science that combines methodological, theoretical, and substantive work. Braudel does not have Marx's 'genius' (Braudel's term), but this is just because on the whole, his concepts *are borrowed*. Some are taken from the French geo-historical tradition. Yet Braudel accepts as fundamental Marx's 'correctness' about questions of the ownership and control of the means of production.[75] His substantive—if brief—discussions of the 'putting-out system',[76] the role of policy,[77] and the essential unity of 'internal' and 'external' reasons for the development of industrial capital owe a heavy debt to Marx.[78] One might speculate that it is because Braudel has an inadequate conception of what Marxism *is* that he does not more readily 'stay with Marx'. This is suggested in his reading of Marx's 'exact words', or the 'strict rule' about base and superstructure, 'which in his eyes seems to make all society swing from one of these structures to another.'[79]

What of the concepts Braudel does favour? Victor Kiernan has rightly suggested that the concept 'world system', which Braudel defends, has at least some advantages over 'mode of production', though it is no doubt rather woolly.[80] It is plausible to suggest that 'world system' does undermine 'mode of production', in the sense that 'mode of production' has always had an uncomfortable dual role to play: it is a 'purely conceptual' object, yet it expresses relations that are embodied in concrete societies. Assuming the notion of embodiment to be unproblematical (as I think it is, given careful specification), there remains a problem about the bounds of the social totalities 'governed' by modes of production. In Marxist literature the *social formations* that seem to fill the role of 'embodiments' most appropriately have no necessary geographical location.

The concept of mode of production, then, may be clear enough, but its ambit is not. This is true even of capitalism, the most 'global' of the modes of production. So the additional idea of world system is useful here: it is *implied* by 'capitalism' *qua* mode of production, but the questions it asks are historical, about the *degrees* of the penetration and the *variable* forms of capital accumulation, given the logical parameters of the concept. Marxists in recent years have (rightly) been concerned with the phenomena of 'combined and uneven' development. This is a notion that involves the possible co-existence of modes of production, and the differential, specific historical forms of class struggle that arise therefrom. 'World system' does not contradict 'mode of production'; rather, it encourages the latter's historical employment at a lower level of abstraction.

Appendix

'Logic' and 'History'
in the Transition Debates

The question of the transition from feudalism to capitalism has figured
prominently in Marxist literature, partly because it highlights the way in
which, for historical materialists, methodological guidelines for historical
analysis entail theoretical questions about the basic concepts of Marxism
itself. For example, Wallerstein's 'world system' perspective has been
heavily attacked *just because* it appears to be historically (that is, methodologically) useful. Ernesto Laclau and Robert Brenner in particular have
attempted to show that whilst it is superficially attractive, Wallerstein's
position is (Adam) 'Smithian'; it is thus assumed to be deeply inimical to
Marxist concepts. In what follows, I shall try to show that, contrary to the
impression conveyed by such decisive refutations, there is much unfinished
business for *Marxists* on these issues. My focus is the problem of the
relation between 'logic and history', a problem that envelops the substantive discussions.

In the now-classic 1950s debate on the transition, Paul Sweezy bore the
brunt of the 'fundamentalist' critique. Brenner's summary is worth quoting
at length.

'In the last analysis, Sweezy's error is twofold. It is to posit that the
producers' relationship to the market determines their operation and development and, ultimately, their relationship to one another—rather than
vice versa. Correlatively, it is to locate the system's potential for development in the capacities of its individual units (thus the emphasis on motivations) rather than in the system as a whole—specifically, in the overall
system of class relations of production which determine/condition the
nature of the interrelationships between the individual units and, in this
manner, their operation and development. For Sweezy, then, it is the
market relation which gives rise to new needs, engenders a "profit motive"

leading to specialization and the development of production, and which forces competition for survival.'[81]

In this summary, it is clear that the general question of what is 'correct' Marxist analysis is superimposed on the more particular matter of the transition. Especially important is the question of the concept 'mode of production'. The debates—whether about Braudel's or Wallerstein's 'world systems', or about Sweezy and Pirenne on 'trade'—become heated because fundamentalists feel the *raison d'être* of Marxism to be under attack. This occurs when historical conclusions are felt to undermine 'the logical development of the categories'.[82] Exactly what the status of the latter is, however, is not actually evident from the contributions of the first set of fundamentalists. Sometimes this is a matter of expression. The following claim of Kohachiro Takahashi, for example, seems to me intrinsically obscure: 'A rational comprehension of feudalism presupposes a scientific understanding of capitalism as an historical category.'[83] But the conceptual problem is not just terminological. Rodney Hilton and Takahashi take the position that the logic of the categories expresses the internal, concrete principle of movement of the modes of production, whatever the appearance-form it may take: 'The dialectics of history cannot go forward without self-movements (the contradictions of inner structure).'[84] This is why there must be a 'prime mover' in a mode of production, and why it cannot, logically, be thought of as *external*. Thus, Sweezy's 'own suggestion that feudalism had no "prime mover", that is no internal dialectic, is in fact non-Marxist'.[85]

Now Sweezy was also accused of seeing 'trade' as the prime mover. Yet there is no contradiction here, because if the prime mover is external (as 'trade' was thought to be), it is not, dialectically speaking, a prime mover at all.

In fact, Sweezy did not regard trade as being 'external' to feudalism. His case was rather that the 'internal' dynamic of feudalism, if narrowly conceived, does not automatically explain its dissolution. Maurice Dobb, in his response, admitted that the matter could not be seen 'as a question of *either* internal conflict or external forces. . . . I see it as an *interaction* of the two; although with primary emphasis, it is true, upon the internal contradictions'.[86]

Part of the difficulty with this complex discussion is that logical questions of causality and contradiction are thought of in spatial terms, 'internal-external'. What is at stake is the relation between the logical categories and historical circumstances. Are the 'occasions' that spark off a logical dynamic part of that dynamic or not? The fundamentalists say 'yes', because the *form* taken by a process is part of its dialectic. But being the form rather than the content, historical occasions *are* in a sense empirical circumstances external to (that is, not logically essential to) the development of the inner process. This is, I think, the context of Dobb's apparent hedging in the last quotation.

Part of Sweezy's argument is that this view of dialectic does not sufficiently grasp how the logic of capitalism—which is purely internal—differs from the 'laws' of feudalism, which are more subject to historical contingency.[87] Sweezy's point is thus also about the varying logics of different modes of production. For Sweezy, feudalism is, logically, more open to external causal factors in its disintegration. For Dobb, external factors, whatever they may be, are logically subordinate to, or are actually part of, internal contradictions; and feudalism is no exception. But the fundamentalists do not accept that, in spite of his uncertainties, Sweezy is also posing the problem of a more adequate conception of the relation of logic to history, namely, that the 'logic' is not something over and above, or even 'inside', its historical 'occasions'. In other words, a more causal than 'essentialist' account of historical development is required, which can avoid the polarity between (dialectical) logic on the one hand and mere contingency on the other.

Actually, Dobb's seminal *Studies in the Development of Capitalism* does not, as is sometimes supposed, offer a clear notion of the function of categories in historical analysis. A number of possible conceptions of that function are suggested in Dobb's account. First, a Weber-like analysis of an 'ideal-typical' kind is advanced. Here, the categories 'illuminate' parts of historical reality, but can never exhaust it: 'In any given period, to speak in terms of a homogeneous system and to ignore the complexities of the situation is more illuminating, at least as a first approximation, than the contrary would be.'[88]

There is also a notion that the 'pure' mode of production approach is actually inferior to empirical generalization on the basis of observed cases: 'In a certain sense one would be right in talking, not of a single history of Capitalism, and of the general shape this has, but of a collection of histories of Capitalism, all of them having a general similarity of shape.'[89] Finally, there is the rejection of these two approaches: 'The conception of socio-economic systems, marking distinct stages in historical development, is not merely a matter of convenience but an obligation—not a matter of suitable chapter headings but something that concerns the essential construction of the story if the story is to be true.'[90]

But this fine formulation is still not clear about whether the stories are true, because they emerge from a certain kind of essential theoretic construction; or whether the relation between a true story of any kind and its construction is an essential relation—that is, not just a contingent 'methodological' coincidence. The former, I take it, is a rationalist or essentialist standpoint that is inimical to the idea of historical contingency—and it is not necessarily Marxist. The latter is a realist conception that requires that historical circumstances are not thought of as simply external accidents—but are not 'internal' either, not given as a matter of pure reason. This conception is entirely compatible with the work of Dobb, Hilton, *et al.* But even the latter are not sufficiently aware of the difference between the two senses of historical 'logic'. Sweezy at least prised them open.

Recent exchanges conform to the lines of the original debate. Indeed, the notion that a fundamentalist view automatically provides a clear understanding of the connection of logic to history appears to be stronger than ever. Brenner defends Dobb's substantive and epistemological positions against Wallerstein's 'neo-Smithian' perspective. Laclau argues that a Marxist approach based on the fundamental concept of 'mode of production' must be kept quite separate from the revisionist 'historical world systems' accounts of Andre Gunder Frank and Wallerstein.[91] Again, the key criticisms by fundamentalists are that in the world-systems theories market relations take priority over those of production and class struggle is largely absent. Similarly, Laclau[92] and Brenner[93] regret the lack of the concept of a dynamic relationship between productive forces and relations of production in the new models. The critics therefore still reject the idea of any 'external' causality in the transition from feudalism to capitalism.

However, in some respects both Laclau and Brenner have had second thoughts on the issue. And when one considers the revisions by Jairus Banaji and Barry Hindess and Paul Hirst (in *Pre-Capitalist Modes of Production*), it is clear that behind the fierce fundamentalist rhetoric all these writers are keen to display, the 'classic' positions are no longer occupied in quite the same way. This realization is important, for it allows Marxists to engage in critical dialogue without the false sense of theoretical self-sufficiency that fundamentalism often engenders. Laclau has expressed dissatisfaction with 'mode of production' as an explanatory category. What had been considered the *virtue* of the concept now becomes the source of its limitations: ' "Mode of production" is an abstract concept and not a stage of concrete historical development.'[94] Consequently, Laclau thinks it desirable to shift from the higher to intermediate levels of abstraction, such as that of the 'economic system'—and thence to 'concrete' social formations. More substantively, Brenner has questioned the Dobbian assumption that feudal crisis led to the replacement of feudalism by the capitalist mode of production.[95] Another important point in Brenner's major reassessment—and here he follows Hilton, as well as Sweezy and Wallerstein[96]—is that the fundamentalist concept of a 'really revolutionary road' along which the small yeoman producers, rather than merchant capitalists, developed into industrial capitalists, is open to serious doubt.[97]

Hindess and Hirst and Banaji make rather more sweeping revisions, though they are said to be nothing of the kind. Without going into great detail, it can fairly be said that while these authors make stimulating criticisms, their own theoretical alternatives are badly flawed or incomplete. Moreover, their exact relation to the historical issues remains unclear, if only because of those theoretical problems. Hindess and Hirst's book valuably weighs against the teleology and reductionism that can accompany fundamentalism. But their own definition of 'mode of production', especially, is problematical and inconsistent. They develop other useful concepts, such as the 'conditions of existence' of relations of production, the 'variants' of the feudal mode, and the 'material causality' of the class struggle: but it is unclear whether these ideas, however 'concrete' they sound, involve historical references or whether they are purely theoretical constructions. In a book that claims to reject 'rationalism' as well as the concept of 'real' history, this problem is inescapable.[98]

Banaji criticizes fundamentalists because he thinks they restrict the crucial category 'relations of production' to the form of exploitation that is preponderant, in a quantitative sense, within a social formation.[99] This restriction ignores instances in which Marx and Lenin refuse to follow that criterion. For Banaji, the supra-historical model of a sequence of modes of production defined as forms of exploitation fails to respect the specificity of the laws of motion of each individual mode of production. The nature of relations of production are not, for him, given by forces of production and so cannot define which mode is really dominant. Rather, the definition of relations follows from the ascertained laws of motion.

But Banaji's positive suggestions are quite obscure, despite his valuable critique of the 'forces-of-production / forms-of-exploitation' connection. To say that the definition of a mode of production cannot fully account for the variety of the *content* of the relations of production is one thing. But it does not follow that relations of production cease to be part of the definition of a mode. Certainly, Banaji's idea that the laws of motion of a mode of production can be stated *prior* to specification of its relations of production is difficult to understand. And what those relations might be if they do not involve characteristic forms of exploitation is a puzzle.

Banaji does posit the need to beware of a rationalist model in which particular economies and societies are 'merely' historical. E. J. Hobsbawm has reminded us that Dobb's model showed the influence of the heavily doctrinal debates in the Soviet Union in the 1920s and 1930s between 'productionists' and 'marketeers'.[100] And of course, Stalin's own *Dialectical and Historical Materialism*, with its rigid schema of the modes of production, for many years cast a shadow over Communist theoretical debate. Laclau and Brenner, free of that context, are aware (as Hilton was then) of the possible relegation of class struggle and historical specificity in a fundamentalist approach. Certainly there is more awareness now that recourse to Marx himself will not necessarily resolve the issues. As I will point out in chapter 8, key notions in Marx—for example that of so-called primitive accumulation—themselves shift between the poles of 'logic' and 'class struggle' or history. Where there is evidence in Marx for the 'internalist' conception of a mode of production, it is often couched in the questionable form of Hegelian 'internal relations'. For example, 'The conditions and presuppositions of the *becoming*, of the *arising*, of capital presuppose precisely that it is not yet in being but merely in *becoming*; they therefore disappear as real capital arises, capital which itself, on the basis of its own reality, posits the conditions for its own realization.'[101] This kind of formulation only compounds the problem of whether the internal logic of feudalism is to be sharply distinguished from, or is itself moulded by, the logic of the growth of capitalism. It gives support to internalist accounts, but they are the weaker for this sort of support. There seems no outstanding reason to dispute Hindess and Hirst's judgement that 'For all the polemical value of [Marx's] chapters, they do not and cannot provide a scientific knowledge of the transition from feudalism to capitalism in England.'[102]

It is a pity that, for all this, Brenner and Laclau should don the fundamentalist mantle in their exposé of the weakness of Wallerstein's *The Modern World System*. The manner of their critique tends to close down the openings for Marxists to develop intermediate concepts. True, Wallerstein is not in any obvious sense an 'orthodox' Marxist. But like Braudel, his concepts are borrowed largely from Marxism, and where his concerns are adapted from Braudel himself, my partial defence of the latter is appropriate. Wallerstein provides a more complex and specific account of feudal crisis than is usual in Marxism, but it remains in important respects close to Hilton's initial formulations, emphasizing production and social relations.[103]

The main criticism levelled against Wallerstein is that of a 'Smithian' concern with the market and trade, a 'circulationism'. However, there is no clear sense in which Wallerstein erects trade into the 'essence' of capital-ism. To be sure, he is keen to emphasize how important bullion and money were in facilitating exchange relations, but, 'It was not bullion alone, but bullion in the context of a capitalist world economy, which was crucial.'[104] Moreover, arguments such as Banaji's must align Wallerstein with the Marxist tradition, since in the latter's 'underdevelopment' paradigm 'coerced cash-crop labour' in the periphery is highlighted just because it is the dominant form of exploitation. Wallerstein's overall framework here appears reasonable. 'The key variable was the emergence of capitalism as the dominant form of social organization of the economy. Probably we could say that it was the *only* mode in the sense that other "modes of production" survived in function of how they fitted into a politico-social framework deriving from capitalism.'[105]

Drawing a parallel between Wallerstein and Perry Anderson's *Lineages of the Absolutist State*, Hobsbawm has endorsed the concern to examine capi-talism, or the expansion of the world economy 'as an economy'.[106] Regret-tably, Hobsbawm does not discuss the way that kind of investigation has been somewhat suppressed by the twin conception of mode of production: first, as a homogeneous form having 'expressions' in different national routes; second, as an economy having the full form of a social totality.

Wallerstein's line of approach is no less important than Hobsbawm's, even if the commanding surveys of the latter's social and political 'world system' texts have not been matched by the former.[107] Wallerstein has tried to see his way round the more 'semantic' criticisms he accuses Laclau of drawing. It would not necessarily be 'revisionism' if Marxists could respond in kind.[108]

Part Three

Historiography

We must put theory to work, and
we may do this either by interrogating evidence (research) or by
interrogating historiography and
other theories (critique).

EDWARD THOMPSON

Marx's and Engels's Historical Writings

I have argued that philosophical analysis of a realist character can sharpen our understanding of what it is that socio-historical knowledge provides, and maintained that historical materialism is the most comprehensively equipped substantive and methodological *corpus* to fulfil those requirements. But caution about the exact significance of these two rather grand propositions is requisite. Although Marxism has contributed to the clarification of realist principles, it does not uniquely exhaust them. On the other hand, the epistemological task of analysing the presuppositions, methods, and general results of substantive accounts is a limited one. Whilst my claim has been that epistemology has a significant bearing on debates, it should not be thought to stand in for the main enterprise of concrete research, and discussion.

Such complexity is well illustrated in the historical writings of Marx and Engels themselves. In particular, those works again raise the question of the compatibility or antagonism between two sides of Marxist analysis. The first is the long-term functional explanation of social processes and relationships. The second is the attention to particular classes, groups, and agents in the more immediate, often political, forms of social conflict. My general conclusion will be that Marx's and Engels's substantive work provides no unilateral prescriptions. It is, on the whole, marked by shifting emphases and unresolved assertions of analytical priority.

1. Reading History

In parts of some of the 'historical' writings, real history is but 'the expression' of historical laws. The *Communist Manifesto* constructs a scenario of a spiralling march to communism. More than most of Marx's texts, it constitutes a 'reading' of history. Of course, some guiding principles can be gleaned from it: 'the history of all hitherto existing societies is the history of class struggles'.[1] But as a text fashioned for struggle, the *Manifesto* adopts a rhetoric of 'inevitabilism': 'We see, therefore, how the modern bourgeoisie is itself the product of a long course of development, of a series of revolutions in the modes of production and exchange.'[2] 'Its fall and the victory of the proletariat are equally inevitable.'[3] This rhetorical note is not unique to the *Manifesto*. It can be found in all Marx's writings, even in the most apparently unphilosophical works, like the *Eighteenth Brumaire*. And, as Stuart Hall as aptly said,[4] there is an 'echo' of the *Manifesto* in *Capital*: in fact, it is rather a loud and recurring echo.

One of the unresolvable problems in interpeting Marx is the extent to which his often Hegelian manner follows into the heart of the Marxian *content*. This is best examined in *Capital*, but it is clear from the *Manifesto* that the *results* of a historical process seem to be carried within it as an 'internal' presence, or an 'internal' logical connection. Modern industry, for example is said to produce the proletariat as its 'special and essential product'.[5]

Yet this can surely be rephrased without the teleology so as to stand as an acceptable historical proposition. The authors of the *Manifesto* are clear that the sweeping surveys of history that provide Communists with their theoretical conclusions have not been 'invented'. 'They merely express, in general terms, actual relations springing from an existing class struggle, from a historical movement. . . . All property relations in the past have continually been subject to historical change, consequent upon the change in historical conditions.'[6] Clearly, without their Hegelian cloak, these sentiments form 'reasonable' empirical generalizations. In other words, no more than *Capital* is the *Manifesto* simply a 'reading' of history, if by that term is meant a thesis that is unfalsifiable in principle. However, as in the discussion of fetishism and the 'historical tendency' of capital accumulation in *Capital*, a Hegelian movement of 'appearance and essence' is adopted whereby 'surface' phenomena, being the manifestation of their deep essences, tend to be regarded as derivative *in all respects*. This schema makes it difficult to clearly establish Marx's distinct contribution to the logic of the relation between theory and history.

Turning to *Capital*, a further complication can be noted. In the postface to the second edition, Marx, distancing himself from Hegel, accepts the formulation of a Russian reviewer who stresses the scientific character of the work. *Capital*, for Marx, is critique, but it is critique grounded in an alternative that 'treats the social movement as a process of natural history'.[7] Despite the 'dialectical' movement to which, according to Marx, the reviewer rightly draws attention, the conception of natural law here is inevitably coloured by the predominantly positivist account of science generally held at the time. Perhaps more concerned with factual accuracy[8] than are Hegelian 'laws', Marx expressed his view of science (and he used similar terms elsewhere) as one in which laws work 'themselves out with iron necessity'.[9] It is crucial to register these aspects of Marx. If he was a 'realist', then he often expressed his realism in 'strange' or 'borrowed' language: a mixture of Hegel and positivism. To 'read through' that language in the search for core sentiments is a procedure fraught with difficulties, one of which is that it is dangerously unhistorical. In sum, concrete history often appears in Marx and Engels as the *illustration* of general historical tendencies, expressed sometimes as the Hegelian 'realization' of some trans-historical essence, sometimes as the factual fodder for positivistic abstract law.

In their more practical writings, Marx and Engels can be specific to the point that the invocation of theoretical laws appears otiose. Parties, social forces, and individuals, to be sure, are placed in terms of economic interest, but the latter is not always cashed in terms either of *whole* classes, or of classes in their larger historical 'choreography'.[10]

Marx and Engels typically display elements of both these contrasting conceptions of the way historical processes and long-term outcomes intersect. At times their accounts seem overburdened by the weight of the general theory of history. Leonard Krieger maintains that Marx's mounting preoccupation with economic laws implies 'the futility of historical study'.[11] This is as mistaken as the claims of some Marxists that Marx's 'dialectical' method endorses the contradictions as part of some higher unity.

2. Logic of Capital, History of Capitalism

In order to avoid the erroneous idea that Marx's concern with 'history' somehow represented one (earlier) *phase* in his thinking, let us begin by looking at *Capital*. The arguments of Louis Althusser and E. P. Thompson are instructive here. For, while they stand ostensibly on opposite sides of the theory/history divide, these authors seem to agree about what is going on in *Capital*. According to Althusser, Marx 'does not even study the English example, however classical and pure it may be, but a non-existent example . . . the "ideal average" of the capitalist mode of production.'[12] This is not even an ideal-type which is *compared* to reality, but is 'the mere

conceptuality of his object, and the "average" as the content of the concept
of his object—and not as the result of an empirical extraction'.[13] What
serves as the highest accolade for Althusser is precisely what moves Thompson to repudiate this Marx. 'This mode of analysis must necessarily be
anti-historical, since the actual history can only be seen as the expression of
ulterior laws.'[14]

Althusser and Thompson thus agree about *Capital*; they simply place
different values upon it. Or so it appears. Actually, behind the rhetoric,
there is tacit understanding first, that Marx is not simply engaged in a
logical exercise, and second, that historical materialism would disappear if
it were only logic, or only history. Balibar recalls the purpose of the
concepts: 'once one has formulated its "presuppositions"—it is also necessary to build an actual history with them, quite simply, *real history, our
history*'.[15]

Thompson, for his part, while chiding Marx for not being historical
enough, lets it slip that theoretical tools are necessary after all. Marx's
'achievement' in *Capital* does not '*produce* historical materialism', but it
'provides the preconditions for its production'.[16] This more flexible assessment on Thompson's part allows him to accept too that Marx is not quite
empirically barren. Volume 1, at least, 'is rich in historical hypothesis'.[17]
Thompson and Althusser, despite the ulterior motives of each, duly, if
grudgingly, pay their respects to Marx's complicated discourse.

Marx thus seems to present history either as the 'realization' of laws, or
as the domain in which theory and research necessarily, if uneasily, converge. Marx's use of history for conceptual purposes is therefore varied and
interesting. One kind of historical illustration that is clearly functional for
the explication of Marx's economic concepts is the historical 'sketch' drawn
to illustrate specific features of capitalism. For example, Marx compares
and contrasts the Danubian *Règlement Organique* with the English Factory
Acts. The latter are themselves but a historical illustration of how 'Capital
. . . takes no account of the health and length of life of the worker, unless
society forces it to do so'.[18] The point of introducing the corvée system is to
show that whereas the latter 'presents surplus labour in an independent and
immediately perceptible form',[19] the appropriation of surplus-*value*, unique to capitalism, 'is not directly visible'.[20]

When Marx outlines a general concept before he turns to its specific
form under capitalism, he tends to give concrete examples, but not yet
historical ones. His discussion of use- and exchange-value, and of 'simple
reproduction' are of this kind. Similarly, his account of co-operation is
concretized by hypothetical illustration: 'For example, if a dozen masons

place themselves in a row . . . '[21] Thus, at a high level of abstraction, Marx operates with hypothetical examples, though they are 'realistically expressed'. But the *point* of the 'rational abstractions' is to facilitate more specific analyses. Consequently, the *conceptual* elaboration of a concept, say co-operation, also takes on an increasingly historical mode of presentation. For example, where a labour process is of a fixed natural period, co-operation based on numerical calculation of the required labour is desirable. 'It is owing to the absence of this kind of co-operation that a great quantity of corn is wasted every year in the western part of the United States, and the same thing happens to cotton in those eastern parts of India where English rule has destroyed the old communities.'[22]

These kinds of illustrations are, of course, convenient samples for Marx, with which fully capitalist forms are contrasted. Yet even in these most clearly 'logical' expositions, the thumbnail illustrations achieve something more. Returning to the 'Danubian principalities' case, Marx's intention is not only to highlight the uniqueness of capitalism. If the corvée law 'was a positive expression of the appetite for surplus labour, which every paragraph legalized, the English Factory Acts are the negative expression of the same appetite'.[23] 'Capital did not invent surplus labour.'[24]

In other words, the distinctiveness of capital can be measured only if it is also clear what it has in common with other modes of production. So conceptual illustrations they may be, but even these sketches are required to describe some of the specific historical features of the modes of production. Equally, they facilitate a more general account of historical development: the theory of history and specific historical formations are bound up with one another.

The more substantial historical sketches, such as those dealing with factory legislation, take on a partial life of their own. Here, Marx is not just illustrating his concepts, he is also pitting them against recent history, in an attempt to explain and understand it. His discussions become correspondingly more complicated and more uneven. If his overriding concern is the *typical* forms of capital, the texture of his writing is nevertheless brilliantly observational. I am thinking here of the detailed overviews of the 'sweated' labour processes in the 'monstrous phase' which precedes the production of relative surplus-value, or of the relay system in the factories. These descriptions give full reign to Marx's ample journalistic and sarcastic literary talent.[25]

But there is also a tension in Marx's arguments about the Factory Acts, in chapter 10 ('The Working Day') and in chapter 15 ('Machinery and Large-Scale Industry'). The tension concerns the relation between the 'logic of capital' and 'class struggle'. In the former mode of analysis, ostensibly different conclusions are drawn. For example, 'Capital oversteps not only the moral but even the merely physical limits of the working day.'[26] But, 'It would seem therefore that the interest of capital itself points in the direction of a normal working day.'[27] No doubt these statements can be reconciled, but they do suggest that some damage is done to the specificity of political and industrial conflict by reading into them the 'natural laws' of capital's historical course. In the same vein, the rule of the state and the factory inspectorate is rendered ambiguous. The moral stature of Horner and his colleagues is clearly noted by Marx. But the state that represents 'society' in interposing a 'barrier to the transformation of children's blood into capital' is also, and inconsistently, 'a state ruled by capitalist and landlord'.[28]

In Marx's more concrete mode of analysis, these 'logical' moments are to a large extent reconciled. The ambiguities nestling in the different tendencies within the natural laws of capital are often overcome by statements about the specific, historical outcome. 'The establishment of a normal working day is therefore the product of a protracted and more or less concealed civil war between the capitalist class and the working class . . . in the arena of modern industry.'[29]

Stuart Hall and G. A. Cohen summarize the 'tensions'. Hall argues that the idea that the functional logic 'is one which can be separated from the "logic of class struggle"—two disconnected threads—is definitively disposed of in this chapter (15 of *Capital*).'[30] I hope I have registered, as Hall does, the complexity of Marx's thinking in these sections.[31] But his conclusion seems both an underestimation of the *Manifesto* and an overstatement of the extent to which that text is 'thoroughly transformed' in *Capital*.[32] This is because, especially in chapter 15, Marx extensively (if complexly) develops his propositions of the '1859 Preface'. 'The system of machine production therefore grew spontaneously on a material base which was inadequate to it. When the system had attained a certain degree of development, it had to overthrow this ready made foundation.'[33] 'Machinery revolutionizes, and quite fundamentally . . . the contract between worker and capitalist.'[34]

More so than in chapter 10, Marx is interested here in the material basis or productive forces most suited to mature capitalism. 'The lengthening of the working day . . . permits an expansion of the scale of production without any change in the amount of capital invested in machinery and buildings.'[35] 'Machinery produces a surplus working population which is compelled to submit to the dictates of capital.'[36]

We can thus agree with Hall that Marx really sets to work 'the notion of dialectical development',[37] but the extent of the deep complementarity of Marx's two 'threads' postulated by Hall seems to me exaggerated.

Cohen also posits harmony in Marx's account of class struggle and natural laws. His reason for this, in contrast to Hall's more dialectical approach, is that 'Class insurgency is more likely to achieve its object when the object has functional value. . . . A reform essential to capital's survival can also qualify as a "victory of the political economy of labour over the political economy of property".'[38] But the implication of Cohen's remark is that class insurgency achieves its object only when it has a functional value either for capital or for the burgeoning productive forces of socialism. There is no suggestion that the struggle for 'the political economy of labour' could even attempt to secure victory without the pre-established co-operation of the level of productive forces. In any case, Cohen acknowledges that Marx 'establishes no bond uniting' the causal influence of the working-class movement with the functional need to curb the passion of capital for a limitless draining of labour-power. It therefore seems to me that whatever the value and coherence of the solution *Cohen* provides for Marx, Marx's own ambiguities need to be stated.

The same tensions appear again in the closing chapters of *Capital*.[39] For the most part, Marx presents 'primitive accumulation' as the *historical* precondition of the capitalist mode of production. Marx's presentation of the process is correspondingly in the 'historical' mode—full of description, details, and varieties of 'class struggles'. And it is laced with moral outrage: 'capitalism comes [into the world] dripping from head to toe, from every pore, with blood and dirt'.[40]

Marx's review of the expropriation of the agricultural population (chapter 27) and of the bloody legislation against vagabondage (chapter 28) is inspired history: 'the history of their expropriation, is written in the annals of mankind in letters of blood and fire.'[41] His vehemence does not necessarily contradict the scientific temperament: space is found to trace the genesis of the farmer (chapter 29) and of the industrial capitalist (chapter 31).

It is not therefore only a matter of 'history from below'. Primitive accumulation, however, whose 'secret' is forcible expropriation, is not altogether free of the tentacles of capital-logic just because it historically predates capital. Of course, in Marxist literature this has been discussed as part of the *transition* to capitalism. In Marx's account, 'the historical process of divorcing the producer from the means of production'[42] forms the 'prehistory of capital'. However, although primitive accumulation is not part of the capitalist mode proper, the 'capitalist era' is held to date 'from the sixteenth century'.[43] The historical genesis of capitalist production involves the regulation of wages, by which means workers are forced into a condition 'suitable for making a profit. . . . This is an essential aspect of so-called primitive accumulation.'[44]

For Marx, then, 'preconditions' are not just historically contingent. That is to say, they are not part of the 'strict' logic of capital; but 'primitive' accumulation is no chance affair. This duality is grasped best in the concept of the 'presuppositions' of capital,[45] which refers both to logic and to history. The logical aspect of primitive accumulation might be thought of as the internal logic of *feudalism's* decline, or of the *transition* from feudalism to capitalism. However, either option is, for Marx, typically part of the long-term logic of capitalism (if not of capital proper). The 'metamorphosis' by which the 'isolated, independent working individual . . . is supplanted by capitalist private property . . . decomposed the old society'.[46]

In the famous chapter 32 of *Capital*, Marx outlines the 'historical tendency of capitalist accumulation'. He places the expropriation that is capital's 'point of departure'[47] in the same logical process as the departure of the expropriated capitalist. 'What is now expropriated is not the self-employed worker, but the capitalist who exploits a large number of workers.'[48] Just as at a certain stage of its development, the old mode of production 'fetters' new forces in 'the bosom of society' and 'has to be annihilated . . . is annihilated', so the immanent laws of capitalism take their own course 'with the inexorability of a natural process'.[49]

'The monopoly of capital becomes a fetter upon the mode of production which has flourished alongside and under it. The centralization of the means of production and the socialization of labour reach a point at which they become incompatible with their capitalist integument. This integument is burst asunder.'[50]

The discussion shows once more how difficult it is to separate 'history' and 'theory' in Marx, as if one had clear analytic priority. There is little doubt, though, that the 'logic' has become more a trans-historical pattern than a statement of complex, overdetermined tendencies. Part of the fault lies in the dominant conception of the forces of production, and it illustrates the sense in which I claimed earlier that functional explanation untempered by careful causal reasoning becomes a philosophy of history in the more speculative sense. We need not *reject* the thesis of forces of production merely on this basis. For example, it is legitimate and important to argue that fundamental constraints are imposed on social structures by the character of the means of production. The adoption or development of a particular material basis for the labour process, of a certain level of science and the effects on the technical division of labour which that entails, can only encourage the preservation or transformation of social relationships. But Marx, in passages like the above, sometimes inflates the depth of this tendency, and assumes its automatic transmission through other relatively autonomous factors and tendencies. Here, talk of 'fetters', of social relations 'cast off like skin',[51] of the pre-given functional fit between class struggle and the level of the forces, of the inevitability of socialism—this terminology leads to the suppression of historical concreteness and the assertion of an a priori schema or universal drama.

3. Political Analysis

Marx's more 'conjunctural' writings are, obviously, rather different from the analyses of the *Manifesto* and of *Capital*. His texts on France particularly stand out as the more *political* of Marx's sustained works. *Class Struggles in France*, the *Eighteenth Brumaire of Louis Bonaparte*, and *The Civil War in France* are in fact very different sorts of accounts. It is partly with Engels that responsibility lies for suggesting (in his preface to *The Civil War in France*) that the last two were classics of the same kind. They do deal with one general problem (though, even here, they vary): to what extent can concrete political situations be adequately described in terms of 'class interests'. This problem is not quite the same as that which lies within the analyses in *Capital*, namely the historical exemplifications of the processes by which forces of production are fettered or impelled forward. Rather, it is an analogous one: class 'interests' refer to the long-term allegiance of individuals *qua* members of classes to a system of economic production. They also refer to the specific objectives that classes, *qua* particular fractions or forces, work for in political conjunctures. There is no necessary dialectical unity of these two conceptions. The first without attention to the second results in class reductionism. The second, on the other hand, need not be a Marxist idea if taken alone. The *Eighteenth Brumaire* best shows Marx's ability to bring these two levels together. Nevertheless, even that work has unsatisfactory passages, and leaves some unresolved questions—especially about 'class interests'.

Gwyn A. Williams has shown that *Class Struggles in France* is a fractured text.[52] Part 3 was written during the immediate period of the upheaval in Paris in 1848. Part 4, by contrast, is altogether more reflective, distanced, even disillusioned. As a whole, it is characterized by the explicit ascription of class interests to the combatants according to a sharp analytical distinction between bourgeoisie and proletariat. This polarization raises a question about the historical aptness of the categories: can France at that time be adequately described in terms of the logic of a fully developed capitalism? It also exhibits the difficulties of a mode of analysis of political conjunctures that deals primarily with long-term *economic* class interests.

In Marx's discussion of the issues and participants, social and political groups are often held unproblematically to 'represent' their 'objective' class position. The exploited classes, for example, are given an analytically identical basis: 'It is evident that [the peasants'] exploitation differs only in *form* from that of the industrial proletariat. The exploiter is the same: *capital*.'[53] Similarly, the fractions of the bourgeoisie, through the 'agent' of 'chemical fusion'—the National party—are identified as one class-unity. Marx considered differences between Orleanists and Legitimists irrelevant, since the 'synthesis of the Restoration and the July Monarchy' represents 'nothing other than the perfected and most purely developed rule of the whole bourgeois class.'[54]

The 'intermediate' classes, since they fall outside the principal class confrontation, are given short shrift. Despite the fact that there was 'a mass hovering between the bourgeoisie and the proletariat, whose material interests demanded democratic institutions',[55] Marx allows the petty-bourgeoisie little independent political capacity. They are typically regarded as vacillators.[56] The lumpen-proletariat, for Marx, 'form a mass quite distinct from the industrial proletariat. It is recruiting ground for thieves and criminals of all sorts'.[57]

Roger Price has argued that Marx underestimated the participation of the lumpen-proletariat in the June days.[58] We need not support the extent of his general revisions of Marx to see that Marx overdraws the features of class-polarization (more appropriate to the English case) in the less developed, still substantially artisanal Parisian social formation.

Class Struggles in France, despite this schematic account of its problems, is a very detailed set of observations. At other moments, Marx is well aware of the complexities of the case. Though he ascribes a bourgeois essence to the National party, he declares it to be without any great economic basis within its class.[59] And he also argues that the republic was not so much the realization of class interests as 'a compromise between the various classes'.[60] Despite the heightened struggles, which do show the *first* 'great battle between the two great classes which divide modern society',[61] that battle was early enough to ensure that compromise was part of the Bonapartist outcome. Louis Napoleon 'precisely because he was nothing . . . was able to signify everything'.[62]

The subdued tones of Part 4 of *Class Struggles in France* reveal an interesting shift of perspective. Previously, in accordance with his sometimes schematic analysis, Marx had postulated an appropriate revolutionary consciousness in the proletariat: 'the proletariat rallies ever more around *revolutionary socialism*, around *communism*'.[63] And: 'the proletariat did not allow itself to carry out a *revolt*, because it was about to carry out a revolution'.[64] There was even some expectation that the peasants would come to be aware of their genuine interests: 'There were various symptoms of the gradual revolutionizing of the peasants.'[65] With the benefit of hindsight, Marx later was more bitter: 'the history of the last three years has sufficiently proved that this class is absolutely incapable of any revolutionary initiative'.[66] As for the proletariat, Marx has hope rather than expectation, and it is based on more 'structural' (but equally inexorable) factors: 'A new revolution is only possible as a result of a new crisis; but it will come, just as surely as the crisis itself.'[67]

The Civil War in France does not display the same detail as *Class Struggles in France*. However, its tone and circumstances bear a close resemblance to that earlier text. It is a controversial work. Hobsbawm calls it a 'magnificent pamphlet' whose object was 'to instruct revolutionaries of the future'.[68] At the other end of the political spectrum, Ludwig von Mises has asserted that it is 'pure invention', slander against the alleged democratic backing for the suppression of the Paris Commune.[69] And it is, of course, the main cited source of Lenin's theory that the capitalist state must be 'broken', 'smashed', and replaced by one consisting only of workers:[70] 'the working class cannot simply lay hold of the ready-made state machinery, and wield it for its own purposes.'[71]

It is difficult, and perhaps illegitimate, to examine *The Civil War in France* in a discussion of historiography, for it is a work with very clear political objectives. Also, we should not expect all conjunctures to display similar complexity. If the work is a statement of support and prognostication[72] rather than a reflective analysis, that is because it is addressed to the General Council of the International in circumstances of horrific 'class terrorism'. Actually, Marx is aware that the latter is perpetuated by the Thiers regime, not simply the bourgeois state.[73] Nevertheless, having acknowledged that the pamphlet is not theory or history so much as a weapon in the struggle, some generalizations can be made about the conception of history it employs.

My comments, given that criterion, are in fact rather negative.

Although there is no need to deny the necessity for a 'popular' conception of history with the help of which people can be mobilized, in this work Marx's teleological mode is again in evidence and should, at some level, be subject to criticism. There seems, for example, insufficient contextual discussion of the events of the Commune. In a letter to Kugelmann, Marx feebly and uncharacteristically refers to the presence of the Prussians as the 'unfavourable accident of the case'.[74] But missing, too, is even the briefest discussion of previous conjunctures, or of the ideological field, or of the nature of the peasantry (unlike Marx's writings on 1848).

But the principal problem with Marx's analysis is what Nicos Poulantzas has termed the over-politicization of ideologies: the ascription of political essences to classes as if they were 'numberplates' worn on the backs of the participants.[75] Despite defeat, Marx asserts, the working class 'knows' that long struggles are necessary for its emancipation. The worker's 'historical mission' is to 'set free the elements of the new society with which the old collapsing bourgeois society is pregnant . . . the higher form to which present society is irresistibly tending'.[76] Here again is the 'echo' of the *Manifesto* and of chapter 32 of *Capital*. First, through the very rhetoric of combat, a philosophical teleology of history is operated that can only undermine specific historical and political analysis. Second, generalizations are made about state forms. The state, *in general*, is conceived instrumentally as the 'engine of class despotism', as a 'parasitic excrescence'.[77] It represents, for Marx, the unconditional dominance of capital over labour. Third, political forms and class fractions are replaced as the main object of empirical attention by personalities. Adolphe Thiers is 'that monstrous gnome'.[78] Several extended passages in this vein reveal Marx's brilliant capacity for character-assassination. But it is a mode that works by evocation rather than analysis, and one is bound to say that at times this penchant represents a flaw in Marx's theoretical temperament. It is well represented throughout texts such as *The Holy Family*, *The German Ideology* (part II), and *Herr Vogt*.

The Eighteenth Brumaire is the text in which Marx, more comprehensively than before or after, draws out the connections and tensions between the different 'levels' of a social formation.[79] Like the final section of *Class Struggles in France*, Marx's analysis is *post hoc* and his temper reflective. Unlike the first three sections of the former text, the day-to-day struggles do not appear as mere expressions of long-term, abstract allegiances, nor are they clashes of autonomous political ideals. More so than in Marx's other writings, a class pattern can be seen in the political kaleidoscope; it is not imposed upon it. No doubt, as Price often remarks, Marx overplays his hand. Yet, the fact that a modern scholar, for all his seeking, can find little to wholly disagree with in Marx's account, is testimony to the remarkable integration of levels of abstraction achieved by the *Eighteenth Brumaire*.

One of the characteristics of the work, which Poulantzas emphasizes, is Marx's concern to periodize the republic in terms of political forms 'below' the level of the 'regime'. That is, he deals in phases of the parliamentary republic, not in terms of the 'bourgeois republic' as such.[80] Marx also stresses a set of forms of state (non-interventionist, for example) that are not quite theoretically consonant with the forms of regime. Unlike *Class Struggles in France*, the *Eighteenth Brumaire* does not deal in class reductionism at the *expense* of specific political groups and institutions.

However, Marx does not at all succumb to the view that declared allegiances and intentions are to be taken at face value. On that score, Louis Napoleon would have to appear as a statesman or strategist of some ability,[81] or the Montagne as the defender of 'the eternal rights of man'.[82] Marx warns us against 'superficial appearance'. 'In historical struggles one must make a still sharper distinction between the phrases and fantasies of the parties and their real organization and interests.'[83] Class reductionism is not the procedure of so relating these two sets of phenomena. Rather, reductionism occurs when we see in 'the parties' *only* the expression of 'interests' held to lie outside political and ideological forms and organizations, in the mode of production. This is a fine distinction, of course, but it is a crucial one if any kind of determinate assessment of the historical shape of political conflict is to be possible. According to Price, for example, Marx's *class* criterion does not directly distinguish, as he thought, Legitimists and Orleanists. But Price clearly accepts that the influence exercised on the Chamber by the 'big bourgeoisie' outweighed their limited presence in it.[84]

Marx recognizes the independent power of the ideological struggle. For example, the 'fanaticism for order' was politically crucial, despite having an 'inconsiderable' economic basis.[85] 'All interests and social institutions are transformed into general ideas, and debated in that form.'[86] Marx is, understandably, not entirely consistent on these questions. This has to do with the persistence of the possibility of class reductionism (present in any such analysis). Marx is aware that the Bonapartist solution is a product partly of the resonance of the slogan 'France demands tranquillity' among *all* classes, especially the peasantry. If the latter's deeper interests were not served by Bonaparte, the symbols and connotations of Bonapartist ideology certainly seemed to represent them.[87] Marx is also aware that the appeal to 'order' is a product of the disintegration of political alliances and, even in the bourgeoisie, 'a feeling of weakness'.[88] The question of the political

168

representation of classes is thus not an easy one; but a distinction must be made between the following paradoxical formulation and the assertion that comes after it.

The bourgeoisie 'confesses that its own interest requires its deliverance from the peril of its own self-government'.[89] And: 'The French bourgeoisie was thus compelled by its class position . . . to liquidate the conditions of existence of all parliamentary power, including its own.'[90] The metaphors of the first formulation ('confesses', 'deliverance') capture the reality of the crisis and the ideological field. Yet it is clear that the 'solution'—whether the bourgeoisie knows it or not—is conducive to long-term bourgeois interest. This is different from the second assertion, because the latter presents the solution as a matter both of compulsion and of the immediate identity between the will of the bourgeoisie and its economic interests. Consequently, the 'crisis' appears as little more than a fake, engineered by the dominant class.

The distinction may seem pedantic, but without it one would have to endorse Marx's frequent collapse of historical specificity into a past-future continuum: 'But the revolution is thorough. It is still on its journey through purgatory. It goes about its business methodically. By 2 December 1851, it had completed one half of its preparatory work; it is now completed. First of all it perfected the parliamentary power in order to be able to overthrow it. Now, having attained this, it is perfecting the *executive power*, reducing it to its purest expression, isolating it, and pitting itself against it as the sole object of attack, in order to concentrate all its forces of destruction against it. And when it has completed this, the second half of its preliminary work, Europe will leap from its seat and exultantly claim: "Well worked, old mole!".'[91]

This is, of course, a wonderfully imaginative and stirring scenario. But the metaphor, the anthropomorphism, and the vast monism on which it depends belong to literature or speculative philosophy of history, not to history conceived as 'scientific' explanation.[92]

4. Marx's Other Half

Modern Marxist historians have rightly called for a proper appreciation of Engels as a historian.[93] Undue prominence has been given to his more general methodological statements. On the other hand, this in turn sets up a rather unfair division of labour between Marx and Engels. If the latter is Marx's 'other half', it is not merely because both of them engage in theoretical history in a complementary way. The strengths and limitations of Marx's work that I have touched on here are also present in the output of 'the General'.

Still, Engels does seem to provide a less subtle combination of respect for empirical detail and the long-term generalization. *The Condition of the Working Class in England in 1844* may be an 'embryo' of historical materialism, but it is also in some respects an exemplar. Engels there achieves an impressive social history within the framework of a theoretical perspective on the development of capitalism as a whole. It is the latter aspect, not the combination as such, that marks the book as an 'early' or undeveloped Marxist account. As Hobsbawm points out, *The Condition of the Working Class* is neither purely descriptive, nor 'labour history'. It is a graphic portrayal of almost the whole of working-class life, and of a class in struggle as well as in suffering.[94]

The text is nevertheless framed by an overly functionalist concept of technically-induced shifts in the mode of production. In at least two respects the model of class-polarization is too simply constructed. First, the proletariat, 'called into existence by the introduction of machinery',[95] is sharply contrasted in a superficial description of pre-capitalist class formations with pre-industrial workers, 'comfortable in their silent vegetation'.[96]

In contrast to this image, the 'factory hand' is portrayed as the most active and intelligent of workers,[97] the *good* side of the dark process of industrialization. Second, and related to the latter point, Engels imbues the working class—in spite of his close description of divergent labour processes and 'inevitable' depravity[98]—with a staged progression of consciousness, from criminality[99] to violent revolution, 'which cannot fail to take place'.[100] 'The approach to Socialism cannot fail, especially when the next crisis directs the working men by force of sheer want to social instead of political remedies.'[101] That social revolution, when it comes, and as a matter of class logic, will prove the French revolution to have been 'child's play'.[102]

There is no need to unduly criticize the first social history of the Marxist tradition. It is in many ways an outstanding book. My intention has been rather to show that Engels perhaps conceived the relation of his political generalizations to his historical analysis too much in terms of the empirical 'proof' of more 'logical' assertions.

In *Germany: Revolution and Counter-Revolution*, Engels outlines the differences between the French and German conjunctures in 1848. The text ultimately argues that the German revolution was premature, above all because the struggle between capital and labour was undeveloped. The revolution was therefore bound to be dissolved or distracted from its course. From a logical point of view, Engels notes the exceptional or contingent character of the struggles in Germany, but exceptions do have 'rational causes' and can prove the rule. They 'give us a clue as to the direction which the next, and perhaps not very distant, outbreak will import to the German people'.[103] These logical reflections are grounded in a thorough survey of the different classes (the lack of a native bourgeoisie was especially important). The details of the vacillations of the Frankfurt Assembly and the nature of the leading groups, too, are provided. The main problem with the kind of prognosis in which Engels (and Marx) indulge is not that they are illegitimate, but that in some of their declarations (often made in hope), explanation and *prediction* are misleadingly implied to stand on an equal footing.

Engels showed a keen interest both in Germany and in the problem of 'exceptions'. In *The Role of Force in History* both these interests merge, though the substantive achievement is rather slight. For example, the problem of armed force and military politics—something still not adequately confronted by many Marxists—is given a standard 'class' treatment. Engels well illustrates the paradox that having created the conditions for the bourgeois *economy* against the will of the embryonic bourgeoisie itself, Bismarck's regime stunted the political power of that class.[104] Ironically, by the time significant representation was seen to be necessary, Bismarck's bogey—the industrial proletariat—had emerged as a massive economic and political counter-force. Engels captures the ambiguity and specificity of Bismarck's 'Caesarism'—as much personal dictatorship in the absence of clear class politics as an example of the latter itself. But Engels takes this as a confirmation of, more than a problem for, class analysis. Regimes, he reasons, require an economic foundation, without which they sooner or later cease to be effective. Since the Junker class was 'doomed to extinction', so was Bismarck (being a Junker).[105] The argument is surely too schematic, citing long-term necessities at the expense of more transient, but considerable, political forces.

The Peasant War in Germany is Engels's *Eighteenth Brumaire*. It was intended to throw light on the balance of forces in 1848, which in respects was analogous to 1525. Yet Engels concludes that the two conjunctures are 'essentially different'.[106] The intention and development of the argument are therefore interesting as to whether historiography can provide 'lessons' without forcing historical parallels.

The analogy, as Engels presents it, runs deep. The 'traitors' of 1525 are the same as those of 1848–49, but on a 'lower level of development'.[107] The three-tiered class structure in the country (aristocracy, knights, and peasants) has its parallel in the cities (patriciate, burghers, plebeians). This is the presumed equivalent to the nineteenth-century divisions between the landowners, bourgeoisie and peasantry/proletariat. In both conjunctures class struggle was clothed in the 'shibboleths' of religion,[108] and the clergy was class-divided.[109] The petty-bourgeoisie and the lumpen-proletariat, as ever, were, respectively, 'vacillating' and 'absolutely venal'.[110] To cap it all, there was a proto-dictatorship of the proletariat under Münzer in Thuringen.

However extensive the analogy, Engels insists that the peasantry was fundamental to feudal Germany in a way it could not be in 1849. Much of the book is taken up by an assessment of the systematic peasant revolts and their aftermath.[111] If Marx and Engels are too swift to dismiss and condemn the peasantry in the *modern* era, the latter-day peasantry could not be said to 'resemble' that of the period of the Peasant Wars. Indeed, if the analogy was more than an aid for comparative analysis, historical materialism would be refuted, since identical situations could then be deduced from essentially different modes of production. It is therefore important to realize that Engels did not postulate such an identity, despite his attribution of similar structures and political consequences (for example, the 'unripeness' of proletarian order in both situations[112]). The analogy is intended to register a lack of common content as well as similarities in form. It seems to me more appropriate to consider *The Peasant War in Germany*, well researched and concrete though it clearly is, as an experiment in both applying and testing historical materialist categories. For example, like Marx in *Eighteenth Brumaire*, Engels considers the class representation of strata and groups that 'appear' on the political scene, whether in armed or ideological combat. Similarly, the forms of religious ideology and their political significance are connected to definite kinds of proprietorship of the land. The exercise cannot be counted as a clear success, but it is an ambitious analysis and an impressive historical description. And it shows the necessity of historical assessment in Marxism based on the *unity* of analysis and description.

I do not propose to go into the detail of Engels's most controversial book, *The Origin of the Family, Private Property and the State*. I want instead to view it as a pivot around which the problem of reading historical processes in relation to secondary *texts* can be hinged, since Engels's book is an undisguised reading of Morgan's *Ancient Society*. According to Engels, Morgan, in his own way, rediscovers the materialist conception of history.

In particular, Morgan is cited in support for the idea that the state is the product of class society, which arises with the growth of material production. Engels logically connects these ideas to advanced communism, where the state will just as surely disappear. This entire historical movement is governed by 'blind laws of elemental force'.[113]

Such generalizations, Engels maintains, are vindicated by empirical evidence. A question arises here: what if the evidence is found to be faulty? It is plausible that in Morgan's work Engels sees a theoretical conception in its 'practical state', and *this* is why Morgan, and not other ethnologists, is important to Engels. Similarly, many modern Marxists defend *Engels* on this basis: it is the theoretical framework that, perhaps, is crucial, because both Morgan and Engels have in all probability got many facts wrong.[114] Feminists have also wondered how to assess some of Engels's assertions. He argued that there was, at least in part, a causal connection between the enforced transition from matrilineal to patrilineal descent and the shift from communism to class society. Despite the general agreement that this hypothesis is mistaken in important respects, Engels's reflections have been defended by feminists as *methodological* precepts. For example, 'The overthrow of mother right was the world-historic defeat of the female sex.'[115] Rosalind Delmar regards this sentiment as a necessary part of a socialist analysis of women's oppression.[116] More empirically, Kathy Sachs has argued that Engels's main ideas about the correlation between the decline of the public rights of women and private property were right. Clearly, as a general proposition, there is much truth in this. Equally plausibly, Sachs argues[117] that the ending of the condition of separate economic spheres and ideological discourses for men and women requires an end to the division between family and society, if not quite advanced communism.

The matter is not so simple, however. From a feminist point of view, it might be said that Engels ignores the oppression of women in matrilineal societies. Engels agrees that reproduction is not simply an economic question, but his tendency is to regard it as a *biological* process.[118] Liz Brown goes so far as to argue that matriarchy, as Engels borrows the term from ethnology, is a purely *legal* category. She accuses Engels of transposing particular data about institutional arrangements in a variety of societies to a general 'humanist theory of history', having man's development as its genealogical focus.[119] We may choose to disagree with Brown's description of Engels's historical materialism, but her criticism raises an important issue all the same. She writes: 'The question of women's oppression is thus produced in *Origins* merely as an effect of the need for the materialist history to bind together disparate ethnological materials into a coherent totality.'[120] Now on one level, this is well wide of the mark. Engels had a great respect for both research and facts. It is more likely that he believed that the facts of science spontaneously and progressively confirmed historical materialism than that he sought to make them do so willy nilly. But this does not resolve the problem that generates discrepancies between facts and 'coherent totalities', namely that we often—as Engels did—read *real* history by reading *texts*. And the latter, as Engels's work shows, is inevitably a 'symptomatic' or theoretical process. For Brown, texts and the facts they generate appear to be indissolubly bound together, incapable of being brought under a generalization arising from another discourse.

The problem of reading for facts also affects the Marxist interpretation of Engels himself. How could he have supported Morgan, who was wrong? One argument (Paul Hirst's) is that Engels was simply mistaken: in fact, Morgan bears no relation to the *real* Engels, because the former, unlike the latter, is a humanist. His interest is Man, not classes. And Morgan is an idealist, not a materialist: he asserts the primacy of *Mind*.[121] Another argument is Emmanuel Terray's. According to Hirst's caricature of Terray,[122] it runs as follows. Engels, being a founder Marxist, can be trusted. So something in the real *Morgan* must be good. Terray therefore locates three discourses in Morgan: an evolutionist, a democratic, and a Marxist discourse; and he highlights the last.

This complex exchange is of interest, because Terray accepts the truth of Engels's symptomatic reading of Morgan. Hirst, according to his anti-evolutionist position within Marxism, condemns Morgan, but refuses to see the truth about the evolutionist elements in *Engels*—or in Marxism generally. It seems to me that just as Brown is mistaken to find something altogether wrong in the discrepancy between facts and discourse, so these authors' symptomatic readings share a refusal to accept different sorts of discrepancies between various *interpretations* of a theory—either between their own and Engels's interpretations, or between Engels's and Morgan's theory. Some light emerges if it can be maintained that theories need not be regarded as unchanging or complete constructions.

There are elements in *Ancient History* that do support Engels's historical materialism. Morgan begins from the idea that circumstances, and especially subsistence technology, shape the character of culture, ideology, and politics. Hirst's attribution to Morgan of 'mentalism' turns out to be as much a case for his materialism: 'The slowness of this mental growth was inevitable, in the period of savagery, from the extreme difficulty of compassing the simplest invention out of nothing . . . in such a rude condition of life.'[123] On the other hand, Hirst credits Morgan's 'problematic' with too much consistent rigour; in fact it is much more eclectic. His 'ethnic periods' are more cultural totalities than modes of production; at times, he stresses the technical determinations of progress, yet that progress is held to be written by the hand of a Supreme Intelligence.[124] Morgan also combines a sense of reverence for 'misty antiquity' with the task of positivist knowledge.[125]

As for Engels, both Terray and Hirst exaggerate his theoretical consistency. Engels shares with Morgan some (though by no means all) aspects of evolutionism and even positivism. The point is that ideal accounts of what historical materialism should provide are bound to differ from historical materialism in practice. Just as historical research might be at odds with Engels's grander generalizations in some respects while not necessarily discrediting his theoretical approach, so particular applications of historical materialism will not be 'given' in the theory's general formulas. The latter may even be modified in application by theoretical or empirical developments over time. It is what allows us to continue to regard Engels as a historical materialist of a high order, though our examination of some of his (or Marx's) 'applications' will often be critical. Historical materialism provides a series of definite but general theses: their historical embodiment is never given in advance. If there could be a complete harmony between the logic of the categories and concrete situations, historical materialism would be of no value. If there was a harmony between the interpretations of Marxism given by people in very different contexts, there would be little productive and cumulative critical engagement. It has been the purpose of this chapter to indicate some of the problems in the work of the founders of historical materialism concerning the relation between theory and history. The modified sense of Marxism that emerges from an examination of those problems does not encourage a one-way 'solution' to those problems, either in the direction of a theoretically pure Marxism, or in that of a fully 'empirical' history.

Soboul and French Revolution Historiography

The French revolution is a useful topic on which to mount an historio-graphical examination involving more than one level of abstraction. The key texts reveal a welcome recognition of the importance of methodology and ideological preferences, as well as a concern for evidential veracity. Moreover, it is a debate in which, until recently, neo-Marxist kinds of accounts have been considered highly relevant. Albert Soboul's work in particular displays the bold lines and internal discrepancies of a schematic historical materialism. But some of his opponents, for their part, employ arguments resting on pluralist or individualist assumptions of an equally a priori kind.

It is therefore a question of some urgency whether, and if so under what conditions, a 'middle ground' can be occupied, and whether a broadly Marxist standpoint need fear the prospect. In its central structural features, French revolution historiography is fairly typical of other major substantive controversies in history. The scholarly minutiae of 'normal history' (to adapt Kuhn) are vital only in so far as they connect with larger explanatory and ideological issues.

In a range of seminal works embracing both massive research and short, sharp polemic, Albert Soboul has put forward a Marxist interpretation of the revolution, emphasizing productive forces and bourgeois revolution. On several occasions we have had cause to doubt whether there can be a paradigmatic Marxist model that is either fully representative of Marx's best practice or internally consistent. The interpretation of history that runs through the *Communist Manifesto*, the '1859 Preface', and such texts as Stalin's *Dialectical and Historical Materialism* is often, and with some reason, cited as a theory that abstractly schematizes Marx's work, and so distorts it. I argued earlier that a 'theory of history' was defensible, but only in so far as it did not stifle recognition of particular causal processes in history. The texts referred to often appear to do just that. In his conception of Marxist historiography, Soboul draws too close to the guidelines for historical assertions that those texts seem to encourage.

Characteristic of that view is the idea that contradictions between the forces and relations of production (the former decisive) create the conditions for political and ideological class struggle of a critical nature. This in turn results in the destruction of the old mode of production and the emergence of a new ruling class. Soboul accepts this form of explanation: 'the Revolution is to be explained in the last analysis by a contradiction between the social basis of the economy and the character of the productive forces.'[1] 'The deeper causes of the French Revolution are to be found in the contradictions Barnave stressed between the structures and institutions of the *Ancien Régime*, and the state of economic and social development on the other.'[2] 'Carried through by the bourgeoisie, the Revolution destroyed the old system of production and the social relationships deriving from it, and in so doing destroyed the formerly dominant class, the landed aristocracy.'[3]

Moreover, it is at least partly because of its clear fit with such an explanatory schema that Soboul sees France as the 'classic' case of the bourgeois revolution. Another reason is that it conforms to Marx's more specific claim that the 'really revolutionary way' to capitalism is the *direct* establishment of new production relations.[4] Soboul regards other cases of bourgeois revolution (America, England) to have less clearly broken with the transitional forms (for example, 'putting out') that remain present within an essentially *feudal* economy.

Soboul is adamant that objections to empirical details alone cannot challenge the basic correctness of the model he proposes. He asks us to 'go beyond the superficial aspect of political and institutional history and to seek to consider economic and social realities'.[5] The explanation is therefore inseparable from the defence of a certain kind of epistemology—one that discovers 'realities' beneath surface appearances. Like Marx, Soboul sees this as the only possible *scientific* procedure. In opposition to Alfred Cobban, François Furet, Denis Richet, and other historians who restrict analysis to the contingent, Soboul insists that there must be and indeed is a knowable structure in history, ascertainable by means of its laws of tendency. We are therefore (logically) in need of *theory*: 'History cannot progress unless it is based on fundamental concepts clearly worked out.'[6] In sum, Soboul's general outlook ties together a theory of history, an epistemology, and a particular account. The theory of history is historical materialism in the sense referred to. The account claims that the French revolution exhibits, in its unique way, the central features of the classic bourgeois transition. The epistemology, however, is as yet unclear. Everything depends on the extent to which the general theory or concepts *dictates to* and thus *constrains* other empirical and analytical factors. If the historical conjuncture appears to be little more than the realization of a trans-historical pattern, the explanation will be *rationalistic* and *essentialist* and thus unacceptable. Alternatively, an (epistemologically) *realist* explanation may be on offer whereby essential mechanisms are indeed posited, but not confirmed in advance or *in toto*. So the *degree* of comprehensiveness and exhaustiveness of the explanation (and thus its usefulness) may be a matter of genuine debate.

Soboul's proclivities, however, at any rate as expressed in general or epistemological statements, are not altogether open. From the outset he draws a distinction between problems of a 'general order' and those of a 'specific nature'.[7] This address establishes a somewhat formal and external relation between general laws (about transitions, for example) and cases (France). Moreover, his generalizations seek to emphasize, in a manner characteristic of Soviet 'diamat', the historical necessity or inevitability of the 'bourgeois' revolution. Classes are the carriers of this necessary movement. 'At the end of the eighteenth century the system of property holding and the organization of agriculture and manufacturing were no longer relevant to the needs of the new burgeoning productive forces and were seen to hamper the productive process. The authors of the *Manifesto* wrote that "these chains had to be broken. They were broken".'[8]

Consequently, Soboul has no difficulty allowing that the popular masses and the lower bourgeoisie were simultaneously the motor of the revolution and its unwitting victims. The popular masses: 'Spring 1793 witnessed the opening scenes in the drama in which the imperatives of bourgeois revolution were finally to destroy the popular republic that the Sans Culottes confusedly desired. These were the first signs of the irreconcilable contradictions between the aspirations of a particular social group and the objective state of historical necessity.'[9] The lower bourgeoisie: 'the Robespierrists tried to overcome the basic contradiction between the exigencies of the equality of rights proclaimed in theory and the actual consequences of economic freedom. . . . This imposing attempt, dramatic even in its powerlessness to succeed, allows us to gauge the irreducible antagonism between the aspiration of a social group and the objective state of historical necessity.'[10]

But although doomed to failure, the popular movement was not, historically speaking, unsuccessful: 'It had helped to promote historical advance by the decisive assistance it had lent to the bourgeois revolution.'[11] Thus the necessity of the revolution confers upon its carriers (victors and victims) a historical *progressiveness*. And because France is the 'classic' bourgeois case, the nation *as such* (its unification being an essential condition of capitalist development) becomes the object of some reverence for Soboul. It certainly allows him unjustifiably to play down the 'classic' features of the English and American transitions, and to erect 'The Revolution' as a kind of trans-historical power: 'The Revolution, child of enthusiasm, still excites men and women. . . . Still admired and feared, the Revolution lives on in our minds.'[12] Not an obviously Marxist description this, and it is as well to remember the quite overtly chauvinist position into which Stalin's version of 'histomat' developed. Of course, no simple correspondence is intended here. But Soboul's account employs a certain *teleology* that lends itself to the assertion that broad historical processes have an identity and a 'home' beyond the agencies and conditions of their making.

One further aspect of this teleology should be pointed out before examining the tensions between materialism and essentialism in Soboul's history in more detail. I have tried to point to Soboul's allegiance to a progressive logic of history that, while largely independent of class forces, can nevertheless confer value upon them, even in defeat. Now, part of the *progressive* nature of bourgeois revolution, in the orthodox Marxist schema, is that it is a necessary condition for further socialist transformation. Thus, Soboul tends to regard the bourgeois revolution not as having succeeded at the expense of the defeated popular movement, but as being the *contradictory unity* of alliance-and-division, of simultaneous bourgeois exploitation and egalitarianism. Despite the dominance of a single 'logic' of capitalist development, there is here an *inner* logic of a suppressed nature. Its tendency is toward fuller historical advance, namely socialism. The sansculottes embodied something of this. Above all, it is *Babeuf* who, for Soboul, represents this inner logic, this future-within-the-present. Babeuf's historical value thus far exceeds his limited contemporary support and success. Soboul makes much of him for that reason. In sum, Babeuf, the popular movement of 1793, the aspiration to real equality: these are as much part of 'the Revolution' and its 'Heritage' as 1789, Thermidor, and Napoleon.[13]

The necessity and logic of revolution in Soboul is therefore both multi-faceted and inexorable. But just as we found no reason to be satisfied with the determinism plus 'dialectical contradiction' in diamat, so it is hard to see that the complexities of Soboul's conception of historical tendency undermine the problems associated with the essentialist epistemology that influences both his empirical analysis and his polemics with 'revisionists'.

1. The Transition: Feudalism –
   What's in a Name?

In several key areas, Soboul's insistence on the 'classic' nature of the bourgeois revolution in France creates both empirical and conceptual problems. Conceptually, these have to do with the sense in which the bourgeois revolution was a capitalist revolution breaking from the feudal mode of production; and the identification of classes and their representation at the political level. More empirically, a number of historians have asked: Did feudalism exist? Who exactly were the bourgeoisie? Did the nobility survive? Was it not perhaps an anti-capitalist revolution? Was not the Jacobin-Sansculottes alliance a deviation from the main course of the revolution produced by contingent circumstances (for example, the war)? In my view, there is no clear division between empirical and conceptual questions of these kinds, and critics of Soboul who profess only *empirical* resolutions to them, such as Cobban, cannot be said to offer any theoretically satisfactory alternative. This does not mean, however, as Soboul seems at times to think, that their questions are irrelevant and purely destructive.

Soboul provides a number of interesting formulations on the nature of the bourgeois revolution in France (apart from its 'classic' character). On the one hand, France took the 'really revolutionary way', 'by wiping out every surviving feudal relic'. 'Henceforth, with the entirely new relations of production, capital was removed from the stresses and strains of feudalism, and the labour force became a genuine commercial entity.'[14]

On the other hand, 'Years were to pass before capitalism was definitely established in France. Its progress was slow during the revolutionary period; industry was usually on a small scale and commercial capital retained its preponderance.'[15] These formulations are all-important. They involve some (perhaps esoteric) reflections on the concept of the 'really revolutionary road'.

Granted, Marx uses this idea, but he, too, is open to interpretation on the question, as the international debate on the transition shows. It is Maurice Dobb who offers the clearest account (though this, in turn, has been systematically and exegetically questioned by Robert Brenner). Dobb regards the 'way of compromise'[16] as that by which the petty producer loses control over his labour-power, but *merchant* capital retains dominance over the productive process. Dobb argues that this state of affairs is compatible with, indeed it prolongs, the feudal mode of production. Soboul's account of the French revolution has it both ways: the peasant producer is set free to exploit or be exploited; the feudal mode is thus abolished; yet commercial capital delays the capitalist process. It seems to me that because of the *politically* revolutionary situation in France, Soboul is tempted to assume its conformity to the Dobbian model. It is at odds with Dobb's version. In any case, one need not accept Dobb's theory to perceive some confusion on Soboul's part. To some extent, the question is resolved by the latter's statement that where the autonomy of the capitalist mode is assured, there is a 'classically revolutionary transformation'.[17] On this reading, however, there need be no reference to the sharpness of class struggle or the relative time span involved. England and America, on this account, seem unjustly excluded from the club of classic revolutions.

The looser sense of capitalist revolution that emerges here is more consistent with other of Soboul's scattered references, which are ambiguous. The French revolution, he says, was 'of the greatest importance in the establishment of the capitalist order'.[18] Again, 'the Revolution speeded up evolution, and marked a decisive stage in the transition from "feudalism" to capitalism'.[19] 'A necessary stage in the transition from feudalism to capitalism'.[20] The stage is, in fact, 'opening up the way for capitalism',[21] the 'advent of bourgeois, capitalist society'.[22] Soboul's terminology is slippery, then, and the difficulty with some of his formulations is their tendency to suggest the automatic identification of the 'destruction of feudalism' and a recognizably *industrial* capitalism, which immediately succeeds it. Soboul overlays this view with one that sees the bourgeois revolution in France as capitalist only in the sense that it provides indispensable *conditions* for the transition to a capitalist economy (free enterprise and a labour market, in particular[23]). This latter reading is supported by important claims by Soboul that the post-revolutionary bourgeoisie was a *new kind* of capitalist class. For example, he acknowledges that the war industries themselves seem to have created more recognizable capitalist forms.[24] In some respects, then, Soboul is less 'dogmatic' than he appears, and is entitled to stand in the tradition of less 'orthodox' Marxists from Jean Jaurès to Georges Lefebvre. But his case is neither clear nor convincing. Questions remain: *was* feudalism destroyed, and what were the class relations leading to capitalism, if they did lead to it?

The nature of feudalism and the identification of the bourgeoisie are issues over which Soboul has been strongly attacked as being quite misleading. Alfred Cobban, G. V. Taylor, Elizabeth Eisenstein, and Betty Behrens, to name a few, contend that feudalism in any meaningful sense, and thus a clearly demarcated *economic* feudal class, had ceased to exist by 1789. If a more adequate Marxist account is to be given, it should be acknowledged that Soboul's presentation suffers from real inconsistencies.[25]

One main source of difficulty is the relationship between analysis at the level of the mode of production on the one hand and of 'social formation' on the other. We have seen that this relation is a perennial problem in Marxist theory and that there are some grounds for rejecting those concepts altogether. However, to a large extent not only 'orthodox Marxism' but Marx's *Capital* depends on such a distinction. In mechanical versions of historical materialism, modes of production are conceptual totalities forming a logical sequence with known 'laws of tendency' and forms of transition from one to another. Soboul's general rhetoric—concerning both 'laws' and the transition from feudalism to capitalism—suggests that he employs this kind of model. And we have seen that in his concern to maintain a 'classic' case of transition he plays down the lack of neatness and the incompleteness of the French transition, of which he is in fact otherwise well aware.

This tendency to reduce the complexities of the social formation to the clear lines of demarcation given by a conceptual totality is a form of rationalist theorizing or epistemology. Cobban is thus not wrong to imply that Soboul divides history into 'a few large and homogeneous phases'.[26] One of these phases is feudalism, and in his discussion of pre-revolutionary France, Soboul seems to posit a feudal mode of production at a general level. But his analysis actually deals with the *ancien régime* as a complex social formation, irreducible in any easy way to the 'pure' feudal mode of production.

The general-level statements are quickly dealt with: unless feudalism was a fairly homogeneous and dominant mode of production, the many assertions of its destruction by capitalism in a 'classic' transition are exaggerations at best. The more specific descriptions require closer attention.

French 'society remained fundamentally aristocratic; it was based on privilege of birth and wealth from land. But this traditional social structure was now being undermined by the evolution of the economy which was giving added importance to personal wealth and was enhancing the power of the middle classes'.[27] The question here is whether this kind of statement is equivalent to the growing replacement of the feudal by the capitalist mode of production. In one sense, if a long enough time span is considered (say a couple of centuries), few would dissent from the equation. What is more contentious is the idea, surely implied by Soboul, that such a description adequately expresses the *existence* of a feudal mode of production and its transformation in a relatively short span (in about forty years, perhaps).

It is not easy to resolve the issues posed by contrasting mode-of-production analysis with that appropriate to the social formation. One reason for this is the polemical context in which these key issues have been posed. Cobban *et al.* maintain that feudalism did not exist since the relevant legal categories became increasingly scrambled and irrelevant. In reply, Soboul has rejected such a 'juridical' account, stressing that socio-economic realities are the crux.[28] But it is precisely when Soboul turns to these realities that his own account resembles his opponents'. In his chapter 'The Crisis of Society', Soboul argues that the 'legal structure of society bore no relation to the social and economic realities', because 'the nobility had been reduced to parasites' and the order of the *ancien régime* contained personnel from different classes.[29] But in establishing a more adequate 'class' analysis, Soboul says that 'fundamentally the aristocracy were the nobility',[30] because by the eighteenth century the nobility had little connection with the feudal (legal) system of the Middle Ages. This complicates the matter for several reasons. First, the nobility's feudal dues and exemptions are precisely what Soboul points to as the basis of their exploitation and latter-day reaction. Second, the nobility 'did not constitute a homogeneous social class that showed any real awareness of its collective interests'.[31] Third, 'In [the] move towards commercialism, a section of the upper nobility came closer to the middle class whose aspirations they in some degree shared'.[32] Fourth, Soboul acknowledges that commoners (presumably 'bourgeois') could acquire noble status fairly easily, and that not all *bona fide* nobles could exact feudal rent.

All in all, Soboul is hard-pressed to keep the 'class' analysis of the aristocracy free of 'legal' definitions. Nor has he made a case for the existence of a feudal mode of production on the basis of real economic appropriation. His best argument is quantitative: the aristocracy owned about one-fifth of the land,[33] and one-third of their income came from peasant dues. The latter represented one-fifth of *the peasants'* income.[34] It is difficult to know whether these figures could conclusively establish 'feudalism' as the dominant mode of production (see appendix). Taking his other considerations into account, one is left more with an impression of 'uneven and combined development'. Industry, for example, 'remained slight', but grew, relatively, by 700%–800%.[35] A significant section of the peasantry owned land, while in some areas a rural proletariat was emerging. In yet others, *metayage* predominated.[36] So in terms of the 'manner of exploitation of the land'—Soboul's criterion[37]—a distinctly *feudal* arrangement is at least questionable.

Soboul himself is at times hesitant. He speaks only of 'the surviving traces of feudalism',[38] of 'what remained of feudalism', and of 'feudal vestiges'. In his detailed discussion of the nobility, the 'dominant class' (which constituted 1.5 per cent of the population[39]) appears divided. Part of the upper nobility were moving into commerce, leaving a decaying and poor provincial nobility, and the *noblesse de robe*, as the other 'class fractions'. Soboul sees the impending *extinction* of sections of the provincial and court nobility as the main thrust behind the aristocratic reaction. In the light of his complicated and sometimes confused discourse on the *ancien régime*'s structure, it seems to me that Soboul's most judicious characterization is that the system of agrarian production was 'pre-capitalist'.[40]

These qualifications on Soboul's part, if that is what they are, undermine his 'classic' model to some extent. At the least, they show that generalization at a high level of abstraction (mode of production: feudalism evolving towards capitalism) does not provide easy correspondences at a lower level of abstraction (social formation: *ancien régime*). Certainly, the conception that the productive forces alone are the prime mover is unconvincing, for it cannot easily be squared with Soboul's statement that the 'backward state of agrarian methods and production was in large measure a direct result of the social structure of the rural economy'.[41]

2. The Bourgeoisie: Personnel, Agency, and 'Interests'

Perhaps the strongest 'revisionist' argument is that Soboul's idea that the revolution was led by a capitalist bourgeoisie well aware of its historic interest is a fiction. He has been accused of 'an outrageous indifference to facts and logic',[42] and of relying on an 'act of faith' (Cobban, Behrens). Even Georges Lefebvre's more respectable version (which Soboul largely follows) has, it seems, been exhibited as contradictory beyond repair.[43]

In the related problems of feudalism and the bourgeoisie, the trouble is that Soboul has more than enough 'logic'. Just as feudalism must be portrayed as a 'homogeneous phase' if it is to be thoroughly destroyed, so the destroyers, if they are to inaugurate the 'entirely new relations of production',[44] should appear to be class-conscious capitalists. This logic of the (theoretical) transition dominates Soboul's analysis of the bourgeoisie. 'The bourgeoisie', he writes, 'constituted the most important class within the Third Estate: it directed the course of the Revolution and benefited from it.'[45] 'The commercial and industrial middle class had an acute sense of the social evolution and economic power which they represented. With a clear realization of their own interests, it was they who carried through the Revolution.'[46]

However, as in the case of the aristocracy, Soboul's analysis of the 'class fractions' of the bourgeoisie is not so simple. He identifies four such fractions: rentiers, entrepreneurs, professionals, and artisans and shopkeepers. The first category increased with the growth of the bourgeoisie, but 'their sources of income were widely varied', and 'there was a wide diversity among the rentiers themselves'. In any case, they 'played little active part in economic life'.[47] The professionals, who provided most of the revolution's personnel, were also a 'highly diversified group', some of whom bordered on the aristocracy, and the professions were in no clear sense a new economic force. As for artisans and shopkeepers, it was quite possible for them to 'pass almost imperceptibly into the popular classes in the real sense of that term', and 'in general, artisans were hostile to the capitalist organization of production'.[48]

Of the entrepreneurs, 'the financiers held pride of place'. This fraction relied extensively on the aristocratic-monarchical tax-farming system, and indeed were 'often linked by marriage with the aristocracy of birth'. 'In 1793 tax-farmers were sent to the guillotine'.[49] The position of commercial capital is ambiguous. In Marxist theory, as Soboul says, commercial capital is thought to precede the development of industry, but as Dobb and others have cogently argued, in and of itself merchant capital can retard the movement of the mode of production. Soboul also implies this when he points out that profits 'allowed the middle class to acquire estates, a symbol of social superiority in a society that was still essentially feudal'.[50]

From this summary it can be seen that Soboul has quite definite ideas about what classes should be, and how they should behave. Strangely enough, given the overall schema, his assessment of the existence of a bourgeoisie is cautious: 'Although the rate of expansion of French industry was so very remarkable, the influence of industrial growth on the general expansion of the economy of the country would appear to have been relatively slight.'[51] The strongest statement is, 'Even at the end of the *ancien régime*, there were traces of certain of the characteristics of large-scale capitalist industry.' So far, then, there is no solid case for the existence of a bourgeoisie with clearly perceived interests 'irreparably opposed to those of the aristocracy'.[52]

But because he persists in invoking a bourgeoisie in a more obviously modern sense, Soboul's use of the term itself is dubious. 'Bourgeoisie' is used interchangeably with the social category 'middle class', yet clearly parts of the latter in no way tally with Soboul's 'strict' meaning of the former: industrial or (at a pinch) commercial capitalists. Not only are the incomes and lifestyles amongst Soboul's class fractions dissimilar, their relationship to the means of production is different, too. It is the latter criterion that is crucial for a Marxist analysis, yet that does not satisfactorily confirm Soboul's argument. In his polemic against revisionists who classify intellectuals as outside the bourgeoisie, Soboul ironically has to combine his 'pure' class analysis with a manifestly 'sociological' shopping list of relevant items. 'Bourgeoisie' is a wide term, he maintains, requiring 'multiple class analysis'—'birth, wealth, education and language, clothes, house, way of life . . . . '.[53] In fact, adopting Ernest Labrousse's and Pierre Vilar's 'systematic' criterion (of which Soboul approves)—namely that a bourgeois is 'able to provide his own means of production'—the matter is still unsatisfactory. That definition could include petty commodity producers, for one thing. It certainly includes different kinds of birth, income, and lifestyles.

The difficulties in Soboul's thesis are compounded by his insistence that the peasant and popular revolutions had an anti-feudal essence. 'The peasant and popular revolution', he writes, 'was at the very heart of the bourgeois revolution and steadily carried it forward.' And: 'It is . . . necessary to underline the fact that the basic objective of the peasant movement was the same as the aims of the middle class revolution: the destruction of the feudal system of production.'[54] The peasantry's 'Intervention entailed the radical, though gradual, abolition of the feudal system.'[55]

In these passages a central ambiguity in reductive Marxist discourse is exemplified, namely the elision of a sense of the *objective outcome* of a historical process and the ascription of conscious *objectives*. 'The French revolution is consistent, all of a piece; it remains bourgeois and anti-feudal through all its apparent shifts and vicissitudes'.[56] We have seen how the bourgeoisie itself is assigned a direction and identity consonant with its long-term historical 'interests', though perhaps not in line with its empirical or immediate constitution and consciousness. This has the following dual consequence. First, the logic of the transition requires that all those forces contributing to the social upheaval 'participate' in its progressiveness. Hence Soboul's tendency to ignore or displace the agencies and demands in favour of more objective, structural, relations. But second, and paradoxically, objective processes and 'interests' are fed back into a reading of the agents' motivations, and classes appear as class-conscious unities that *make* revolutions.

Something of this contradictory logic is present in these latter passages of Soboul's. The anti-feudal content of many of the peasants' grievances is difficult to deny, especially in the face of Lefebvre's fundamental researches. But Soboul does not take seriously enough Lefebvre's view that the

peasant revolt was *autonomous* of that of the bourgeoisie. So although both
revolts resulted in the abolition of feudal dues, and although the bourgeois
revolution, while 'classic', would have been less radical without the popular
masses, it is not self-evident that their interests were the same, or that the
masses were 'at the heart' of a bourgeois revolution *simpliciter* and carried 'it'
steadily forward in the absence of any 'typical' bourgeois cadres. 'The
passionate opposition of the popular masses to any form of privilege or class
distinction' is thus compatible with peasant 'hatred of the aristocracy',[57]
but it need not at all mean unity with the bourgeois revolution. The
provincial research of Cobb, the facts of the Vendée, and the arguments of,
for example, Barrington Moore do not support that elision.[58] Soboul himself shows the internal divergences of peasant development. The minority
of rural capitalists emerging from the peasant ranks clearly ran thoroughly
counter to the stable domestic self-sufficiency to which the rural masses
continued to aspire. Marx's famous remark that they resembled 'a sack of
potatoes'[59] in 1848 as in 1789 and E. J. Hobsbawm's comment about
1789—'The peasantry never provides a political alternative to anyone;
merely, as occasion dictates, an almost irresistible force or an almost im-
movable object.'[60]—show that Marxists have a poor opinion of peasant
consciousness.

Soboul shares that tradition. 'At the end of the eighteenth century', he
wrote of the peasants, 'their ideal was that every peasant should own
land.'[61]

3. Jacobins and Sansculottes:
The Political Representation of Classes

Much of Soboul's talk of the 'popular masses', which ostensibly includes
the peasantry, is rather more concerned with the urban masses, and especially the Parisian sansculottes. This group is Soboul's specialism, and it is
the relationship between them and the Jacobins that fascinates him.
Around that relationship Soboul marshalls an account of class power in the
revolution. The distinguishing feature of his analysis is the identification of
political forces with class fractions. The latter are assumed to have identifiable 'interests' transparently represented by political groups and forms of
regime. The sansculottes form a partial exception to this rule, but Soboul's
class analysis is rounded off again by means of what I have called the hidden
inner logic of his account of the popular masses.

Before examining the problems involved in this kind of approach, I should note in passing that Soboul's (too brief) treatment of ideologies and intellectuals is consonant with his 'class' analysis of the state. Both exactly fit a rather stark Marxist concept of 'base-superstructure'. The bourgeoisie's 'ideological spokesmen had elaborated a doctrine which conformed to their social and political interests'.[62] 'The economic base of society was changing and with it ideologies were being modified.'[63] 'They were persuaded that their interests and the dictates of reason coincided.'[64] All this is, perhaps, true enough. But even Soboul feels it necessary to counter the intrinsically misleading mechanism of the formulations, as stated. 'It is no doubt necessary to qualify these statements', he writes. 'The bourgeoisie was a richly varied group, not one homogeneous class. Many of them were totally unaffected by the writings of the Enlightenment.'[65] No doubt, too, much of the aristocracy *was* affected by them.

Problems of an exactly similar kind confront Soboul's condensation of politics and economic location into class unities at the level of the state. On the one hand, given the definition of the bourgeois revolution, its 'irreconcilable' opposition to feudalism, any attempts at political compromise must appear futile. On the other hand, since the inner logic of the revolution points toward popular democracy, any 'bourgeois' resolution must involve some kind of compromise. In turn, then, even the least enthusiastic revolutionaries are in some degree representative of the bourgeoisie or a class fraction of it. This complicated double movement lies behind Soboul's story.

Lafayette, for example, 'brought together the divergent interests of the nobility and the capitalist middle class. So the aristocracy took part in the sudden blossoming of new productive forces'.[66] This hero of two worlds 'was for a year the idol of the revolutionary bourgeoisie'.[67] But because of the feudal essence of the aristocracy and the revolutionary essence of the bourgeoisie, 'the policy of compromise and reconciliation which Lafayette tried to pursue in 1790 had not the slightest chance of success'.[68]

Similarly, in turn, the rule of Mirabeau, the Triumvirate, the Girondins, and the Jacobins are seen by Soboul as inherently contradictory. But for different reasons. Mirabeau and Barnave *et al.*, like Lafayette, were caught in the contradiction between aristocracy and bourgeoisie: they did not perceive the necessary measures required for full bourgeois success. At this point, however, the contradictions are viewed as implanted not just in some bourgeois fractions, but in the very essence of the revolution itself.

'By building the new nation on the narrow social base of the property-owning bourgeoisie, the Constituent Assembly was condemning its life's work to the weaknesses occasioned by its inherent contradictions.'[69] This complication allows Soboul to draw the following paradoxical, even whimsical, conclusions. First, those sections of the bourgeoisie that did not perceive the necessity of uncompromising anti-feudalism for the bourgeois revolution now appear 'logical' in their contradictoriness. They are representative of the bourgeoisie in stopping short of the necessary extremities of revolution. Thus, with the disciplining of the King after Varennes, enough was enough: 'The middle classes who governed France preferred that the nation remained a nation of property owners. For them the Revolution was indeed over.'[70] This about-turn, or dialectical twist, in the argument is not altogether strange. Although we will not pursue it in detail, it is clear that the *reactionary* process from Thermidor to Napoleon and even beyond is equally 'logical', in so far as the process of bourgeois stabilization 'required' it.

Soboul's second crucial deduction is that the Jacobin dictatorship, the alliance with the popular movement, is the agency *par excellence* of bourgeois revolution. And this despite—or *because of*—the Jacobins' limited or indirect representativeness of the bourgeoisie as a whole.

The Girondins, whose political leadership was perhaps the most transitory of all the major 'regimes', occupy the central position in Soboul's explanatory schema. Although the Brisotins were 'second generation' revolutionaries, 'journalists, lawyers, and teachers', they gradually take on the mantle of the quintessential bourgeoisie. 'The Girondins were the representatives of the bourgeoisie'.[71] Their role is thus particularly contradictory, and this is highlighted by the necessary brevity of their rule. In favour of the need for revolutionary war, they showed greater class consciousness of the objectives of the revolution. But their commitment was purely formal, since they would not accept the means requisite to the end: a broadening of their social basis to include the popular masses. The Montagnards, on the other hand, are the fraction most *politically* representative of the needs of the revolution. They are the really revolutionary bourgeoisie.

At this point, Soboul's shifting class reductionism is especially problematic. Many critics find no empirical difference between Montagnards and Girondins.[72] This may or may not be relevant. For example, Daniel Guerin[73] poses the question in terms of the difference between class fractions, so there may be no class differences as such between the Gironde and the Montagne, but considerable sub-class economic tensions. The trouble with Soboul's presentation is once again historiographical and not simply factual. For, yet again under the rubric of 'utterly implacable' struggle,[74] he describes all political or intra-class differences as if they were those of economic classes *per se*: 'What divided these groups was essentially their divergent class interests.'[75] Here again we are referred to those teleological 'interests', the ascription of an 'essence' grounding, but clouded by, superficial political or other aspects. And yet the rigour is only apparent. For example: 'The Girondins were the representatives of the propertied middle classes, the commercial and industrial bourgeoisie.'[76] The first identification in that sentence must be held against Soboul's claim that the pre-Girondin factions wanted to halt the revolution in order to preserve middle-class property. The second and the third are not only rather all-embracing, but also involve the theoretical problems already referred to about the relative weight of different forms of capital in the transition. In any case, Soboul can be more explicit: 'The Gironde . . . the party of the great merchant classes'.[77] 'The Girondins represented the interests of the rich commercial bourgeoisie.'[78]

In short, Soboul's identification of classes and interests is uncommonly slippery: the firmness of tone is not always matched by firmness of conceptualization. Above all, the representation of class interests in political struggle is assumed to be transparent and easily demarcated, even when class associations are 'fractional' rather than total. And this is quite implausible. Thus the fact that the 'spokesmen' of the Gironde are second-generation intellectuals raises no comment or mediation at all. Indeed, rather than explore the ramifications of political differences within a class (such a thing is entirely possible after all), Soboul takes political differences as little more than an index of an essential class split. 'The conflict between Girondins and Montagnards,' he writes, 'bears the mark of class antagonism, in spite of both groups' bourgeois origin, because of the different political choices that confronted them.'[79] The 'relative autonomy of the political', whether expressed in the current theoretical terms of Poulantzas or in Marx's own contemporary political assessment of the forms of regime in 1848–51, is entirely absent in Soboul.

The final series of contradictions are those concerning Jacobins and sansculottes. Soboul's account of the liaison oscillates. On one reading, the Jacobins constitute the truly revolutionary bourgeoisie. They take the risk of a popular alliance in the pursuit of their class interests, and embody a form of state quite different from the sansculottes: a representative bourgeois democracy, as against direct popular democracy. Because of class differences, these forms are in 'irreducible contradiction'.[80] On Soboul's other reading, the alliance is less clear cut. Two factors bear out the second, more complex reading.

First, the Jacobins are not quite so representative of the bourgeoisie as may appear from Soboul's characterization, and this is *because* of their revolutionary nature. Here, the revolution/bourgeois representativeness correlation is inverted.

If the 'first reading' can be maintained on the basis that 'men of the upper middle class' and the 'middling bourgeoisie' belonged to the Montagne,[81] there are sections of the latter that scarcely fit the bill at all. The Montagnards also include representatives of the 'popular classes of society, artisans and shopkeepers, like consumers . . . ';[82] and even middle-class Jacobins were 'ready to place restrictions on the freedom of property ownership and, indeed, on the liberty of the individual' in order to 'serve the needs of the people'. One of the definitive features of Soboul's work appears to break down here: class determination with regard to political programmes. And the ambiguity of his class-identification procedure is again exposed: the Montagne contains representatives of all classes.

Second, the 'contradictions' facing Robespierre, and the political ideal of the Jacobins generally, are far from visibly different from those facing the sansculottes. They shared, Soboul writes, a common pre-capitalist ideal, that of 'a society of small independent producers, peasants, and artisans'.[83] Here, 'every Frenchman should be a small proprietor and an independent producer'.[84] There can be little doubt that some sections of the Montagne were indeed of a different class in every sense from sections of the sansculottes. But there is an extensive social as well as political overlap not easily susceptible of hard and fast economic class analysis. In his less 'popular' treatment of the sansculottes,[85] Soboul is noticeably more subtle. It seems to me that one has to agree with Richard Cobb that Soboul's 'rigorous choreography'[86] is too formalized, if only because it withdraws attention from a crucial part of the 'class logic' of the revolution: the growing conservatism of the Plain, who Soboul allows *also* 'represented the middle classes and believed in economic liberty'.[87]

As in the case of the Jacobins, the dissection of the sansculottes moves from the presentation of a class unity to that of a heterogeneous internally divided *political* force. Soboul does not much stress the popular class element of the Montagne when he seeks a class-representative logic. For the same purpose, he neglects the considerable 'bourgeois' proportion of the sansculottes which Cobb, for example, tends to emphasize. This relative absence in Soboul requires some explanation, especially since it is the *contradiction* of the sansculottes' position that, he maintains, is responsible for its downfall. And one of the elements of the process of defeat is the 'buying off' of many of its leaders: those who presumably developed an 'interest' in political stability.[88]

The popular alliance, for Soboul, was required to force through the bourgeois revolution. In this sense, the popular masses are seen to be 'at the very heart' of the bourgeois revolution, in many ways its prime mover. The sansculottes, perhaps even more than the Jacobins, are in the advance *political* guard of the revolution.[89] This view is one pole of Soboul's choreography: the pull towards real democracy and not just formal/civil or market equality is one aspect of the bourgeois contradiction, and that which links it to the sansculottes. But the other aspect of the sansculottes' contradiction is their backward *economic* aspiration. Robespierre's 'spiritual' conception of society was the left-bourgeois version of the popular ideal of self-sufficient small production.

Here Soboul's sympathy with the masses appears to run thin: they are now presented as a purely transitory phenomenon. They were not, after all, a class. They were governed by immediate material demands (especially bread); they constituted a unity of *consumers* only.[90] Their artisanal consciousness was under the hegemony of the bourgeoisie. They were 'lacking all sense of class consciousness', having 'no clear and precise idea of the nature of labour itself'.[91] The contradictions within both Jacobins and sansculottes—like those *between* them, allowing for nuances—thus account for the 'historical necessity of the Ninth of Thermidor'.[92]

But harsh as Soboul is about the backwardness of the popular movement, he does not restrict its positive features to the cruel irony of mere 'participation' in a 'progressive' bourgeois revolution. Even in its negativity, there is a dialectical 'moment' that carries the seed of future historical counterbalance to bourgeois victory. We have had signs of it in Soboul's characterization of popular anti-feudalism. This aspect is popular anti-capitalism and its hints of advanced socialist consciousness. 'The popular masses', Soboul writes, '*knew what lay in store for them*, which is why they opposed the economic freedom which opened the path to economic concentration and capitalism.'[93] Little as this matches Soboul's earlier argument that the popular struggle was in key respects identical to the bourgeois revolution, he also notes 'the passionate opposition of the popular masses to *any* form of privilege or class distinction' (my emphasis). This is a continuous, if hidden, motif in his history. It enables him to posit an inner logic to the revolution, and to lend a unity of political purpose to the sansculottes, who otherwise appear divided, exhausted, and historically outmoded. In his essay on the logic of state forms, Soboul places popular democracy in sheer opposition to bourgeois representative democracy. The autonomous right of the people to exercise justice is 'deduced' from a 'total conception of sovereignty'.[94] However, the dilemmas of sansculotteism (its necessary link to economic utopias and bourgeois-Jacobin hegemony) prevented it from pursuing this new inner logic of revolution. It is Babeuvism that represents 'a real mutation'.

Despite Babeuf's numerically weak conspiracy, it was a transcendence in the full Hegelian sense: a preservation of the rational elements of sansculottes democracy, without the contradictions by which the latter was bound. The liberating new feature was the beginnings of an identifiable proletariat. Babeuvism showed 'a full consciousness of the revolutionary process', it was 'ideologically adequate to the new society, born of the revolution itself'.[95]

There were contradictions—of course! The circumstances of the period, for example (they were not ripe for socialism). Babeuf's temperament, for another. A third problem is his tendency to 'think in terms of the stagnation of the productive forces'.[96] There is also a certain Blanquism or even Jacobinism whereby the relation of dictactorship to the masses is largely unresolved.[97] This is enough, yet again, to seriously question what is left of the 'logic' by which such moments in the revolution are presented as essential historical meanings. But as so often in Albert Soboul's sustained, complicated historiography, a certain Marxist teleology, born of rationalism, prevails. It carries the logic of one revolution into the hypothetical outcome of another. 'Through Babeuvism, Communism (hitherto a Utopian dream) at last developed ideological coherence; through the Conspiracy of Equals it entered the history of social and political struggle.'[98] 'Thus were born of the French Revolution . . . conceptions . . . of a new social order which would not be the bourgeois order.'[99]

4. Alternative Problematics

This discussion of Soboul has been theoretical and critical, and while I have not engaged in any directly empirical debates, theory and history are not starkly polarized. The criticism presented here thus ought to entail some concrete conclusions, even if the suggestions be only tentative.

It seems to me that Soboul's rationalist Marxism at times encourages a position more dogmatic than is necessary, and at times produces a misleading and inadequate class reductionism. I have pointed to instances in which the very contradictoriness of Soboul's exposition shows his own awareness of the pertinence of 'revisionist' arguments. The latter conveniently fall under theoretical headings: the nature of the feudal mode; the identity and consciousness of the bourgeoisie; the 'interests' of the peasantry; the constitution and function of the sansculottes, and so forth. I would argue that substantial amendment can be made to Soboul's arguments without entailing 'revisionism' in any non-Marxist sense. However, it must be acknowledged that many of the more empirical conclusions of the 'revisionists' must be accommodated, together with the conceptual criticism of essentialism.

Let us take some examples. Taylor's major 'revision'[100] to the effect that there was neither a strictly feudal economy prior to the revolution, nor a significant capitalist class, is a point made by Soboul himself. To grant the fact does not necessarily run counter to the view that the society was moving from feudalism toward capitalism. Similarly, Taylor argues that it was a political revolution with social consequences of a capitalistic nature. Only for Soboul's class essentialism is this notion difficult to accept. 'Political revolution' can be translated as 'revolution with no direct class determination' without loss.

Barrington Moore and Cobban have argued that the revolution was principally anti-capitalist. Furet and Richet have gone as far as to say that the years of Jacobin-sansculottes dominance were a deviation: the revolution had been blown off course. These contentions are scandalous to Soboul. And yet there is no reason why this should be so. The former critics effectively state no more than that there was an anti-capitalist content to many peasant grievances. Indeed, Cobban also argues that the peasantry willingly went along with such capitalistic measures as enclosure, though perhaps for different reasons. The exaggeration of Furet and Richet, on the other hand, may be provocative and sweeping, but they do not point to any conclusions radically different from Soboul's. As we have seen, Soboul is concerned to explain the necessity of 1792 as well as of Ninth Thermidor, and is caught between two persuasive revolutionary logics. But it would not be absurd to maintain with Furet and Richet that in the last resort the bourgeoisie was less revolutionary than Soboul occasionally maintains. Certainly, Soboul could always see the 'logic' of Thermidor as the *preservation* and not simply the 'betrayal' of the revolution.

Individually, then, the objections of the revisionists to the 'classic' account of the revolution are neither startling, nor necessarily at odds with Soboul's own conclusions, as they appear in the more narrative moments of the latter's overview. In sum, four revisionist contentions are acceptable.

1. The bourgeoisie was not a class-conscious unity.

2. In many respects the popular movement had anti-capitalist aspirations as well as anti-feudal grievances.

3. The developments of the Year II were not necessarily a predictable part of the logic of bourgeois revolution.

4. The class identification of and the ascription of class interests to nearly every social force or category in the revolution is a more problematical operation than Soboul allows.

These propositions can be asserted on the basis of a critique of Soboul's rationalism or essentialism. However, it is not clear that on this basis alone one may conclude, as many 'moderate' commentators do, that 'the analytical categories of the established Marxist view have increasingly been shown to be crude and anachronistic'.[101]

Such charges readily degenerate into the more extreme views of Cobban or Behrens. The latter both conclude, on evidence related to personnel in the revolution, that the 'class conflict' approach is no more than an 'act of faith'.[102] But the charges of, for example, J. M. Roberts, can and should be answered apart from more extreme pronouncements, if only because by their very nature the latter seem to imply an altogether more rational and consistent viewpoint that must be independently assessed.

My argument has been that Soboul's account is often crude and misleading. But the 'classic' Marxist view is not therefore simply *wrong*. In some ways, it is Soboul's *Leninist* views that offend most obviously. Henri Lefebvre, for example, has rightly criticized Soboul for introducing a scenario of 'dual power' into the French popular alliance.[103] This refers to 1917, when popular soviets uncomfortably coexisted with representative democratic institutions in Russia. Soboul projects the Bolshevik eulogy of the soviets back to the meetings in the Paris sections in 1793–94. Or again, Soboul champions Babeuf largely in terms of a hypostatized vanguard proletarian party in the Leninist sense.

But Soboul's 'anachronisms' cannot be pushed too far. He convincingly argues against Guerin, for example, that the sansculottes were not a proletariat, despite Guerin's efforts to portray them as such.[104] Indeed, if anyone is guilty of a pure class logic it is Guerin. For him the revolution is also the instantiation of a law: Trotsky's law of combined and uneven development.[105] But while Soboul shares something of this approach, he does not follow Guerin in seeing the war as *simply* capitalist expansionism. Nor does Soboul exaggerate the 'socialist' potential of Hebertism in the uncritical manner of Guerin. Of course, Soboul's version is cloudier and less exciting than Guerin's for that very reason. But the charge of anachronism can be taken only so far.

The crux of the matter is that the revisionists equate Soboul's essential-ism with Marxism *tout court*. In this respect their empirical or *ad hoc* criticisms are part of a more thoroughgoing attempt to displace the Marxist problematic altogether. I must now briefly show that this is so, and that such attempts are unsuccessful.

Attempts to replace one problem by another involve philosophical as well as empirical statements. This may be demonstrated in a number of cases, each of which differs to some extent from the others and which display varying methodological self-awareness.

The most obvious example of an alternative problematic to the neo-Marxist orthodoxy is Crane Brinton's *Jacobins*. Related to his *Anatomy of Revolution*, Brinton's 'new history' (of the 1930s) consciously rejects piecemeal empirical research in favour of socio-historical 'laws'. Concerned with the 'unit' of history and not the human individual, Brinton constructs a typology or psychology of the revolutionary fanatic, the essential lines of which can be perceived across *all* revolutions in history. 'History' in this schema becomes no more than the incidental material for a static, indeed eternal, typology of human nature. The laws relating to the 'fanatic' and the like must ultimately be psychological rather than social. As Brinton openly acknowledges, 'material' causality has no place in his account. This is a very clear example of an alternative problematic. Indeed, it is so clear that there is no real debate: either one accepts a psychological and static view of history or one does not, and at least Marxists and empirical histo-rians share a concern to explain *change*. Whatever value Brinton's typologies may have (they are not devoid of valid observations), they do not broach the explanation of historical movements.

Such thinkers as Crane Brinton, however, recognize that an explanatory framework *is* necessary to any evaluation of empirical data. Many empiricist historians either reject that position or pay mere lip service to it. The most serious critics of Soboul are empiricists, usually of the second variety. As we have come to expect, a concern to put the facts straight does not discourage larger methodological pronouncements. Elizabeth Eisenstein appears to be an exception. She declares her theoretical neutrality in arguing that the bourgeoisie did not intervene in 1788, and is upset that J. Kaplow and G. Shapiro think her partisan.[106] There is some justice in her complaint: after all, she only pointed out that a 'collection of notables and nobodies' were ideologically homogeneous but socially heterogeneous. And yet we have seen that the argument for a 'bourgeois' revolution need not stand or fall on the status or opinions of individuals. The longer-term economic movements, the *content* of the demands, the broad lines of class mobilization: these are the key terms in the 'logic' of the revolution. Soboul's concern to press-gang individual consciousnesses into that class mould may well provoke the revision that in fact the individuals cannot be so manipulated. But neither Soboul's exaggerations nor Eisenstein's disclaimers settle the larger, structural questions. Here Soboul's rationalism is matched by Eisenstein's empiricism, for the whole mode of her critique assumes that questions of social processes can be decided by attending to the particulars of individual belief and action.

George V. Taylor expresses Eisenstein's concern more explicitly. He consciously attempts to go beyond the 'inherent deception' of terms such as class, feudalism, capitalism, etc. [107] Indeed, as Taylor sees it the 'problem is how to rescue data from a language that misrepresents it and imprisons it in categories that can no longer be justified.'[108] Such a view implies that its proponent has access to an alternative language that faithfully represents the data, or (a slightly different metaphor) that liberates it. In reality, the very value of Taylor's contribution *requires* an adequate conception of class, feudalism, and capitalism. His argument is that rentiers were numerically more significant than traders and capitalists in the *ancien régime*, and that while feudalism 'in the strict sense' no longer existed, property was not profit-making. A further, and crucial, factor that persuades Taylor that we are dealing with a 'traditional society' is that a significant section of the middle class shared the aristocratic value-system and concern for status. There are four reasons why this more sophisticated revision is inadequate even in its own terms. First, it attempts a structural economic explanation while at the same time treating the ideological *status* values of groups as one definitive criterion. Second, feudalism and capitalism must be regarded as significant and tenable concepts if the conclusion that non-capitalist, non-feudal wealth was predominant is itself to be significant. Third, a Marxist analysis need not come unstuck over a social formation in transition. The fact that a pre-capitalist economy is a case in which neither the feudal nor the capitalist mode of production can be said clearly to dominate does not invalidate the concept of feudalism or capitalism, nor their central role in establishing the nature of a social formation. Fourth, no mystical choreography is required to show that the *tendencies* of a society point in a clear (capitalist) direction. In short, the relative strength of the revision depends on the extent to which its explicit empiricist methodology is abandoned in practice.

Alfred Cobban is the doyen of revisionism. Although nominally he allows that the facts require an interpretative framework, the latter cannot amount to the assertion of 'laws'.[109] Rather than defend 'the facts' as such,

Cobban mounts a Popperian attack on Marxism. This allows him to dis-
qualify Marxism on philosophical grounds, while enabling him to respect
the empirical research of the Marxist tradition. It is an intelligent gambit,
and scores important points against Soboul's essentialism. Without recapi-
tulating the problems of Popperian epistemology, it is useful to point to
the elisions by which Cobban (like Popper) ties *any possible* Marxist account
to self-confirmatory essentialism: 'Any general theory of sociology must
also be, like Marxism, a philosophy of history. . . . the inherent assumption
in any philosophy of history is that the evolution of humanity is a single
process; but if this is allowed, then there cannot be a scientific law about it,
because as Professor Popper has pointed out, a scientific law cannot be
deduced from a single example. Part of general sociological theories is that
success is built in.'[110] Cobban's whole argument against Marxism rests on
these assumptions. The general theory is allegedly erected against the facts,
such that confirmation is inevitable. A philosophy of history (which resembles a 'secular religion') grounds that general theory, but its defence is
ruled out by Popperian norms.

There is no need to deny that some Marxist accounts, or at least some
elements of them, are open to criticisms of this kind. But far from being a
trenchant critical tool, this vulgar Popperianism is itself inevitably reductionist and self-confirming. It is also wrong. To begin with, 'philosophy of
history' (including empiricism) involves methodological presuppositions
that (in many cases) cannot be reduced to the purely 'speculative' type. In
any case, the phrase in this context implies a realm of pure fact that
Popperian thought itself does not allow. Second, a general theory can allow
different levels of abstraction which respect 'fact' as well as promoting
'theory'. (For example, realism.) Third, historical 'laws' need not be conceived in a positivist manner, requiring constant conjunction of cause and
effect covering many 'instances'. Fourth, conceptions of history do not at
all require that 'humanity' (or anything else) be a unitary subject following
a pre-given evolution.

The substance of these points has been argued in earlier chapters. Their
purpose here is simply to identify the irrevocable philosophical element in
Cobban's position and its dependence on some assumptions that themselves
can be no more than a matter of faith.

Cobban's substantive contributions are inherently ambiguous. Either
they modify the Soboul-Lefebvre version without necessarily requiring a
full-scale critique of their 'problematic', *or* they propose an eclectic and
agnostic alternative, something called 'empirical history'.[111] The latter
logic is more fully expressed by Betty Behrens. The 'ascertainable facts', in

her view, render Marxist concepts redundant. 'Bourgeoisie' and like categories 'yield no clear and verifiable conclusions'.[112] In the light of this, Behrens's call for more useful concepts is purely gestural, because her 'ascertainable' facts are those relating to the self-perception of individual agents, and a refusal to allow the possibility that 'causality' can be identified in any other way than according to the conscious declaration of intention by agents. But in that case, there is no need for 'explanations' at all: the facts are all we need, suitably verified. In this respect, Behrens performs a service, for her defence of 'straight history' lies behind the approach of many historians, whether they consciously intend such a view or not.

Cobban is not so easily tied down. The reviewer in a *Times Literary Supplement* article (7 January 1965), which was later denounced by Behrens (not without justice),[113] fails to appreciate the contradictions Cobban attempts to encompass. Cobban's ambiguity is best captured in his sensationalist general pronouncements. For example: 'The search for the causes of *the* Revolution may well now be at an end.'[114] This view also hints at a radical scepticism (why bother with causes?), but it is in fact a concern to avoid a teleology of the Revolution as the self-moving subject of history.

'The French Revolution is a myth, or rather a number of rival theories.'[115] Again, if one assumes that the rival theories are unnecessary or radically incommensurable and unjudgeable, then the deeply agnostic view is entailed that not only the revolution but all history is mythical. Perhaps Cobban really means only that the French revolution is in many respects the construction of different historiographies. But nothing scandalous follows from this. Theory may be indispensable and the 'revolution' a dangerous hypostatization, but rival interpretations can still be rated according to empirical as well as logical criteria. The identification of a 'myth' in this context is a publicity stunt, a purely verbal or connotative manoeuvre.

Similarly, Cobban's empirical conclusions do not provide an alternative to the 'classic' interpretation. Like Taylor, he shows the weaknesses of Soboul's essentialism. Yet in substance we are left to take the question of classes as an unanalysable and infinite gradation of wealth and status on the one hand, and a recognition of the 'penetration of the countryside' by 'bourgeois' urban financial interests on the other.[116]

Other discrepancies can be enumerated. In an attempt to refute Soboul's view of the peasantry, Cobban says that, ironically, it was the supposedly anti-capitalist peasantry that voted for enclosures of partage (typical capitalist measures). But shortly after this, Cobban notes the widespread protests against large farms amongst the rural masses.[117]

In *critique*, he maintains that 'bourgeoisie', 'aristocracy', and 'sansculottes' are only political categories. When tying his own account together, Cobban does employ class terminology. Indeed, if his views have a theme of substance, it is the *retardation* of capitalism by the revolutionary process. Now this view does not necessarily involve rejection of the Marxist problematic, as we have seen. It presupposes a general context of the transition to capitalism anyway, in which peasant and noble groups mobilize in defence of the *status quo ante* (or at least of some rationale for it). And it does not contest that after the revolution the balance of class power had changed, even if industrial capitalism was still a fair way off. This is the context of Cobban's claim that the successful 'bourgeoisie' was, strangely enough, a landed class.[118] As in R. Forster's case for 'the survival of the nobility', the shift towards capitalist forms is not denied, only its abruptness and transparency at the political and ideological level.[119] For that reason, Cobban's work is extremely useful, providing we are aware of its rather confused methodological status.

The same might be said of critics such as Barrington Moore, whose perceptiveness at the level of class forces is matched by a rather dubious attempt to erect them into a theory of modern history. Moore stresses the adaptation of the upper class to capitalism and the peasantry's sacrifice and hatred for both. This is certainly a good point to make against Soboul's a priori equation of bourgeois and peasant interests. But Moore wants to go on to portray the peasants as 'the chief arbiters of the revolution', knowing well that they were 'not its propelling force'.[120] One reason for this complication is that the book from which the argument comes is a long and persistent attempt to establish that the analysis of the peasantry, although it was the historical victim, is the key to modern social developments.

Richard Cobb's work, especially *The Police and the People,* is perhaps the most impressive detailed critique of Soboul. And yet its own claims are ostensibly modest, including no epistemological or theoretical pretensions. It is also specific, being an analysis of the sansculottes. The book is said to be an 'accident'. Its main concern is to show, *contra* Soboul, that the sansculottes were 'a political accident',[121] but Cobb strenuously denies any concern to be 'scientific'. His book is said to be about attitudes, not movements or thoughts, and proposes to let 'the people speak for themselves'.

But the effect of this subjectivist historiography is significant. The unitary 'rationality' of the Crowd as seen by Georges Rude[122] now appears imposed rather than inherent, and Soboul's formalized schema of the popular alliance is severely if respectfully dismantled by Cobb. In addition, Cobb's view is that the sansculottes—though expressing elements of class conflict—were essentially a political force with distinct moral and psychological features that were as much a product of war emergency as 'the maximum'. He puts their effective term of power at only two to three months.

Apparently a deadly critique, Cobb's impressive research coheres well with much of Soboul's analysis, at least when the failures of the popular alliance are under scrutiny. In particular, the materialist explanation of surge and defeat is stressed' by both historians in terms of death and physical exhaustion. Cobb, however, refuses to accept a logic of revolution such that the popular movement is conceived as an effective, spontaneous and democratic unity. Given Soboul's ambiguities on just these points, Cobb's criticisms make their mark. Together with developing work on the sexual relations of production and reproduction in the popular classes,[123] a more conjunctural materialist analysis seems likely to deepen and revise Soboul's seminal work.

Is *this* then an acceptance of the futility of the classic Marxist approach? Only if we hold—and I do not—that such conjunctural analyses form an illegitimate, or the only, level of abstraction. Again, it is salutary to examine the elements of a different theoretical problematic in Cobb. In so far as he acknowledges that his preference for a subjective historiography *is* subjective, no argument is necessary. One can accept valuable work and formulate an adequate historical materialism in the light of it. But Cobb's views sometimes appear to be grander statements about history as such. He treats personal experience as the matter of history and its sole *raison d'être*. In his book *Second Identity* Cobb rather moralistically denies the intellectual any right to theorize from the experience of his 'lower' subjects. Here, it seems, only a sympathetic and descriptive history is adequate; hence Cobb's concern to portray moralities, temperaments, and mentalities.

As far as popular history is concerned, this emphasis can be admirable. The following lines clearly resemble another classic 'sympathetic' historian, E. P. Thompson. 'I am seeking to depict individuals, swimming desperately in collective currents, attempting to keep their heads above stormy waters and to reach the other shore.'[124] But whereas Thompson is interested in the making of a popular collective identity (especially *class* identity), Cobb is more concerned to assume a background of ordinary apathy, marginality, and individual suffering: 'a collective Diary of a Nobody'.[125] He thus stresses *continuities* (the revolution did not alter male violence to women), and in looking at 'fringe' occupations, the *irrelevance* of major political change. A welcome criticism of celebratory modes in historiography (one thinks of large parts of Whig or labour or Communist history), Cobb's view is nevertheless the product of pessimism and of a refusal to see that 'historic' events, trends, and movements cannot be referred *only* to the subjectivities of 'ordinary' people. The latter expression is still a *category*, and its members, whoever they may be, are also in part the *product* of history.

5. Conclusion

I hope to have offered some support for a non-essentialist Marxist historiography of the French revolution, both through an internal critique of the work of Soboul and through an examination of revisionist arguments where they aspire to an altogether different, and especially an empiricist, problematic.

The resulting theory or conception (or better: set of explanations) is not at all the series of platitudes or generalizations that Cobban forecasts a contradiction-free Marxism would produce.[126] An exemplary, though short, Marxist account is Eric Hobsbawm's.[127] There, a firmly Marxist perspective is mobilized in such a way as to leave itself empirically open. The book from which the overview comes, *The Age of Revolution*, also seems to me to incorporate what is important in J. Godechot's and R. R. Palmer's thesis that France was part of a larger international democratic-political chain of events.[128] Soboul, on the other hand, dismisses their views out of hand as quite incompatible with historical materialism.

In other words, Marxist interpreters have as much interest in establishing empirical facts or data as 'straight' historians. Events and processes are never wholly constructed in theories and ideologies. A central part of explanatory adequacy lies in accounting for what is empirically known. But this also rules out the empiricist assumption—accepted to varying degrees by many revisionists—that discrepancies between facts and theory automatically signify the artificiality or superfluity of the latter. Facts come as 'hard' as Labrousse's cycles or as 'soft' as the self-images of lawyers. They may 'exist', but hardly in splendid isolation. If facts *require* theory, it is in the way that humans need air rather than tobacco.

In conclusion, it is in the accounts of the non-Marxist historians that we find the most serious discrepancies between the priority of fact and opinion and the concern for theoretical explanation. On the positive side, the best of the critiques seem to establish no more than the view that if the bourgeoisie did not make the revolution, it was nevertheless made by it.[129]

The 'orthodox' neo-Marxist view of the French revolution is long-established. It cannot be purely a sign of the times that this is so. Recent revisions certainly lead to a new synthesis in the sense that essentialism, Marxist or otherwise, must be abandoned. But the broad lines of the substantive account and its epistemologically realist form of explanation still hold the field. A respected scholar such as Norman Hampson shares the concern for orders rather than classes, status rather than class consciousness. But the following proposition differs in no important way from the supposedly anachronistic views of a Hobsbawm, or even a scarcely-modified Soboul. 'The reorganization of France by the Constituent Assembly was an attempt to bring French institutions into harmony with the demands of efficient government and a capitalist economy.'[130]

Appendix

More on the
Transition Debates

I referred earlier to Soboul's quantitative support for his thesis about the feudal structure of the *ancien régime* and its suppression by capitalism. Even to offer a 'numerical' proof is, however, a questionable move in Marxist discussion. This is nothing to do with avoiding the 'facts', but rather is a matter of determining the conceptual boundaries relative to which numbers make sense. For example, there is the debate—touched on in the appendix to chapter 7—about whether preponderance of a mode of exploitation is a sufficient condition for the existence of the mode of production associated with it. Banaji accused Dobb of making the connection too readily. On the other hand, Banaji as yet has provided no conclusive alternative. One of Marx's famous 'definitions' of 'mode of production' surely requires *some* degree of quantitative assessment of forms of exploitation. 'The specific economic form in which unpaid surplus labour is pumped out of the direct producers determines the relation of rulers and ruled, as it grows immediately out of production itself. . . . it is always the direct relation of the owners of the conditions of production to the direct producers which reveals the innermost secret, the hidden foundations of the entire social construction.'[131]

It is instructive at this point to mark the nearly exact parallel between the Dobb-Sweezy debate about England and the discussion on the French revolution. Of course, the coincidence occurs because the very concept of 'bourgeois revolution' is an important but problematical category of Marxist thought.[132] In general, Marxists claim that 1640 and 1789 are structurally parallel bourgeois revolutions, and the theoretical arguments among Marxists and between Marxists and 'empiricists' are strikingly similar.

Sweezy, for example, agreed with Dobb that the 'two-hundred-odd years which separated Edward III from Elizabeth' was transitional in character.[133] However, neither was it 'properly' feudal or capitalist. To complicate things, Sweezy (no doubt aware of the dire theoretical consequences for Marxist theory) also said that 'while pre-capitalist commodity production was neither feudal nor capitalist, it was just as little a viable system in its own right'.[134] These considerations could have had France as their reference.

Dobb, for his part, had some sympathy with Sweezy in regarding the social formation as 'complex and transitional'. But in his argument that it is an 'impossible procedure' to posit a distinct mode of production that is neither feudal nor capitalist, the following passage is crucial. It could be transposed word for word into the debate about the *ancien régime*. The point of reproducing it here is to indicate the crucial role of conceptual considerations in Marxism where numerical evidence is scanty or proves little effective.

'The crucial question . . . is this: what was the ruling class in the period? Since . . . there was not yet developed capitalist production, it cannot have been a capitalist class. If one answers that it was something intermediate between feudal and capitalist, in the shape of bourgeoisie which had not yet invested its capital in the development of a bourgeois mode of production, then one is in the Pokrovsky-bog of "merchant capitalism". If a merchant bourgeoisie formed the ruling class, then the state must have been a bourgeois state. And if the state was a bourgeois state . . . what constituted the essential issue of the civil war? It cannot [according to this view] have been *the* bourgeois revolution. We are left with [the] supposition that it was a struggle against an attempted *counter-revolution* staged by Crown and Court against an *already existent* bourgeois state power.'[135] As we noted earlier, similar considerations move Soboul to adopt a rather teleological perspective as a counter to the dilemma of a non-class view or a labyrinthine attempt (such as Sweezy's) to escape the consequences of the harder forms of Marxist theory.

I do not mean to suggest that Soboul and Dobb offer the same account of transition. The former's over-politicized interpretation finds little support in the letter or the spirit of the latter's work, which, if anything, is *under*-politicized. As regards *economic* transformation, Dobb's position is ultimately heavily qualified: 'But as long as political constraint and the pressures of the manorial custom still ruled economic relationships . . . and a free market in land was absent (as well as free labour mobility), the form of this exploitation cannot be said to have shed its feudal form—even if this was a degenerate and rapidly disintegrating form.'[136]

This seems to strike a sensible, if somewhat contorted, balance, and it wisely leaves specific quantitative questions open. It is also worth pointing out that Dobb's formulation does not easily fit Hindess and Hirst's accusation that his account is simply teleological.[137] They argue that Dobb sees transition as the automatic product of the inner contradictions of the old mode. There is, of course, some truth in this charge (and it can certainly be levelled against Soboul). But the remarks above should provide the qualifications Hindess and Hirst characteristically omit. In any case, their own recipe for 'transitional conjunctures' has its own problems: 'It is necessary to consider the specific forms and conditions of class struggle as they appear in determinate social formations dominated by determinate modes of production.'[138] Prior as this is to Hindess and Hirst's subsequent rejection of Marxist concepts such as 'mode of production', we are entitled to ask how to establish that a dominant mode exists, to what extent it dominates, and how determinant it is of the forms and conditions of class struggle. Hindess and Hirst's rather abstract formulas do not necessarily go beyond Dobb, nor do they resolve the issues with which he grappled.

10

The Theory of the
Labour Aristocracy

The idea that a labour aristocracy arose in Britain in approximately the third quarter of the nineteenth century has been the subject of renewed interest amongst historians, for a number of related reasons. In some versions, particularly Marxist ones, the theme carries a heavy explanatory burden. Thus, although it depends on empirical research of very specific kinds, the question of the 'labour aristocracy' also embraces debates about the entire pattern of modern capitalist development, especially during the nineteenth century. Moreover, it illustrates the variations within the Marxist tradition, notably Leninist and Gramscian interpretations.

Unlike, for example, the case of the French or English revolutions, or even that of the making of the English working class, our present subject relates to modern capitalism. It should therefore be a fuller test of Marxist categories than 'earlier' historical issues. Also, since the bourgeoisie is no longer so 'progressive', debates about the forms and functions of a stratum of labour elite have a sharp political edge, for they involve questions of reformism and the alleged 'betrayal' of the working class by its ostensible leaders. Finally, the topic illuminates the relations between historical analysis and current sociological findings and methods concerning 'embourgeoisement'.

In sum, the question is particularly suited to a treatment linking epistemological to ideological options, via the levels of historical content and methodology. Also, the debates again raise the question of the relationship between realist philosophical assumptions and a broadly Marxist account.

Since useful summaries exist,[1] the literature on the labour aristocracy may be approached in a classificatory rather than descriptive or chronological way. I will first outline the Marxist approaches and try to assess how compatible are the forms of causality prescribed by some of them. The 'classic' thesis,[2] which traces its lineage to Lenin, emphasizes economic causation, and makes political ascription clear. The 'revised' thesis is upheld by Marxists more influenced by the recent opening up (or closing down) of Marxist tenets.

The key feature of the concept of the labour aristocracy, at least in its classic form, is that it is inescapably explanatory. If the idea is tenable at all, it points to a causal sequence, and thus cannot be simply empirical or descriptive. Some Marxists have tried to avoid the moral connotations and contemporary uses of the term. This broad intention leads to the 'revised' thesis.

However, the logic of the classic thesis cannot do without the connotations revisionists dislike. The literal meaning of the phrase seems to require that it refer to a clearly identifiable stratum in the working class with unrepresentative wealth and elitist values. Its causal employment implies that in some sense the labour aristocracy is responsible for the retardation of the class as a whole, and that this is politically or morally reprehensible. We thus find a paradox: in order to be explanatory, the theory of the labour aristocracy must *retain* the cluster of descriptions and values implicit in its metaphorical character. Conversely, merely in rejecting the term, revisionists may be offering a very different set of explanations or arguments.

The difference between the classic and modified perspectives can be further clarified. It is useful to reintroduce the notion of different levels of abstraction here, for it will guide the rest of the discussion. The concepts of Marx's *Capital*, for example, contain very-high-level abstractions such as production-in-general, or surplus labour, or co-operation. Lower-level abstractions would be surplus-value, the tendency of the rate of profit to fall, or increasing centralization of capital. But these abstractions are still high-level in that they specify the mechanisms and tendencies of capitalism *as such*, what we might call capital-logic. One central problem in Marxist theory is in what way capital-logic guides lower-level abstractions, the ones that refer to historically specific phenomena. The danger of 'reductionism' arises when the connection between higher- and lower-level descriptions is treated in a positivistic manner, in other words, when cases are regarded as instantiations of universal correlations. In the realist view, by contrast, such laws as there are operate tendentially as a consequence of the real causal mediation of a number of different and irreducible processes.

Another relevant characteristic of capital-logic is that it deals in 'personifications'.[3] Capitalists or workers are typified according to their structural location in the contradictions of capitalism, which alone can serve as the basis of typical behaviour. This does not rule out, for example, psychological or 'motivational' traits, but those traits, too, are typical. For example, Marx speaks of the 'voracious appetite' of the manufacturer for surplus-value.[4] He thus uses personifications to illustrate the logic of capital; it is less certain that he would recommend without qualification the use of capital-logic to deduce only personifications from specific groups of people.

The labour-aristocracy debate is a good example of a problem in which such questions loom large. In the classic position, the labour aristocracy is not itself the object requiring explanation, but the *explanans*. The *explanandum* is really the failure of the working class to be revolutionary, for which the labour aristocracy is held partly responsible. However, a further explanation (at a higher level of abstraction) accounts for the causal role of the labour aristocracy, namely the super-profits of imperialism, by which means the labour aristocrats are 'bought off'. John Foster's work elaborates these further structural conditions, adding to imperialism certain changes in the labour process, and inserting, at an intermediate level of abstraction, the will of the bourgeoisie.

The main interest of the revisionists is in the existence and character of the labour aristocracy itself. Revised versions, unlike the classic thesis, are about the elite stratum, and not directly about proletarian retardation. Nor does the revision assume a 'natural' sequence whereby proletarian consciousness becomes revolutionary, only to be betrayed by its upper stratum. This, of course, is a broad generalization, but some classic theses almost say as much. In sum, the revised position does not seek to fully explain the phenomenon in question merely by showing the operation of the logic of the higher level of abstraction in and through the lower.

Despite the bold lines of this sketch, the question, Which is the more genuinely Marxist approach? is neither easy to answer nor particularly enlightening. As we will see, the revisionists do not abandon a 'structural' perspective. Similarly, classic theses suppose a remarkable degree of subjective or motivational causation. We may cite Foster's emphasis on the desire of the ruling class to 'liberalize', or Lenin's scorn of the venality of the labour aristocrats. Also, it might not be too much to say that the gullibility of the mass of the working class is assumed as well. But if classic versions tend unduly to collapse the different levels of abstraction, in fairness it should be noted that in trying to play down the 'betrayal' theory and capital-logic, the more empirically open revised positions run the risk of ceasing to be explanatory at all.

1. Classic Approaches

By employing the terms 'classic' and 'revised', which themselves will be scrutinized, we can capture the strong element of dispute in debates about the kind of theoretical problematic Marxism is. In fact, there is no *theory* of the labour aristocracy in Marx or Engels. There is one in Lenin, with whom it takes its 'classic' form. Yet even Lenin's theory is not altogether clear. His main concern was reformism in the working-class movement as a result of imperialism. In terms of a historical *period*, Lenin took imperialism to be a global phenomenon, especially from the 1890s. This is considerably later than the high period of the British labour aristocrats. But 'imperialism' is also a general theoretical category, and it might be asked whether Lenin intended it to be part of capital-logic, a stage through which each capitalist country must necessarily pass. Only if we take Lenin's theory in its full logical sense will it be thought to have an immediate exemplification in the British labour aristocracy.

It is certainly Lenin who gave the theory its characteristic bite: 'This stratum of workers turned bourgeois, or labour aristocracy, who are quite philistine in their mode of life, in the size of their earnings, and in their entire outlook, is the principal . . . social (not military) *prop of the bourgeoisie* . . . the labour lieutenants of the capitalist class, real vehicles of reformism and chauvinism.'[5]

Lenin is explicit that it is their receipt of a share of the profits of imperialism that makes 'a section' of the British proletariat become 'bourgeois',[6] and he cites in support Engels's well-known statement of 1858 to the same effect. Yet three points show that Lenin's detailed ideas are vague. First, he is unclear about *who* is bought off or how it is done. Who is bought off? Sometimes it is 'labour leaders', or 'the upper stratum of the labour aristocracy'.[7] These are not necessarily the same, but even so it seems that the aristocracy is somewhat wider than the bought-off section. Elsewhere Lenin refers to the upper strata of *the workers*: 'the bulk of the membership of co-operatives, trade unions, sporting clubs, and numerous religious sects'.[8] If this is the 'bribed section' (of the *class* rather than the elite stratum), then it can be 'a fairly considerable minority'. Lenin's concept of an aristocracy, following the Webbs', comes partly from the British context, which predates imperialism except in a very extended sense. But his illustrations and qualifications weaken his initial thesis. In addition to the unclarity about the scope of the 'bourgeois' stratum, the mechanisms of control postulated are sometimes conveniently dispersed: bribing goes on 'in a thousand different ways, direct and indirect, overt and covert'.[9]

It is not difficult to see how Lenin's specific thesis could be generalized, and perhaps he meant it to be so. His use of Engels is indicative. In fact, Engels's letter to Marx of 1858 has nothing to do with imperialism. Nor does it say very much. But in the 1892 preface to his *The Condition of the Working Class in England*, Engels provided an account of the aristocracy of labour recognizably closer to the concerns of British historians. Writing of the remarkable advances of the skilled workers organized in unions, he notes: 'They form an aristocracy among the working class; they have succeeded in enforcing for themselves a relatively comfortable position, and they accept it as final. . . . They are very nice people nowadays to deal with . . . for the whole capitalist class in general.'[10]

Yet there is no theory of imperialism, 'buying off', or of a betrayed proletariat. Engels argued that the benefits arising from 'the period of England's industrial monopoly'[11] may have been disproportionately divided, but that 'even the great mass had, at least, a temporary share now and then'. Within the Marxist tradition, the fusion of Marx, Engels, and Lenin has undoubtedly led to the assumption that their ideas and political invective were identical on many counts. The question of the 'labour aristocracy' is one such occasion. It seems to me that the causalities offered by the various 'classics' are, when drawn out, somewhat different.[12] Further, the characteristic vehemence of Lenin and his readiness to see betrayal in Menshevism and reformism has been (with confusing results) projected backwards in time. Both these points can be illustrated briefly.

When reviewing developments in the German working class in the 1920s, Max Adler, an able Marxist, had recourse to the concept of the labour aristocracy. He was struck by the loss of the unitary character of labour and the 'embourgeoisement' of the 'so-called labour aristocracy'. Like Lenin, he attributed their class 'betrayal' to a further, structural 'transformation in the capitalist process', namely imperialism.[13]

However, Adler was not satisfied with the 'voluntarist' implication of making the labour aristocracy the main causal explanation. In this, he actually did make a *general* point of Marxian thought more akin to Engels. 'Reformism in the proletariat', he wrote, 'is not just a problem of leaders but of the masses, and if only for this reason the phenomenon of the "labour aristocracy" is one of great significance, since it is the surface manifestation of a current which is also present in the masses. It would be fundamentally misleading, therefore, to identify the labour aristocracy with so-called "bosses".'[14]

With this statement the nature of the labour aristocracy becomes *part* of a more general analysis of proletarian differentiation and subordination. It is not itself the explanation for incorporation. Adler does not appear to regard his two arguments as counterposed, but he clearly rejects an explanation in terms of motivational greed or conspiratorial betrayal. Yet the labour aristocracy thesis encourages the latter.

Theodore Rothstein's book *From Chartism to Labourism* (1929) takes imperialism to be an inadequate explanation of British developments. He offers instead the gradual decline in price levels in the last quarter of the nineteenth century. But the characteristic tone and form of explanation in Rothstein are Leninist (leaving aside the fact that the labourism in question had its heyday in the *third* quarter of the century). 'From militant proletarian', writes Rothstein, 'the English worker turned petty bourgeois.'[15] Essentially, such a transformation was due, Rothstein argues, to the 'economism' of the 'hirelings of capital', the labour leaders and aristocracy who 'diverted the labour movement from revolutionary to opportunist, from proletarian to middle class, from political to trade-union lines'.[16] Rothstein does not accept imperialism as the cause of degeneration, but transposes Lenin's entire Bolshevik polemic against reformism to the mid nineteenth century. His account is thus anachronistic and essentially voluntarist. On all counts this is quite the reverse of the analysis of Max Adler, who nominally accepts Lenin's theory. In other words, even in the confident assertion of Leninism the problem arises of whether 'structural' and 'motivational' causality are compatible.

In any event, the necessary political attributes of social groups are questionably woven into the very fabric of 'class analysis'. At a purely theoretical level, Guillermo Carchedi exemplifies this operation. His analysis shows how disagreement about fundamental concepts of Marxism can be bound up in the historical fate of the labour aristocracy. According to Carchedi, the labour aristocracies, 'While members of the working class on the level of production relations, become middle class (or better said, petty-bourgeois) when distribution relations, superstructures, and class struggle are considered.'[17] The aristocracy of labour 'contaminates' the other sections of the proletariat with their bourgeois ideologies and practices, even if not purely by design.[18] Carchedi thus suggests that the aristocracy belongs to the working class, but not to the proletariat proper, because their class practices in politics are not those of the proletariat ('Joining the revolutionary party, etc.'[19]), nor do they develop a proletarian class consciousness.

As a nominal Leninist and a contemporary Marxist academic, Carchedi ostensibly rules out economic reductionism. His *identification* of classes is meant to be only the basis for a more complex *definition* of class, in which political and ideological components have equal weight with the strictly economic. Like Poulantzas's work, Carchedi's search for systematic 'complexity' is impressive in some ways. But actually, as in the case of the labour aristocracy, the results are historically barren; theoretically, they can be as fatalistic as any 'vulgar' economism, for built into his conception of the true proletarian is a Leninist definition of correct Marxist politics. And because Carchedi regards political and economic criteria as inseparable, these 'definitions', which are actually political idealizations and assessments, take on a dangerously 'objective' appearance.

Thus the labour aristocracy is *necessarily* bourgeois in Carchedi's scheme, and only truly class-conscious workers ('the revolutionary party, etc.') are real proletarians. This is very convenient for the vanguard, but the superficial appeal of back-stabbing labour aristocrats is not enough, even in theory, to convince us that the 'mass' of the class is governed by Carchedian or Leninist ideas of proper class consciousness. Historically, this has not been so, and labour aristocrats *have* been revolutionaries. Moreover, the automatic 'contamination' of the bulk of the class is, historically, more problematical than it may seem to be at a high level of abstraction. While there is no need to blame Lenin for Carchedi, there is a similar 'over-politicization' of categories in much Leninist thought, not always to good effect. It seems to me possible to argue that classes are *economic* classes only, and that while the 'correspondence' of certain cultures, conditions, and ideas may, over some considerable time-span, be traced, the matter is historical rather than logical.

I have tried so far generally to identify some theoretical problems with classic approaches, such as the question of the object of explanation; the definition of the sociological boundaries and historical reach of the concept 'labour aristocracy'; the kinds of causality involved; and the question of the ascription of economic-political essences in the analysis of classes or strata. In fact, none of these issues appear in their 'pure' form in the historians' work (with the exception, perhaps, of that of John Foster). More common is a concern to focus attention on the identification of the labour aristocracy, together with *some* account of its political effects.

The historians most influenced by the classic thesis seem to have little doubt that Lenin's general views can be adapted to an earlier period and that the existence of the stratum presents no great problems. Rather, the task is to fill out the historical circumstances of its function in Britain. Thus E. J. Hobsbawm (like Rothstein) takes up the labour-aristocracy thesis from Lenin, not as a phenomenon specific to imperialism, but as a 'special case of the general model of economism'. On the basis of Victorian parlance, Hobsbawm regards the existence of the 'aristocracy' as given. The problem is to adequately identify its 'character and social and political consequences'.[20]

Royden Harrison, too, does not question whether the *terms* as used in pre-imperialist decades may imply that the *theory* is inapplicable. His *Before the Socialists* is about the political contribution of the elite of the working class to reform and Lib-Labism. If the theory of the labour aristocracy is artificial, Harrison writes, 'then the analysis in this volume is faulty at its core'.[21]

John Foster, the most orthodox Leninist amongst the historians, regards nineteenth-century Britain as the test case of Lenin's theory, and is happy to accept that it implies that mid-century capitalism must be regarded as imperialist.[22] But the *object* of Foster's analysis, and to some extent of Harrison's, is the watershed of mid-century, the point at which revolutionary class consciousness gives way to the economic differentiation and quiescence of the proletariat. All the classic-influenced historians assume that the upper stratum—the aristocracy—effects the stabilization of the system. Keith Burgess, for example, says that the aristocracy mediated conflict by performing the function of capital,[23] and all agree that the result was the pacification of the working class.

Before examining the different explanations, we should note that, although the object of analysis is agreed and assumed, problems of definition and scope continue to worry the historians. To begin with, the rather simple question should be posed, Can we identify the labour aristocracy in economic terms alone? Hobsbawm gives the most cogent response, taking the regularity and level of wages as crucial, and providing data to show the marked existence of differentials. The *source* of the differential is less clear. For Hobsbawm, it is the level of the industrial reserve army and fixed capital, together with specific pressures of craft-exclusiveness.[24] For Burgess, it appears additionally to be part of the savings made by capital from the aristocracy's performance of management functions. Harrison, more straightforwardly (and following Engels), attributes the rise in real wages—of which the aristocracy took 'the lion's share'[25]—to the overcoming of capitalism's growing pains and Britain's 'unquestionable predominance in the world economy'. Finally, Foster regards the higher wages as coming from imperialist super-profits garnered from exported capital.

But the main criterion Foster employs concerns the production process rather than distribution. He isolates the newly found authoritarian role of labour aristocrats with respect to work tasks. Hobsbawm himself says something on the same lines,[26] linking control over the labour process to co-exploitation (and thus approaching Burgess's argument). On the other hand, Foster rejects any easy connection between either miseration and radicalism or higher income and conservatism. In this respect he goes beyond Hobsbawm, who relies, ultimately, on some such equation.

Second, if the economic criteria by which the aristocracy is identified seem unclear and insufficient, the historical breadth of the concept is questionable, too. Hobsbawm sees its 'classic period' as 1840–1890. But although in the period up to the 1840s 'it is doubtful whether . . . we can speak of a labour aristocracy at all',[27] he implies that his main criterion, wage level and regularity, is applicable 'throughout the century'.[28] This squares with E. P. Thompson's evidence that the first half of the century saw the formation of the working class, including its aristocratic stratum.[29] At the other end of the period, Hobsbawm regards the aristocracy in the 1890–1914 years to be 'substantially of the same type and composition' as in its classic period.[30] Although he notes large changes as well as 'survivals' of privilege, Hobsbawm gives no conclusive reason why the model should cease to be applicable after 1914.

John Foster, by contrast, openly advocates that it can and must be applicable. In his (1976) article, Foster postulates the idea of a 'Labour aristocracy – Phase II'.[31] Briefly, he argues that in the period up to the general strike (and presumably after), the revolutionary consciousness of the proletariat was retarded in a manner logically similar to the 1850s. The mechanism of retardation, however, was dissimilar. Rather than a section of the class being bought off 'through the market' (as in the earlier phase), the class organizations (the unions) as a whole were 'educated', and their leaders incorporated.

All in all, the labour aristocracy has had a long life. There is even a case that it is highly pertinent today. Gavin Mackenzie's study of American unions,[32] and the material on 'embourgeoisement' in Britain shares at least this assumption with the Marxist historians: that higher income levels encourage conservatism and dampen, or educate, the intrinsic militancy of the rank and file. 'The political and economic positions of the labour aristocracy reflect each other with uncanny accuracy', writes Hobsbawm.[33] More needs to be said on the politics of labour, but the sociological boundaries of our concept remain to be considered.

Hobsbawm's essay estimates that the aristocracy accounts for 10–15% of the working class. He also argues that the aristocracy is not equivalent to skilled workers, and even less so to the amalgamated unions. This is important, not only because the Webbs, with their 'new model', propagated that idea,[34] but also because it appears, from Hobsbawm's point of view, to be a confusion common to scholarly and popular Marxist writings. Harrison, for example, equates the labour movement in general with the 'aristocrats', 'the organized'; the plebeians are therefore the 'unorganized'.[35] Rothstein, Burgess, and Tony Lane take up a similar stance. In his more 'popular' text, Lane, for example, consistently identifies the aristocracy with the 'top-hatted trade unionist'.[36] Interestingly, the classic Communist popular history is less scathing and more circumspect. A. L. Morton states that the skilled unions catered to the aristocracy, thus leaving room for a more exact identification.[37] Even Hobsbawm is ambiguous about classification. He sees the 'upper' boundary of the aristocracy merging into the lower middle-class. He also identifies a (changeable) 'super aristocracy',[38] and a sizeable group between the aristocrats and the labourers, shading into both.[39] Harrison, while speaking of a 'profound gulf' between aristocracy and plebeians, acknowledges a 'large intermediate group' in that apparently empty space.[40]

No doubt the 'plebeians' could be stratified, too. Hobsbawm merely cites Baxter's fairly arbitrary line of those who earned less than 20s (40% of the working class) to designate the 'lower stratum'. More recently, Hobsbawm has allowed that an overall division between poor and respectable would be useful for some purposes, though if that concession may leave the aristocracy thesis unscathed, it surely reduces it importance.[41]

He has also argued that 'the superficial observer might sometimes see the working class merely as a complex of sectional groups and grades with their social superiority and inferiority, without observing the major divisions'.[42] But Hobsbawm's own criterion of male wages could be said to be rather sectional and economistic, and it leaves out matters of family circumstances and regional differences. Moreover, 'social superiority' is also part of the problem of the labour aristocracy, so in either case it is not so obvious what the 'major differences' actually are. Even in its closest, most statistically explicit presentation, the concept is slippery and possibly misleading. And if, as John Field has observed,[43] contemporary usages of the term were also at odds with each other, then identification of the labour aristocracy, either historically or conceptually, seems bound to be impressionistic in various degrees. Yet it continues to be used as a causal theory. Hobsbawm is characteristically circumspect, but his work is still intended as a vindication of the theory, which is taken for granted by Rothstein, Harrison, and Foster as accounting for the roots of the blight of labourism and reformism. As James Hinton has pointed out,[44] this prohibits more detailed socio-economic analysis of the class as a whole. It also denies political and ideological factors their own power to generate allegiances, though Harrison, for one, admits that 'a whole complex of inter-related changes . . . lie behind political developments'.[45]

John Foster's work systematically raises the questions of the compatibility of structural and 'motivational' causality. It is worth pausing on his version of the classic thesis. To simplify, Foster's argument is that the limited working-class consciousness of the early proletariat (until about

1830) gave way to a revolutionary consciousness in a period of crisis for the bourgeoisie (1830–47). This was followed in turn by a phase of 'liberalization', which, although it corresponded to a new stage of capitalist expansion, was the product of a deliberate response by the bourgeoisie to the revolutionary threat. It should be said that Foster's argument is about Oldham only. However, it is clear that his model is meant to be of general value,[46] and that in comparison to Shields and Northampton, Foster regards Oldham as an exemplar of capitalist development in key respects.

In a pioneering comparative analysis, Foster demonstrates that tradition, material conditions, or unionism, of themselves, did not imply revolutionary consciousness. Rather it was the 'logic' of the industrial structure that laid bare the capitalist mode of exploitation. This in turn produced the crucial factor that cemented the alliance between the political 'vanguard' and the working class: the intellectual conviction that a different society was desirable. However, with inexorable logic, the same 'economics of class consciousness' spurred the bourgeoisie to re-impose social control by creating a labour aristocracy. The aristocracies (in cotton, coal, and engineering) redivided the proletariat. A sectional, subordinate working class was maintained thereafter through institutions such as friendly societies, Sunday schools, and mechanics institutes. The return of chauvinism in the 1850s and 1860s and a programme of social amelioration are cited by Foster as further evidence of the success of the ruling-class offensive.

A number of empirical complaints have been lodged against Foster's account, from both Marxist and non-Marxist historians. Foster's own modest claim to provide 'rough backing for more impressionistic findings' is certainly a poor gloss on his stridently Leninist argument.[47] Yet the main difficulty is the theoretical apparatus constructed, without which the account would be pedestrian.

One major problem about the Leninist framework is its anachronism. The small beginnings of the export of machinery are taken without warrant to be imperialism.[48] The wages of the aristocrats must therefore be regarded (dubiously) as part of the super-profits of imperialism. The initial stabilization of the capitalist system (Hobsbawm) is taken by Foster to be the first of its inherent death-pangs, with crisis as the symptom. Further, as Martin Nicolaus makes clear,[49] the theory of the aristocracy under imperialism requires that the elite be paid at a higher rate than the value of labour-power. Foster gives no argument that this could be the case in his period.

Gareth Stedman Jones[50] has rightly argued that the Leninist formula of trade-union consciousness leading to class consciousness is distorted by

Foster's use of a pure, unhistorical concept of alienation, drawn from the early Marx. This concept logically ties the discussion to the absence, but necessary return, of a lost essence to potentially fulfilled humanity. Stedman Jones sees this schema as responsible for Foster's overemphasis on the intellectual unity of the vanguard and masses in the 'revolutionary' period in Oldham. Stedman Jones's points are pertinent, but do not completely satisfy, because for all their differences, the Leninist schema and the alienation schema share important features. Both tend to posit a 'true' or 'correct' politics and consciousness arrived at in stages defined, almost, by a teleological end-point: the paradigmatic 'revolution'. Both thus tend to reduce ideology to a uniform condition of falsity, not admitting of degrees or having specific 'natural' conditions. In addition, both envisage a single, qualitative leap from ideology to non-ideology.

The real problem with Foster's (and to some extent Lenin's) theory is its yoking together of arguments about the necessary logic of capitalist development with the assertion of the primacy of political design. Poulantzas has captured this theoretical phenomenon in his assertion of the 'invariable duo' of historicism: economism implies voluntarism, and vice versa.[51] To illustrate: Foster assures us that the 'decisive factor'[52] in the growth of consciousness was intellectual commitment. Yet this turned out to be a product of the structural development of capital. He has difficulty in convincing most readers that his empirical evidence displays that kind of commitment. Again, monopoly and imperialism are part of the logic of accumulation, but 'liberalization' is the conscious product of the bourgeoisie. Finally, the labour aristocracy, a phenomenon of the market and the labour process, is both the instrument and agency whereby the organizations of the class 'remained virtually under enemy control'[53] for fifty years.

This set of explanations collapses levels of abstraction: consciousness and its effectivity are guaranteed by the necessary logic of the mode of production. Material circumstances are impregnated by political schemata, and consciousness is reciprocally given in the capital-logic. Here, what have been referred to as 'over-politicization' and 'economism' amount to much the same thing.

2. Revisionist Perspectives

There seems to be a tendency in the classic approaches towards theoretical essentialism: the assignment of empirical phenomena to parts of a rather heavy-handed logical sequence. What I have heuristically termed 'revision-ism' is not untheoretical, but it suspects both the form and level of the theory in classic views of being too reductive. Since they remain within Marxism, the two approaches do share much. But the distinction is worth making, because in the work of revisionists there is much less commitment to the idea that the 'labour aristocracy' theory is, in all respects, explana-tory. 'I would not argue that the emergence of a labour aristocracy is the key component of an explanation of the stabilization of Victorian society.'[54] 'The term has often been used as if it provided an explanation. But it would be more accurate to say that it pointed towards a vacant space where an explanation should be.'[55] 'It is not valid to introduce the role of a corrupt labour aristocracy as special pleading to explain the absence of revolution-ary politics.'[56]

The object of explanation in the classic view—retardation—is ques-tioned here. The means of explanation—the labour aristocracy—is down-graded if not rejected. And the assumption behind many classic views—the tendency of the proletariat to develop revolutionary consciousness—is dis-carded. However, *if* the points made by revisionists are theoretical and not mere empirical preferences, some alternative 'problematic' (not necessarily in the hard Althusserian sense) would seem to be required. Here the debates become interestingly varied, since each of the quoted revisionists is committed to explanatory history.

The first point to notice is that the term 'labour aristocracy' is retained and accepted as a 'social and ideological phenomenon'.[57] 'The labour aris-tocracy must be understood in a precise historical sense', writes Gray.[58] The title of Geoffrey Crossick's book, *An Artisan Elite in Victorian Society*, conveys a similar impression. Second, of the revisionists, only Gray (and he is closer to the classic versions) lays out an extensive analytical framework. True, Stedman Jones's article is only a review, and he is entitled to be negative. But it is a major piece, and in any case he has agreed that *something* needs explaining. Further, he seems to allow that there is a problem of 'labour aristocratic attitudes'. In any development of his posi-tions, we would be entitled to ask a number of questions. Despite his admirably 'materialist' analysis, what is the material basis of the 'social and ideological' phenomenon he recognizes? Or again, while we could agree that certain attitudes went beyond particular strata of the labour force, why continue to use the term 'labour aristocracy' if it did not have a basis and a function in working-class development? Stedman Jones rightly points us away from abstraction towards the 'general political and ideological con-juncture', but it would be unfair to the classic views if it were implied that they had no historical purchase outside of abstraction.

Crossick's contribution is also 'negative'. It has a tentative object of explanation, 'relative mid-Victorian stability'. However, and paradoxically, the argument is that the subject of his research—an identifiable labour elite in Kentish London—makes only a small and misunderstood contribution to that stabilization. Stability was 'the result of a process of continuing struggle, in which the features of a class society determined the outcome in only the most generalized sense'.[59] If this sounds more like an abdication than an argument, it should be said that Crossick really deals with a more limited problem. In fact, he accepts[60] that there was a striking change of temper in working-class political and social organizations between 1850 and the 1880s, and the emergence of an elite stratum. The point is rather that from his own work and from his rejection of Foster-like arguments, Crossick advances the idea that the 'labour aristocracy achieved its position through struggle and conflict, not capitulation'.[61]

Crossick's view seems to differ from Gray's in that the former sees the aristocracy as only one amongst several explanatory factors of stabilization, though this is rendered questionable by Crossick's other statements, for example that his book 'examines a major element in the lessening of social tensions, the emergence of a labour aristocracy'.[62] More emphatically, Gray continues to place the concept at the centre of Marxist concerns.

At the level of the object of explanation, then, the classic case has been modified, but it still exerts pressure: it has not been explained away. A similar conclusion can be drawn on the question of the identification of the elite. Here the revisionists, despite their criticisms of Foster, have taken much from him. He began to introduce questions of authority at work, inter-marriage, and housing patterns, and questions of organizations and leisure, in preference to the yardstick of income alone. In this respect, there is also continuity, and not simple disjuncture, from Hobsbawm to Crossick.

Recently, Gray has summarized and pursued the case against Hobsbawm's concentration on earnings. In his research on Edinburgh, Gray found it difficult to establish clear wage patterns; rather than being complementary categories, high wages, regular income, and authority at work often work against each other. The 'economic' criteria alone are thus by no means straightforward. Crossick feels able to identify an aristocracy in London without having much earnings evidence at all. Their common sentiment would appear to be, 'There is no necessary reason why high-wage earners should form an exclusive social group with aspirations and values distinct from others'.[63] Both argue that skill (and unionism, too) is an insufficient measure of the aristocracy. Indeed, Gray has noted that the definition of a skill is both technologically variable and a product, in part, of collective bargaining by strong unions. The revisionists implicitly refuse to extend the concept of the 'aristocracy' much beyond the mid-Victorian decades: that would be to risk a general sociological reduction of the kind exhibited by certain classic theories.

The emphasis on identifying a 'social stratum' rather than an 'economic elite' is important, but should not be exaggerated. To begin with, no classic account denied that the values and politics of the elite were the crucial question. In any case, Gray's widening of the conception of 'economic determination' is not at all assumed to undermine the proposition that there *was* an economic basis to artisan culture and ideology. And Crossick, whose account in many respects is ambiguously 'Marxist', declares: 'The economic basis of the labour aristocrats' position underpinned all else, and the stratum formation would have little relevance without it.'[64]

Moving on to the third and fourth of my theoretical 'guidelines', it is clear that the pattern of explanation also determines the degree of political necessity ascribed to the 'aristocracy'. The key feature of the revisionists' view in these respects is the assertion of a 'relative autonomy' in the spheres of politics, ideology, and culture. In this they follow the predominant climate in Marxist theory generally. By 'relative autonomy' I do not mean Nicos Poulantzas's theory that the state requires autonomy in order to secure its long-term functionality for capital. That is a more specific and, arguably, an independent question. I have in mind rather the fairly simple idea that the pattern of capitalist economic development 'determines' the other social levels only in the sense that it imposes limiting conditions or constraints on the forms and outcomes of struggles. This is really the crucial point behind the entire revisionist argument.

Consequently, the general, structural, 'logic of capital' is not in question: it lies behind all significant social phenomena, including the labour aristocracy. Revisionists consequently have no difficulty in accepting a background, conditional causality at a fairly high level of abstraction. 'Industrially', writes Stedman Jones, 'what Foster imputes to the emergence of a labour aristocracy was in fact nothing but the effect of a restabilization of the labour process on the basis of modern industry.'[65] This point is not to suggest that Foster was not determinist enough. It is rather, I take it, intended to structurally explain the labour aristocracy (and other things) without predetermining more concrete questions by fusing structural and motivational causality (as Foster does). Gray makes a similar point: the labour aristocracy was 'just one form of a far wider process of adaptation to the given environment of industrial capitalism'.[66]

In other words, the fact of capital restructuring is not in doubt. The idea that it was primarily a deliberate decision involving the ideological incorporation of 'aristocrats'—*that* conclusion is rejected. Thus Gray and Crossick are most keen to establish the wider social conditions within which labour aristocratic values develop. For Crossick: 'If it depended fundamentally on its economic position, it [the 'aristocracy'] constructed its social situation on an additional complex of diffuse and normative characteristics.'[67] And Gray: 'The formation of the labour aristocracy . . . is the outcome of differential socio-economic experience, as this was handled through the available ideologies and actively interpreted in terms of life-style and imagery.'[68]

It is by now commonplace to observe a certain instability in the term 'relative autonomy'. In some cases, such as Poulantzas's political 'region', functionalism only *appears* to be overcome. In others, the autonomy seems so great that determinations dissolve altogether. While Gray's adaptation of Gramsci's concept of hegemony remains recognizably Marxist, Crossick's similar stance leads to more eclectic, and even empiricist, conclusions. Both historians present much description to portray the 'rationality' of the labour aristocrats' aspirations to respectability, moderate affluence, and decent conditions. But they also lend that 'rationality' a certain amount of sympathy. They argue that Hobsbawm's blurred line between labour aristocrats and the middle class was in fact surprisingly stable, that 'bourgeois ideas' were as much transformed as they were swallowed whole, and that similar values were also accepted by the bulk of the working class. Such militancy as the class showed, the aristocracy participated in. They were responsible for the *preservation* of class institutions as much as for their 'incorporation'.

In Gray's work, however, due respect for such achievements does not prevent harsh judgement, or at least realistic assessment. The 'ideas' involved remained those that accommodated the class to capitalism. Bourgeois hegemony was negotiated, certainly: status claims had to be won in the context of strong class pride.[69] But the style and language of the strata, the tendency to privatization, elitism, patriotism, and the absorption of watered-down middle-class culture—these elements ensured a 'corporate' or subordinate consciousness. Robert Gray has revised the classical Marxist theory, but in the end his conclusions are not outside its traditional causal patterns: 'The labour aristocracy thus implanted accommodative responses to capitalism, and subsequently transmitted them to a broader class movement.'[70] Judging by his more recent reflections, Gray would want to place more emphasis on the need to examine other issues: technical changes in the labour process, sexual division of labour and power, ruling-class responses, and so on. But he has not rejected the above conclusion.

Crossick, too, does much to rehabilitate his elite. His account of 'negotiation', however, is a little less weighted than Gray's. Crossick locates the aristocrats' 'respectability' firmly 'within a specific working-class socio-economic situation'.[71] Here, the refusal of patronage, the demand for decent standards, the pride in manual work, and the solidarity of the 'mutual' are not to be sneered at. Kentish London aristocrats did not allow independence and respectability to contradict, for instance, social drinking. The culture may have been accommodative, but it was distinctly working class.

Crossick's revisionism, then, is more radical than Gray's. He is aware of the peculiarities of his area of London: its lack of an aggressive bourgeoisie, or a Chartist tradition, and its lack, too, of sharp class conflict. Indeed, the stress on the locality is refreshingly concrete. But it is not without its dangers. For one thing, Crossick seems as keen to raise his research into a paradigm as Foster is to champion Oldham.[72] In some ways, if one had to choose, Foster's option has a more persuasive rationale. But more specifically, Crossick places the locality at the heart of his *methodology*. He argues that 'it is unreal to ask whether the communities in question were typical or representative, for that issue is in the last resort unresolvable'.[73] Now, the Marxist mode of analysis employed by Crossick and his reference to a necessary 'typology of urban development' would suggest that Crossick claims more for his study than his more 'particular' statements imply. But he constructs his own 'firm explanatory framework': 'It is based on that explicit argument, that the ideology and behaviour of the skilled elite derive from particular forces.

'The activities and values of the labour aristocracy in Kentish London derived from the perceived experience that they drew from their own lives and traditions, and from the forces operating upon and around them.

'The economic and social system of industrializing Britain was not seen by the workers as a totality, but only as they themselves experienced it.'[74]

These statements are puzzling in the extreme. One strand suggests that experiences are irreducibly particular. This may be so, given suitable elaboration, but I personally doubt it. But *that* claim does not prevent analytic generalization. However, is there not a second strand here to the effect that an *account* of the values of the elite can be conducted only in terms of its own experience? Crossick makes much of the constructive and normative character of 'aristocrat' consciousness.[75] He speculates on their subjective need to feel superior,[76] and insists that meaning-systems are relative to the values of those who construct and participate in them.[77] Such asides, I think, together with the cryptic assertion of 'particularist' criteria quoted above, indicate that a phenomenological method, as opposed to a causal account, is being recommended. If this is not entirely mistaken, we might speculate that Crossick's position, unlike Gray's, abandons the very concept of ideology and determination required by any explanatory thesis in the Marxist tradition: the aristocrats' reformist tendencies cease altogether to be a problem of any kind. Given Crossick's verbal acknowledgement of the object of analysis, we may doubt this intention and refuse to draw those conclusions. But for all the book's important contributions, a 'firm explanatory framework' is *not* provided.

3. Critics and Alternatives

I have tried to argue that the 'revised' thesis of the labour aristocracy, for all its criticism of the classic thesis, retains some of the latter's key features. Consequently, the comparison reveals the double-edged character of the debate: as a debate *within* Marxism about economic causality and historical specificity, the positions can be in sharp counterposition. However, revisionists are quick to deny that their views fail to be explanatory, 'structural', or recognizably Marxist. In the complex case of someone who appears to go distinctly beyond the theory (Crossick), the Marxist element of the analysis disappears into a rather eclectic set of categories. A distinct form of explanation, in other words, seems less important and not obviously present. I would therefore disagree with Robert Gray's judgement, 'It is . . . misleading to see the debate about the labour aristocracy as a confrontation between Marxist historians and those of other persuasions.'[78] It seems to me appropriate to ask: what do other critics of our 'theory' say? What are their alternatives? What, after due consideration, are the explanatory merits of the *Marxist* concept 'labour aristocracy'?

Gray's comment is useful in directing attention to the fact that the reductionist forms of some classic versions are akin to certain sociological views about 'embourgeoisement' and 'social control'. In addition, the criticisms of the Marxist theory made by historians are not necessarily mistaken. However, beginning with the latter point, we must carefully distinguish empirical agreement from deeper explanatory differences (and sometimes vice versa). There are three forms of historians' response.

Some historians would accept the theory, providing empirical or institutional limitations were placed upon it. Thus H. A. Turner's important study of the cotton industry is seen as confirming the generalization that 'aristocratic' organization retards the formation of mass unionism and the radicalism associated with it. Turner here defines the aristocracy in a fairly general way, as skilled organized workers. Also, there is no assumption that the adaptation to the system is correlative with the potential for overthrowing it. But at times Turner almost says as much,[79] and he uses 'the theory of the labour aristocracy' as the title of a central part of his book. This indicates that his work is quite *compatible* with the Marxist account, though he is not explicitly a Marxist.

Other historians share some of the terms and empirical judgements of the theory's advocates, while operating within non-Marxist explanatory frameworks. T. R. Tholfsen's argument, for instance, shares much of the revised thesis. Though radicalism was 'blunted and the subculture softened', there was no total surrender to middle-class values.[80] Tholfsen explicitly favours 'hegemony' over 'embourgeoisement' as a concept, and emphasizes that class antagonism remained part of the aristocracy's (and the union's) existence.[81] However, as Crossick has observed, Tholfsen's book is 'fundamentally idealist'.[82] Tholfsen thus shares the revisionist view that cultural forces 'cannot be reduced to the status of manifestations of something else presumed to be more fundamental'.[83] Also, his point that revisionism leaves doubt about what remains of classical Marxism is well taken. But Tholfsen goes on to reject the primacy of the economic, and of class structure, altogether. This is partly a theoretical mistake: the conclusion is a fallacious deduction of the kind that assumes that if the structure is not a *sufficient* condition of explanation, then neither is it *necessary*. More fundamentally, Tholfsen favours explanation in terms of inherited cultural and ideational forms. Thus the 'Enlightenment legacy' plays a teleological role, working both with and against class and other factors in the persistence of radicalism. 'The left' and other terms thus appear as trans-historical entities. Tholfsen also manifests a marked preference for explanation of a 'culturalist' kind: mid-Victorian culture reveals a 'structure of feeling' or even *conscience collective*, which is analysed through its 'expression' in high culture: art and literature.

Tholfsen's explanations thus lie well outside Marxism, and tend to be idealist in character. However, it is not the *fact* that a writer uses alternative 'problematics' to Marxism that renders the work unsatisfactory. Rather it is the tendency of certain contradictory frameworks to produce puzzling and inconsistent historical arguments. For example: 'Despite their *total commitment* to consensus values, the friendly societies had by no means abdicated their *critical* faculties or abandoned their quest for *genuine independence.*'[84] Another case in which an idealist framework does not rule out particular conclusions similar to those of revisionism is Harold Perkin's *The Origins of Modern English Society*. Perkin agrees, broadly, that the working class was educated in various social modes to accept and thus help create 'the viable class society'.[85] However, in contrast to his handling of classes in terms of teleological 'ideals', Perkin acknowledges that within the dominance of the 'entrepreneurial ideal' the skilled unions could not escape the economic *class* character of the institutions and thus inevitable class conflict.[86]

The third variety of historical response is to reject the empirical conclusions *and* the theoretical analysis of the classic version, at least. For revisionists, some of the examples in this heuristic subdivision actually belong to the previous kind. The two principal critics have been Henry Pelling and A. E. Musson.[87] Pelling argued that the classic thesis, as proposed especially by Hobsbawm, did not succeed in identifying a labour aristocracy. Giving reasons substantially similar to Gray's and my own, Pelling spotted differences in the definition and use of the term according to explanatory context, and refused to accept the wage criterion as an indicator of family circumstances. In addition, he opposed the implicit identification of the aristocracy with conservatism by recalling the leading role played by skilled artisans in radical and socialist struggles.

The revisionist thesis, it seems, can accept some of Pelling's criticisms. Hobsbawm, on the other hand, rejected them, attempting to demonstrate that Pelling's case is contradictory.[88] If a stratum could not be identified, how could it be deemed more militant than the rest of the class? This rejoinder of Hobsbawm's is not persuasive, however. Pelling rejected the category of 'labour aristocracy', not the notion of skilled workers, and he rightly suggested that the latter played some role in the classic thesis. If the other components of the criterion are less than clear (in Pelling's view), then it is legitimate for him to cite counter-evidence about the politics of artisans as a problem for the classic thesis. Hobsbawm may disagree, and it may be wrong as a generalization, but there is nothing contradictory about it.

Musson's complaints are rather more extensive. It is not unfair to say that he has something of an obsession about the theory of the labour aristocracy. He certainly spends much energy reiterating his case against.[89] That case has essentially three components, though Musson produced a number of more empirical protests against more specific texts (such as Foster's). First, the claims for the revolutionary potential and subsequent quiescence of the working class are false. Second, the union movement has always been riddled with sectionalism. The mid-century decades and the unionism that developed are, in Musson's view, in no way exceptional to the history before or after. Third, the theory places an unfair moral judgement on the political achievement of so-called aristocrats. If the first two points are true, then in Musson's view we may regard the aristocrats' prevention of insurgency as a contribution to a rational society.

With Musson's open objections, the full range of the divergences between 'problematics' is revealed. That is to say, epistemological and political dimensions appear as part and parcel of an historiographical dispute. Foster's reply is indicative of the incommensurability of Musson's view with the classic approach. Foster offers a *restatement* of his case rather than accept that his positions might require modification. This is because Musson's claims that the mass movements of 1834 and 1842 were not political in character are simply wrong, in Foster's opinion. As an epistemological flourish on which to rest his case, Foster takes a stand for dialectical materialism as the scientific approach to history: 'In contrast, the biggest of all ideological traps would seem to be presented by the type of empiricism that marks Musson's view.'[90] Even if revisionists would be less keen to declare their faith, Foster at least has seen that the criticisms of Musson, and to a lesser extent of Pelling, are attacks on the kind of explanation characteristically offered by Marxists. (It is strange that Foster also thinks Musson has failed to challenge the basic conceptions of his book.) Both Musson and Pelling implicitly reject the idea that it is possible to speak of a class as such, much less its political development or tendencies. The classic view is therefore held to be methodologically nonsense.

In many respects the critics' complaints are compatible with revisionist accounts: both reject the illicit assumptions of the classic view in favour of a historically specific description of sectionalism as a process as 'rational' as solidarity. Similarly, revisionists and critics agree upon the importance of the popular cultures and communities, in redress for over-concentration on the labour process. Above all, both hold that forms of consciousness cannot be automatically assumed on grounds of economic class alone. Nevertheless, some key differences continue to divide the two approaches.

The critics do not, for example, offer any explanation at all. Or rather, if they do, it rests on the assumption that sectionalism within the working class is trans-historically endemic. The categories that guide Musson's or Pelling's analysis are therefore methodologically individualist: persons or groups are preferred to classes, ideas to ideologies, and facts to tendencies. Foster is thus right to say that the premises of the critics are empiricist, and they must conflict at some level with the Marxist concept of explanation, even a 'soft' version of it. The points the critics make must be fully measured in an explanatory framework; but in principle, their work eschews that kind of framework.

Before drawing some conclusions, further remarks are required to clarify the status of the 'aristocracy theory'. They concern the sociological categories 'embourgeoisement' and 'social control'—sources of much confusion in this debate. For example, Musson accuses Foster of subscribing to the former thesis.[91] M. J. Piva notes the 'irony' that Marxist historians champion the labour-aristocracy theory while Marxist sociologists are the most vocal opponents of 'embourgeoisement'.[92] Social control is, if possible, a more malleable term. Both have to be distinguished from other kindred terms such as 'affluence', 'deference', 'respectability', and perhaps most important, 'incorporation'. What is embourgeoisement, and can it be part of the labour-aristocracy theory in either of its variants? Engels's oft-quoted remark about the 'bourgeois' working class encourages such an assimilation. And Raphael Samuel makes an explicit identification between the labour aristocracy and embourgeoisement. But my conclusion depends on a distinction within 'embourgeoisement' theory as much as in within the theory of the aristocracy.[93]

In what I take to be its strict form, 'embourgeoisement' theory states that in advanced or successful capitalism (or 'industrial society'), most, or at least part, of the working class becomes affluent and, in terms of values and status, merges with the middle class. Now it is important to note that this is an argument about the *disappearance* of the working class. Either an arbitrary level of 'affluence' must be designated, or a definition of class in terms of *status* is required, or some combination of the two. The key feature is a non-Marxist definition of class, and the claim that 'we're all middle class now'.

A different account is possible, in which the working class still exists, but has acquired middle-class values. Such a view *is* compatible with a labour aristocracy thesis, for example Samuel's 'classic' position. Strictly, it is a theory of *incorporation* not embourgeoisement. Piva, who proposes to enlighten historians by means of sociological insight, does not establish this clearly. If 'embourgeoisement' really included 'incorporation', it would hardly be informative. The strict embourgeoisement view, in turn, which depends on an account of stratification in terms of status, is relatively unhistorical and perhaps idealist, in the sense that the main reality is held to consist in values and impressions.

Incorporation theory is closer to the classic aristocracy position, but it need not be the same. Foster, for example, requires only that political quiescence result from the imposition of cultural controls. He is not committed fully to the view that the control was wholeheartedly complied with. Incorporation theory seems to require a supine working class, and for that reason, too, it is incompatible with revised views, which (provided 'hegemony' is properly used) highlight struggle and conflict in the process of 'accommodation'. To assert the corporate and subordinate consciousness of the working class is not to say that the latter is unproblematically incorporated. In so far as any 'embourgeoisement' account would agree with this, it is wrongly labelled. On the whole, it is quite untrue that the 'similarities between the analysis of the labour aristocracy and the embourgeoisement of the working class are remarkable'.[94] Only in one account (Hobsbawm's) is there an assumption that higher income levels produce political conservatism. *Contra* Piva, Hobsbawm does not then draw the 'embourgeoisement' conclusion, that Marxist class definitions are increasingly useless analytically. On the contrary.

'Social control' is also a difficult category to fathom. Stedman Jones[95] has traced the pedigree of the concept, and rightly argues that a functionalist model of the social system is its theoretical prerequisite, the equilibrium of the system being its normative assumption. To get a flavour of the dominant problematic, here is E. A. Ross, writing in 1910: 'If the units of a society are not reliable, the waste and leakage on the one hand, or the friction due to the checks and safeguards required to prevent such loss on the other hand, prove so burdensome as to nullify the advantages of high organization and make complicated social machinery of any kind unprofitable.

'Men are therefore in chronic need of better order than the natural motives will provide.'[96] The social control necessary to maintain functional equilibrium can be of a collective, moral, or political, coercive nature (or both). It has no specific historical reference whatever, and it seems to rule out a characterization of society based on conflict and contradiction. 'Social control', on this model, is not at all close to Marxism.

From a more historical point of view, A. P. Donajgrodski[97] has tried to render the term compatible with 'hegemony', 'conflict', 'deviancy theory', and other things. He hopes that it can be used with facility by right and left alike, that it can refer to conscious and unconscious processes, and that it can assert the necessity of scrutinizing many social institutions and causalities. In one sense, Donajgrodski is faithful to the eclecticism of the concept—but that should be a reason for rejecting its sweeping historical employment. Richard Johnson has aptly described 'social control' as a concept in search of a theory.[98]

As a more historical than functionalist term, 'social control' is implicit in Foster's work. He regards the aristocracy of labour (and the state) as instruments of social control for the capitalist class. No general model of society is being advanced here, only a conception of *capitalist* domination. Thus, mechanics institutes, friendly societies, and other cultural institutions complement the authoritarian structure of the labour process in being the vehicles through which the bought-off aristocrats cement their role and control the values of the working class. The revisionist thesis, of course, opposes such a characterization: aristocratic institutions also involve struggle, and the entire class, to some extent, has been 'sold' aristocratic values. Gray, for example, has rejected the vulgarization of 'hegemony' into 'social control' in a functionalist manner.[99] The Marxist variants, then, are opposed to the general concept of social control, albeit in different ways. Of course, if *any* conjuncture, short of cataclysm, is 'under control', then Marxist accounts, along with many others, will be applicable. But once again, that would be small basis for explanation.

However, in an otherwise very useful survey of the debates, H. F. Moorhouse appears to claim that on the above basis, all Marxist theories stand or fall together. Moorhouse is keen to condemn both revised and classic theses for their 'simplistic theory of development of class consciousness.'[100] He argues that Gray sidesteps rather than confronts the problem, because in the end the Marxist theory *is* about social control. It is, for Moorhouse, unclear, confused, and contradictory. It should be noted at the outset that social control, like embourgeoisement, can be loose enough to include any means of domination, however mediated and contested. A tie-up between Marxism and functionalism on this score alone is hardly convincing.

Second, there is the question of Moorhouse's alternative. This is important, because in his manner of analysis and his other sociological work,[101] he conducts a useful critique of non-Marxist accounts of the working class, arguing that it has never been 'incorporated' into capitalism. Rather, there are always real possibilities of radical action, and embryonic forms of alternative social organization.

With reference to the nineteenth century, Moorhouse argues against the use of a 'subjective' dimension in explaining working-class 'compliance'.[102] Naturally, Gray objects to this, because it disputes the role that even Marxists allocate to 'normative' factors in the negotiation of hegemonic values.[103] Moorhouse further asserts that bourgeois control of enfranchisement from 1867 to 1918, amongst other things, meant that the working class participated in the system without any chance of achieving power. Its acceptance of the status quo was therefore largely pragmatic; any internalization was gradual, and never wholly effective.

Several conclusions emerge from this exchange. First, Moorhouse's criticisms of the labour-aristocracy theses are not essentially about the form of explanation. Despite appearances, then, his critique is not a logical attack. He rejects the object of explanation as he understands it, namely the failure of the working class to be revolutionary. He also attacks the mode of explanation as being of the social-control type, and he dislikes the suggestion that the class was party to it through normative self-betrayal. Moorhouse's alternative thus tries to dispense with the concept of *ideology*. A social formation is managed through struggle and practical reason, not (even partly) through false consciousness. This view, like others of a similar persuasion, [104] is a welcome reminder that domination is seldom total, that material factors 'spontaneously' generate ideational forms that cannot easily be socially 'shared', and so on. But *in fact*, Moorhouse does accept a degree of 'internalization': he merely wants to ensure that 'objective' considerations prevail. Moreover, he is in no position to criticize the object of explanation of the 'aristocracy' theory, because as we have seen, in some versions the object is not revolutionary failure, but a certain type of capitalist stability. And Moorhouse's account is also an attempt to explain that causally.

Alistair Reid is therefore quite right to attribute a variant of the social-control perspective to Moorhouse himself. [105] Rejecting embourgeoisement, the explanation Moorhouse offers is actually similar to Foster's: control is class struggle, and there are always 'triggers' (Foster's term) that can provide proletarian alternatives. Moorhouse does not accept the labour aristocracy as the causal factor. But his own emphasis on electoral management is certainly as 'conspiratorial' as the former. It must surely entail mechanisms of 'objective' constraint at lower levels of social causality, including the institutions of the working class.

4. Epistemological Summary

An earlier chapter argued that if problems in philosophy of history were to assume their proper significance, they would have to be linked more closely with substantive questions. Epistemological assumptions are not *directly* evidenced in historical arguments about, for example, the French revolution or the labour aristocracy. I have, therefore, tried conscientiously to treat the topics in their own right, with due respect for the details of historical debate. It is through the choice of general social categories and empirical methods that epistemological preferences are expressed. To hope for a less complex discussion would be to return to the view that philosophy can analyse historiography from an external and privileged position, a view that I dispute.

Yet it is also clear that the protagonists in these debates adopt forms of explanation and criteria of proof that do involve epistemological perspectives. I said that some Marxist versions of the labour aristocracy theory 'collapsed' different levels of abstraction as if to show how the essence of history reveals itself. It is not the case that John Foster, for example, always adopts a rationalist or essentialist model of explanation, but the *logic* of many of his arguments could nevertheless be so described. A series of particular experiences and conditions are conceived as forming a *single* object requiring explanation (for example, incorporation or revolutionary failure). The *causes* of that failure are to be sought in the schema in which the structural development of capital and forms of political consciousness form a logical sequence or unity. Accordingly, the labour aristocracy is instrumentally conceived as the medium or agency whose existence both secures and reflects the higher-level logic.

On the other side, the non-Marxist critics, and at times the revisionists, focus on a *range* of empirical phenomena. In many respects those phenomena are taken at face value. Sectionalism in the working class, for example, might be thought to be 'natural', the mere inevitable result of the conflict between irreducibly individual interests in their historical circumstances. Theoretically, on the logic of this view, there is nothing much to explain. Methodologically, the task of the social historian is to describe social changes and continuities as they appear. On the rationalist model, empirical discrepancies are not, of themselves, a problem. On the second— empiricist—view, the very particularity of circumstances, together with the prospect of Marxist reductionism as the alternative, is sufficient to deem theoretical explanation ill-equipped for historical study.

Seldom is this polarity starkly posed in the debates, but it underlies the sharper formulations. Revisionist Marxists attempt to register the specificity of political and cultural formations, and so object to the harder Marxist arguments. But structural explanation—to do with the tendencies of the capitalist mode of production—are indispensable to the revised position, though they are further 'in the background'. Moreover, as the accounts laced with sociological concepts indicate, superficial acceptance of the participants' own view of their 'status' and function can also lead to an a priori, a historical belief in the equilibrium of the system ('consensus', for example, or, more historically, the 'entry into citizenship').

What conclusions can we draw from this? It is, I think, the revisionist Marxist account that, in principle, provides the most suitable form of explanation. In other words, explanation in terms of underlying structural movements is indispensable: they materially determine and set limits to the kind of cultural and ideological repertoire available to class fractions, and probably to the labour aristocracy in particular. However, structural factors alone cannot specify the cultural or ideological character of the labour aristocracy. Nor can its causal role in 'stabilization' be thought of as given (though it may still be pronounced).

I said that in *principle* the revisionist account is better than its rivals, because, in principle, realist explanations are 'more adequate' than rationalist or empiricist ones. It must be said, however, that *in practice* explanations that look as if they conform to realism (as the revisionist view does), may not *satisfy*. There are two main reasons for this. First, the attempt to combine empirical specificity and grander theory is both difficult and provisional. The terms of the labour-aristocracy theory, for example, are inexact and seem to require heavy qualification. Moreover, as a longstanding theory, it may hinder the formulation of other informative (and formally realist) explanations. Gray[106] suggests, for example, that the aristocracy-plebeian division is also that of men-women, but since this might be thought to be 'non-Marxist', labour-aristocracy theories might resist it.

Second, it seems that issues about social and historical structure can be decided only at a relatively high level of abstraction. The 'long-term' is therefore the most apt perspective from which to conduct realist explanation in historiography. On this score, differences between 'essentialist' and 'flexible' Marxisms may be much less important than on specific matters where the 'application' of historical materialism is under contention. Whilst it is no doubt entirely appropriate that political strategies or historical research should not be dictated by the logic of history, the lack of any clear guidelines for such 'application' remains a problem. There may inevitably be some friction between general theory and specific analyses. That must be one main conclusion, and it also illustrates real differences between epistemological certitude and historical investigation.

Conclusion

The vast majority of Anglo-American academic historians seem to be both in their practice and in their relatively rare moments of theory causal pluralists, and the history of history over the past fifty years has shown them to be endlessly hospitable to new types of candidate for causal efficacy.[1]

I have tried to argue that 'abstract' philosophical questions and 'concrete' historical issues are intimately connected. That they appear otherwise is partly the product of an artificial, sometimes jealously guarded, academic division of labour. It also has to do with the fact that the majority of professional philosophers have been causal pluralists. Philosophers have been reluctant to accept that science provides knowledge of real, structured, material processes. In history, the dominant view is that competing ideas, provided they are well documented, can be regarded as equally valid perspectives on the multifaceted realm of past human affairs.

For historical materialism, causal pluralism cannot be supported. However, the acceptance of Marxism as a defensible set of beliefs has been long overdue—and not only for political reasons. Marxism is regarded, variously, as functionalism, economic determinism, or the pragmatic suppression of difficult intellectual and practical issues. All these accusations are based on the view that Marxism is a causal *monism*, that it claims that there is but one set of factors, in nature or history, that determines everything else. In his otherwise important article, Alasdair MacIntyre fuels this preconception by citing, for example, Marc Bloch's objections to monism as evidence for even *Bloch*'s pluralism. This is misleading, because Bloch does not (on the whole) support pluralism, and MacIntyre does not defend monism.

My own inclination is to uphold aspects of both positions, for it does not · undermine the value of a conception of *structural causality* to emphasize that it has two 'moments'.

First, like the natural world, history has a determinable shape or structure. The latter is related (especially) to the kind of material causal processes that historical materialism, more than other traditions, has highlighted. However, unlike natural science, historical knowledge must in principle be incomplete, because the relations it seeks to analyse are between human beings who are themselves causal agents who materially change history. This is no reason for epistemological despair, but it does mean that there are no determinist explanations of specific 'conjunctures'. Structural principles must be complemented by, or even include, notions of individual action, natural causes, and 'accidental' circumstances. Historical outcomes depend on them, too. Nevertheless, material and social relations can be long-term, effective real structures that set firm limits to the nature and degree of practical effect that accident and even agency have. It is not true, therefore, that historiography can sustain either a single causal explanation or an infinite number of them.

The idea that the choice between pluralism and monism exhausts the question of historical causality is therefore far too restrictive. Here, despite their many differences, the dominant paradigms in both philosophy and history have colluded. Philosophers have not as a rule been realists, or if they have, they have not been sufficiently vocal about it. The residual dualism between positivism and idealism has thus been difficult to dislodge. And the less epistemological strands of modern philosophy have not noticeably advanced matters; approaches to history, for example, that set great store by the logic of *language* rather than knowledge, often construct an artificial conception of what historians say they do (for example, that they only narrate).

Or rather, it is artificial in the sense that philosophers convey the impression that historians do not employ philosophical conceptions in their empirical work. Historians themselves will tend to confirm that impression, but that does not mean that it is right. G. R. Elton's recent statements on the 'Historian's Social Function' form an extreme but indicative example of how to reinforce a certain kind of intellectual or philosophical hegemony (that of abstract empiricism) whilst remaining deeply hostile to the idea of theory or presuppositions. The note of panic in Elton's concern is a welcome sign that here, as elsewhere, there may be—to use Gramsci's terms—a crisis in hegemony. In support of what he calls 'thesis-free' empirical history, which he takes to be mortally opposed to philosophical 'determinism', Elton maintains that the historian succeeds by multiplying causes. He 'throws away Ockham's razor and grows his epistemological beard, sprouting in all directions'.[2] For Elton and, one supposes, for other historians, these ideas are tied to an *ideological* position: causal pluralism is taken to be part and parcel of 'democratic' values. Elton says that the historian is 'trained to freedom';[3] and 'possessed of intellectual freedom, he must resist the imposition of intellectual dictatorship and its social consequences'.[4]

Something of the political implications of debates on the logic of histor-iography is revealed in this declaration of faith. The claim expressed by Elton, together with the philosopher's professional scepticism, continues to be opposed by Marxists, and rightly so. One main objective of this book has been to show that ideologically motivated views such as Elton's have slender intellectual foundations. I have argued that epistemological and theoretical questions are inescapable, both in the historians' methodologi-cal statements and in substantive debate. Many historians might hesitate to endorse Elton's ringing assertions about the historical discipline, and that is important. But I hope to have made a stronger case, namely that histo-rians should adopt a realist frame of analysis. In so doing, they would have more explicitly to recognize the strengths of historical materialism.

Similar conclusions about philosophy are indicated. Marxists have much to learn from specialist philosophy. But, as a rule, philosophers avoid substantive commitment and historical contextualization. This is particu-larly unacceptable in philosophy of history. Marxism, through its connection with scientific realism, poses some fundamental criticisms for 'philosophical' accounts of the historical domain.

The other major aim of the book has been to remedy the lack of a sustained discussion, in current Marxist work, of problems of historiog-raphy. My arguments have been threefold. First, philosophy has an impor-tant function in the formation, clarification, and defence of substantive concepts. There is, or should be, no serious case within historical material-ism for an exclusive choice between 'theory' and 'history'. When mounted on an 'anti-philosophical' platform, that argument cannot be long sus-tained. However, although Marxism requires realist premises, there is no singular Marxist philosophy. The need to borrow from and contribute to general philosophical developments consequently leaves open the possibil-ity that Marxism may become over-philosophical. Since this possibility entails the risk of what I have termed 'substantivism', and must surely demote the significance of historical research, Marxist philosophers must be self-critically sensitive to the dangers of 'theoreticism'.

Finally, some of the problems that arise when long-term causality and historical specificity come together have been investigated. The defensi-bility of historical materialism as a theory of history and an account of particular epochs tempts Marxists to underestimate the real causal power of transient struggles, whatever their outcome. This temptation arose both for Marx and Engels and in more recent Marxist historiography. My gener-al stance in this book—and its justification—is that a realist conception of explanation can assist both the empirical moment in historiography and its theoretical structure. But to hope that particular research projects can be theoretically insulated against error, polemic, or doubt is both unrealistic and undesirable.

References

Preface

[1] The words 'history' and 'historiography' are notoriously difficult to separate when the former means the writing of history as well as historical reality. I am not convinced that the ambiguity can be systematically avoided, so I sometimes use one term, sometimes another, hoping that the context makes the meaning plain. The reader will decide whether or not this strategy succeeds.

[2] Notably Perry Anderson in his *Considerations on Western Marxism*, London, NLB, 1976. Anderson's stark contrast between a Bolshevik tradition of militant-intellectuals and current *déclassé* professors, together with his general political assessments, seem to me exaggerated.

Chapter 1

[1] J. V. Stalin, *Essential Writings*, London 1973.

[2] G. V. Plekhanov, *Fundamental Problems of Marxism*, London 1976, p. 23. See also the misleadingly titled *The Development of the Monist View of History*, Moscow 1956.

[3] J. Dietzgen, *Philosophical Essays*, Chicago 1908, p. 293.

[4] Otherwise, they are very different kinds of books, as we might expect. For 1930s Marxism, see T. A. Jackson, *Dialectics*, London 1936, or J. B. S. Haldane, *Marxist Philosophy and the Sciences*, London 1938. For the academic Marxism coming out of the Radical Philosophy movement of the early 1970s, see J. Mepham and D-H. Ruben (eds.), *Issues in Marxist Philosophy*, 3 vols., Brighton 1979.

[5] For example, Karl Popper, *The Open Society and Its Enemies*, vol. 2, London 1966. H. B. Acton, *The Illusion of the Epoch*, London 1955. A more up-to-date philosophical assessment is Herbert Fiegl's, 'Critique of Dialectical Materialism', in J. Somerville and H. L. Parsons (eds.), *Dialogues in The Philosophy of Marxism*, Connecticut 1974.

[6] V. Kelle and M. Kovalson, *Historical Materialism*, Moscow 1973, p. 75. In science, Lysenko's biological investigations discredited Marxism. See D. Lecourt, *Proletarian Science: The Case of Lysenko*, London, NLB, 1978.

[7] *Historical Materialism*, p. 18.

[8] *Historical Materialism*, p. 25. (It is a quotation from Brezhnev.)

[9] For example, Blakeley, *Soviet Scholasticism*, Boston 1961, or J. M. Bocheński, *Diamat*, Boston 1963.

238

[10]Ted Benton, 'Natural Science and Cultural Struggle: Engels and Philosophy and Natural Science', in *Issues in Marxist Philosophy*, vol. 2.

[11]F. Engels, *Dialectics of Nature*, Moscow 1934, p. 17.

[12]F. Engels, *Anti-Dühring*, Peking 1976, pp. 172-3.

[13]*Anti-Dühring*, p. 159.

[14]*Dialectics of Nature*, p. 114, p. 257f.

[15]One of the main critical moves of dialectical materialism is to charge that its rivals are 'metaphysical'. This makes distinctions difficult, but I would not want to suggest that dialectical materialisms were always mechanical or dubiously metaphysical, nor that it can all be put down to the Soviet political system. In *Economic Problems of Socialism in the USSR* (Moscow 1952), Stalin chided a certain Yaroshenko for being undialectical. Loren Graham has argued in *Science and Philosophy in the Soviet Union* (London 1971) that Soviet scientists were keen to develop dialectical materialist principles without much reference to Stalinist politics.

[16]In his letter to Conrad Schmidt of 5 August 1890.

[17]For the typical combination of modest and grand declarations in Engels see *Anti-Dühring*, in which materialism is said to be 'a simple world outlook' (p. 177), then 'nothing more than' the 'science of general laws of motion and development of nature, human society, and thought' (p. 180).

[18]*Historical Materialism*, New York 1965.

[19]V. I. Lenin, *Materialism and Empirio-Criticism*, Moscow 1970, p. 114f and p. 248f.

[20]A. Pannekoek, *Lenin as Philosopher*, London 1975.

[21]L. Althusser, *Lenin and Philosophy and other Essays*, London, NLB, 1972.

[22]R. Edgley, 'Dialectic: the Contradictions of Colletti', *Critique* 7, 1977.

[23]See Milton Fisk, *Nature and Necessity: An Essay in Physical Ontology*, Bloomington 1973.

[24]Plekhanov, *Fundamental Problems*, p. 94.

[25]Ibid., p. 96.

[26]Engels, *Dialectics of Nature*, p. 215.

[27]Fisk, 'Dialectic and Ontology', in *Issues in Marxist Philosophy*, vol. 1.

[28]Edgley, 'Dialectic', p. 51.

[29]Fisk insists that things are naturally contradictory in the full sense: 'The entity is contradictory precisely in that, as an entity in its own right, it is one, and yet, as an entity with multiple aspects, it is not one.' ('Dialectic and Ontology', p. 121.) As a contribution to the ontology of complexes, this is fine. But it is also an unnecessary riddle, for an entity with many aspects is not too many entities; nor, if the aspects are contradictory, will they be held by the entity at the same time or in all respects.

[30]Colletti again skews the terms of the issue on this question. He knows that Kant's and Hegel's conceptions of logic differ, and he wants to say that real opposition can accommodate dialectical contradiction without much loss to the latter. Yet Colletti continues to equate or identify dialectical with logical contradiction. There is no need for this, except to give a reality-status to some logical-dialectical contradictions, such as the theory of alienation which Colletti espouses. It makes his claim that Marx was a Kantian rather than Hegelian look a bit strange.

[31]Popper, *The Open Society*, p. 155.

[32]G. A. Cohen and H. B. Acton, 'On Some Criticisms of Historical Materialism', *Proceedings of the Aristotelian Society*, Supplementary Volume, 1970.

[33]Kolakowski, *Main Currents of Marxism*, Oxford 1978, vol. 1, p. 369.

[34]John Plamenatz, *German Marxism and Russian Communism*, London 1953.

[35]*Main Currents*, vol. 1, p. 369.

[36]*Main Currents*, vol. 3, p. 524.

[37]Hindess and Hirst, *Mode of Production and Social Formation*, London 1977; A. Cutler *et al.*, *Marx's 'Capital' and Capitalism Today*, vol. 1, London 1978.

[38]P. Hirst, *On Law and Ideology*, London 1979, pp. 18-21.

[39] S. Gaukroger, *Explanatory Structures*, Brighton, 1978.

[40]*Explanatory Structures*, p. 57. Hindess and Hirst, *Mode of Production*, pp. 77, 79.

[41]Hirst, *On Law and Ideology*, p. 19.

[42]Ibid., p. 21.

[43]London 1975, p. 308f.

[44]G. Lukács, *History and Class Consciousness*, London 1971, p. 1.

[45]These well-known aphorisms are from, respectively, Marx's postface to the second edition of *Capital* (Harmondsworth 1976),/Engels's letter to Schmidt 5 August 1890, Lenin's 'What the "Friends of the People" Are', *Collected Works*, vol. 1. Moscow 1972.

[46]*History and Class Consciousness*, p. 46.

[47]G. Williams, 'In Defence of History'; K. McClelland, 'Some Comments on Richard Johnson', *History Workshop Journal* 7, 1978.

[48]E. P. Thompson, *The Poverty of Theory and other Essays*, London 1978, p. 252.

[49]Ibid., pp. 236-7.

[50]Korsch, *Karl Marx*, London 1938, p. 21; *Three Essays on Marxism*, London 1971, p. 65.

[51]Korsch, *Marxism and Philosophy*, London, NLB, 1971, pp. 70-1.

[52]Korsch, *Karl Marx*, p. 216.

[53]*Karl Marx*, p. 168, p. 223; *Marxism and Philosophy*, p. 47, p. 111.

[54]D. Sayer, *Marx's Method*, Brighton 1979. P. Corrigan, H. Ramsay, and D. Sayer, *Socialist Construction and Bolshevik Theory*, London 1978.

[55]For example, G. A. Cohen, *Karl Marx's Theory of History: A Defence*, Oxford 1979; W. Shaw, *Marx's Theory of History*, London 1978; J. McMurtry, *The Structure of Marx's World View*, New Jersey 1978; Allen Wood, *Karl Marx*, London 1981.

[56]G. D. H. Cole, *The Meaning of Marxism*, London 1948, p. 13.

[57]J-P. Sartre, *Critique of Dialectical Reason*, London 1976.

[58]E. Bloch, *On Karl Marx*, New York 1968, p. 114.

[59]New York, 1973.

[60]B. Ollman, *Alienation*, Cambridge 1971.

[61]London 1970, p. 97.

[62]H. Lefebvre, *Dialectical Materialism*, London 1968, p. 132.

[63]*The Hidden God*, London 1964. *The Human Sciences and Philosophy*, London 1969.

[64]C. Caudwell, *The Crisis in Physics*, London 1939; *Illusion and Reality*, London 1946.

[65]K. Marx and F. Engels, *The German Ideology*, London 1969, p. 52.

[66]Sohn-Rethel's *Intellectual and Manual Labour*, London 1978, is the most thoroughgoing in this respect. Bourgeois science is not wrong or distorted, according to Sohn-Rethel, but it represents the highest form of mental labour in class society. Epistemology guarantees the false objectivity of science, and the 'eternal' status of logic and mathematics. Sohn-Rethel claims that Galilean laws of inertial motion are

the formal homologies of the movement of commodities in circulation. Newtonian space and time are empty, devoid of their material contents, just as exchange relations are. The indivisibility of matter parallels the infinite transactions that money facilitates. Sohn-Rethel argues that the whole market/science complex is a natural-historical phenomenon. What he says may be true, but the 'homologies' are very broad, and he does not assert a direct causal relationship between thought and the market.

[67] Roy Bhaskar, *The Possibility of Naturalism*, Brighton 1979, pp. 14-15.
[68] A. Gramsci, *Selections from the Prison Notebooks*, London 1971, pp. 347-8.
[69] Ibid., p. 465.
[70] Ibid., pp. 445-6.

Chapter 2

[1] F. Parkin, *Marxism and Class Theory: A Bourgeois Critique*, London 1979; E. P. Thompson, *The Poverty of Theory*.
[2] Althusser has remarked that Colletti's 'best efforts' are directed towards a 'historicist but non-humanist reading of Marx'. *Reading Capital*, London 1974, p. 134. This is probably to damn with faint praise. Colletti, for his part, says in 'Marxism and the Dialectic' (*New Left Review* 93, 1975) that Althusser's determination to denounce 'alienation' leaves him with only a 'few pages' of Marx to support his notion of a scientific break.
[3] Colletti, *Marxism and Hegel*, London, NLB, 1973, p. 119.
[4] Ibid., p. 103.
[5] Colletti, 'Introduction' to Marx, *Early Writings*, Harmondsworth 1974; and G. Della Volpe, *Logic as a Positive Science*, London, NLB, 1980, p. 176.
[6] Althusser and E. Balibar, *Reading Capital*, London 1974, pp. 59-60.
[7] See also Della Volpe, *Logic*, p. 197.
[8] *Marxism and Hegel*, p. 134.
[9] Althusser, *For Marx*, Harmondsworth 1969, pp. 82-93.
[10] *Reading Capital*, p. 77.
[11] Ibid., p. 182.
[12] Ibid., p. 34.
[13] Ibid., pp. 178-9.
[14] Marx, quoted in *Reading Capital*, p. 41, p. 87.
[15] *Reading Capital*, p. 180.
[16] For more on this, see chapter 3.
[17] In his *Essays in Self-Criticism* (London, NLB, 1976) Althusser admits all these problems. He brings philosophy back into historical materialism as generalization or as 'class struggle in theory'. He eases the science/ideology distinction, and allows that his earlier Spinozism and structuralism led to distortions. On the other hand it is not clear that Althusser has abandoned his earlier views, or that he has since developed a 'synthesis' in which his present dilemmas might appear less intractable. See G. McLennan, 'Will the Real Louis Althusser Stand Up', *Radical Science Journal* 6-7, 1978.
[18] Hindess, *The Use of Official Statistics in Sociology*, London 1973.
[19] Lenin, *Materialism and Empirio-Criticism*, pp. 56-7.

[20]Mandel, *Late Capitalism*, London 1976, p. 10.

[21]A. Hussain, 'Crises and Tendencies of Capitalism', *Economy and Society*, vol. 6, no. 4, 1977, p. 441, p. 459.

[22]B. Fine and L. Harris, *Re-reading Capital*, London 1978, p. 71.

[23]Bhaskar, *A Realist Theory of Science*, Brighton 1978, second edition; *The Possibility of Naturalism*, Brighton 1979.

[24]Sayer, 'Science as Critique: Marx vs. Althusser', *Issues in Marxist Philosophy*, vol. 3.

[25]*A Realist Theory of Science*, pp. 29-30. *The Possibility of Naturalism*, pp. 6-10.

[26]Ruben, *Marxism and Materialism*, second edition, Brighton 1979, pp. 201-7.

[27]Keat and Urry, *Social Theory as Science*, London 1975.

[28]Benton, *The Philosophical Foundations of the Three Sociologies*, London 1977.

[29]*A Realist Theory of Science*, pp. 29-30; *Philosophical Foundations*, p. 171; *Marxism and Materialism*, p. 5. For a more substantive materialism, with some attendant dilemmas, see S. Timpanaro, *On Materialism*, London 1975.

[30]In his 'A Note on Justification', *Philosophy and Phenomenological Research*, vol. 37, 1976-7, Ruben suggests that it is the correspondence theory that defines knowledge, but the coherence theory of truth that provides the criterion of justification. 'Reflection' is too restrictive to do justice to that sort of distinction.

[31]*Marxism and Materialism*, pp. 23-7.

[32]Ibid., p. 24.

[33]Ibid., p. 21.

[34]Della Volpe, *Logic*, p. 157.

[35]Bhaskar, *A Realist Theory of Science*, p. 247.

[36]*The Possibility of Naturalism*, p. 73.

[37]*A Realist Theory of Science*, p. 249.

[38]Ibid., p. 249.

[39]In Marx and Engels, *Collected Works*, vol. 1, Moscow 1975.

[40]The postface to the second edition of *Capital* is especially important in this respect. Only after having decisively broken with Hegel and philosophy could Marx so self-confidently announce himself a 'pupil' of that 'mighty thinker'. *Capital*, pp. 102-3.

[41]*Early Writings*, pp. 65-70.

[42]*The Holy Family*, Moscow 1956, pp. 78-9.

[43]Ibid., pp. 48-9.

[44]*The Poverty of Philosophy*, Moscow 1976, p. 184.

[45]'Critique of Hegel's Philosophy of Right', *Early Writings*, p. 244.

[46]*The German Ideology*, p. 48.

[47]*Early Writings*, p. 423.

[48]These are discussed again in chapter 8.

[49]*Reading Capital*, p. 24.

[50]Sayer, *Marx's Method*, p. 102.

[51]S. Hall, 'A Reading of the "1857 Introduction": Marx's Notes on Method', *Working Papers in Cultural Studies*, 6, 1974.

[52]A. Collier, 'In Defence of Epistemology', *Issues in Marxist Philosophy*, vol. 3.

[53]Benton, *Philosophical Foundations*, p. 167.

[54]Hall, 'A Reading', p. 152.

[55]Sayer, *Marx's Method*, p. 94.

242

56*Reading Capital*, p. 41.
57Benton, *Philosophical Foundations*, p. 166; Hall 'A Reading', p. 157.
58Marx, *Grundrisse*, Harmondsworth 1973, p. 100.
59*Grundrisse*, p. 101.
60Ibid., p. 101.
61Ibid., p. 102.
62This idea is close to a number of positions developed within Marxism. In *A Philosophy for Modern Man*, London 1938, Hyman Levy propounded a concept of scientific 'isolates'. Della Volpe and Colletti speak of 'determinate abstractions'. H. Rose and S. Rose adopt a similar view of Marx's theory of science in their 'The Problematical Inheritance', *Political Economy of Science*, London 1976. E. Laclau tries to adapt the notion of levels of abstraction for political analysis, in *Politics and Ideology in Marxist Theory*, London, NLB, 1977.
63*Grundrisse*, p. 108.
64Ibid., p. 101.

Chapter 3

1See P. Corrigan, H. Ramsay, D. Sayer, *For Mao*, London 1979.
2Engels, *Anti-Dühring*, pp. 364-5.
3Ibid., p. 344.
4Ibid., p. 357.
5G. A. Cohen, *Karl Marx's Theory of History: A Defence*.
6For example, B. and S. Webb, *The Decay of Capitalist Civilization*, London 1923; R. MacDonald, *Socialism and Society*, London 1908; P. Snowden, *Labour and the New World*, London 1921.
7W. W. Rostow, *The Stages of Economic Growth*, second edition, Cambridge 1971.
8 M. Cornforth, *Historical Materialism*, London 1976 (revised edn), p. 52.
9N. Poulantzas, *Political Power and Social Classes*, London, NLB, 1973, p. 15.
10*Reading Capital*, p. 225.
11Ibid., p. 304.
12Hindess and Hirst, *Pre-Capitalist Modes of Production*, London 1975, p. 312.
13D. Sayer, *Marx's Method*, p. 86; cf. Simon Clarke *et al.*, *One Dimensional Marxism*, London 1980; Bob Young, 'Science *is* Social Relations', *Radical Science Journal*, 5, 1977.
14Cohen, *Karl Marx's Theory of History*, p. 31.
15Ibid., p. 63, p. 90.
16Ibid., p. 98.
17Ibid., p. 112.
18Ibid., p. 79.
19Ibid., p. 80.
20Ibid., p. 45.
21W. L. Adamson, *History and Theory*, vol. 19, no. 2, 1980, p. 194.
22*Karl Marx's Theory of History*, p. 29n.
23Marx, *Grundrisse*, p. 700.
24*Karl Marx's Theory of History*, p. 42.
25Marx, *Grundrisse*, p. 278.

[26]*Capital* Volume 1, p. 304.

[27]*Karl Marx's Theory of History*, p. 98.

[28]Ibid., p. 198.

[29]Ibid., p. 155, p. 162.

[30]Ibid., p. 98.

[31]Ibid., p. 153.

[32]Ibid., p. 153.

[33]Ibid., p. 156.

[34]Ibid., p. 170.

[35]Ibid., p. 165.

[36]A. Giddens, *Central Problems in Social Theory*, London 1979, pp. 162-3 (modified).

[37]*Karl Marx's Theory of History*, p. 177.

[38]Marx, *Capital* Volume 1, p. 1035.

[39]*Karl Marx's Theory of History*, p. 149.

[40]Ibid., p. 171.

[41]C. G. Hempel, 'The Logic of Functional Analysis', in B. A. Bródy (ed.), *Readings in the Philosophy of Science*, New Jersey 1970, p. 138.

[42]E. Nagel, *The Structure of Science*, London 1961, p. 422.

[43]*Karl Marx's Theory of History*, p. 261.

[44]Jon Elster, 'Cohen on Marx's Theory of History', *Political Studies*, vol. 28, no. 1, 1981, p. 126.

[45]*Karl Marx's Theory of History*, p. 250.

[46]Ibid., p. 284.

[47]Cohen, 'Functional Explanation: Reply to Elster', *Political Studies*, vol. 28, no. 1, 1981, pp. 133-4.

[48]Nagel, *The Structure of Science*, p. 535.

[49]*Karl Marx's Theory of History*, p. 206.

[50]Cohen, 'Functional Explanation', p. 135.

[51]R. Harré, *Social Being*, Oxford 1979, pp. 162-3.

[52]M. Mandelbaum, *The Anatomy of Historical Knowledge*, Baltimore 1977, p. 99.

[53]D. Shapere, 'Scientific Theories and Their Domains' in F. Suppe (ed.), *The Structure of Scientific Theories*, Urbana 1974.

[54]G. C. Homans, 'Bringing Men Back In', in A. Ryan (ed.), *Philosophy of Social Explanation*, Oxford 1973.

[55]Ruben, 'Marxism and Dialectics', *Issues in Marxist Philosophy*, vol. 1, p. 76.

[56]In both the 'Speech at Marx's Graveside' and 'Karl Marx', in Marx and Engels, *Selected Works*, London 1968.

[57]Marxist economists of a 'revisionist' hue have maintained that it *is* wrong, or at least unhelpful. See I. Steedman, *Marx after Sraffa*, London, NLB, 1976. Cohen has now declared against it, having abstained in *Karl Marx's Theory of History*. See Cohen, 'The Labour Theory of Value and the Concept of Exploitation', *Philosophy and Public Affairs*, vol. 8, no. 4, 1979, reprinted in Steedman, Sweezy *et al.*, *The Value Controversy*, London, NLB, 1981. However we vote on that question, the theory of capitalism and the theory of history in Marx are not logically bound together.

[58]This is also Geoffrey Helman's candidate. In 'Historical Materialism', *Issues in Marxist Philosophy*, vol. 2, Helman sets out adequacy conditions for such 'core

principles'. His method is more systematic than mine, but my conclusions are close to his.

[59]See Mario Bunge, 'Do The Levels of Science Reflect the Levels of Being?', *Metascientific Queries*, Illinois 1959.

[60]See Raymond Williams, *Marxism and Literature*, Oxford 1977, p. 84.

[61]See Erik Olin Wright, *Class, Crisis and the State*, London, NLB, 1978, p. 21.

Chapter 4

[1]Bhaskar, *The Possibility of Naturalism*, p. 2.

[2]C. G. Hempel, 'The Function of General Laws in History', in P. Gardiner (ed.), *Theories of History*, Glencoe 1958.

[3]W. H. Dray, *Laws and Explanation in History*, Oxford 1957; 'The Historical Explanations of Action Reconsidered', in P. Gardiner (ed.), *The Philosophy of History*, Oxford 1974. The term 'reactionist' was coined by M. Mandelbaum to refer to the movement against Hempel's model: 'Historical Explanation: The Problem of "Covering Laws"', *History and Theory*, vol. 1, no. 3, 1961, p. 229.

[4]Collingwood, *The Idea of History*, Oxford 1946, pp. 165-176.

[5]*The Idea of History*, p. 170. Collingwood himself, though in key ways a realist, believed that the uniqueness of history lay in the re-enactment within the historical mind. *The Idea of History*, pp. 307-8.

[6]A. Schutz, 'Problems in Interpretative Sociology', in Ryan, *Philosophy of Social Explanation*.

[7]Dray, *Laws and Explanation in History*, p. 20.

[8]Hempel, *Aspects of Scientific Explanation*, Glencoe 1965, p. 42.

[9]Dilthey, *Selected Writings*, (ed.) H. P. Rickman, Cambridge 1976, p. 201.

[10]O. Neurath, 'Foundations of Social Science', in O. Neurath, R. Carnap, and C. Morris (eds.), *Foundations of the Unity of Science*, Chicago 1970.

[11]O. Neurath, *Empiricism and Sociology*, Boston 1973.

[12]F. Suppe, 'Introduction', *The Structure of Scientific Theories*. See also T. Nickles, 'Introduction', *Scientific Discovery, Logic and Rationality*, Boston 1980.

[13]K. Popper, *The Logic of Scientific Discovery*, London 1972; *Conjectures and Refutations*, London 1963.

[14]K. Popper, *Objective Knowledge*, Oxford 1972.

[15]An important summary colloquium is I. Lakatos and A. Musgrave (eds.), *Criticism and the Growth of Knowledge*, Cambridge 1970.

[16]Suppe uses this term, meaning something like 'world-view'.

[17]*Patterns of Discovery*, Cambridge 1958.

[18]Suppe, *The Structure of Scientific Theories*, p. 157.

[19]*Patterns of Discovery*, p. 86.

[20]Ibid., p. 90.

[21]T. S. Kuhn, *The Structure of Scientific Revolutions*, Chicago 1962.

[22]T. S. Kuhn, 'Second Thoughts on Paradigms', in Suppe (ed.), *The Structure of Scientific Theories*.

[23]I. Lakatos, 'Falsificationism and the Methodology of Scientific Research Programmes', in *Criticism and the Growth of Knowledge*.

24'Falsificationism', p. 174.

25P. Feyerabend, *Against Method*, London, NLB, 1975.

26Feyerabend, *Science in a Free Society*, London, NLB, 1978.

27J. Curthoys and W. Suchting, 'Feyerabend's Discourse Against Method: A Marxist Critique', *Inquiry*, vol. 20, no. 2, 1977; P. Feyerabend, 'Marxist Fairytales from Australia', *Inquiry*, vol. 20, no. 3, 1977. Reprinted in *Science in a Free Society*.

28Feyerabend had in fact been amongst the first modern critics to launch 'An Attempt at a Realistic Interpretation of Experience', *Proceedings of the Aristotelian Society*, 1957-8.

29D. Shapere, 'Notes Towards a Post-Empiricist Interpretation of Science', in P. Achinstein and S. F. Barker (eds.), *The Legacy of Logical Positivism*, Baltimore 1969, p. 130.

30Hanson, *Patterns of Discovery*, p. 64.

31Suppe, *The Structure of Scientific Theories*, p. 216.

32H. Putnam, 'What is Realism?', *Proceedings of the Aristotelian Society*, 1975-6, p. 193.

33Putnam, 'What is Realism', p. 194.

34Shapere, 'Towards a Post-Empiricist Interpretation', p. 125.

35Shapere, 'Scientific Theories and Their Domains'. Shapere's model captures the most useful connotations of Althusser's concept of a 'problematic', but is also more flexible.

36M. W. Wartofsky, *Models: Representation and the Scientific Understanding*, Boston 1979, p. 10.

37Fisk, *Nature and Necessity*. In 'Materialism and Dialectic', *Critique* 12, 1980, Fisk describes Putnam and other realist-inclined philosophers as 'idealists'.

38M. Hesse, *The Structure of Scientific Inference*, London 1974, p. 301.

39These are Wartofsky's terms, *Models*, p. 16.

40G. H. Von Wright, *Explanation and Understanding*, London 1971, p. 22.

41*Explanation and Understanding*, p. 137.

42See Wright, 'Determinism and the Study of Man', in J. Manninen and R. Tuomela (eds.), *Essays on Explanation and Understanding*, Boston 1976.

43New York 1965.

44M. G. Murphey, *Our Knowledge of the Historical Past*, Indianapolis 1973.

45L. Pompa, Review of White, *Inquiry*, vol. 11, 1968.

46L. Krieger, in S. Hook (ed.), *Philosophy and History: A Symposium*, New York 1963, p. 137.

47L. Stone, 'The Revival of Narrative: Reflections on a New Old History', *Past and Present* 85, 1979.

48See Haskell Fain, 'History as Science', *History and Theory*, vol. 9, 1970. Alasdair MacIntyre has developed a very broad and interesting view of the 'narrative' structure of the significance of scientific and social change: 'Epistemological Crises, Dramatic Narrative, and the Philosophy of Science', *Monist*, vol. 60, 1977.

49W. G. Gallie, 'The Historical Understanding', *History and Theory*, vol. 2, 1963, p. 168.

50Ibid., p. 177.

51A. C. Danto, 'Narrative Sentences', *History and Theory*, vol. 2, 1962-3.

52W. H. Dray, 'On the Nature and Role of Narrative in Historiography', *History and Theory*, vol. 10, 1971.

[53]M. White, 'The Logic of Historical Narration', in Hook (ed.), *Philosophy and History*, p. 127.

[54]Dray, 'On the Nature', p. 169.

[55]For example, F. J. Teggart, *Theory and Processes of History*, Berkeley 1941; J. H. Randall, *Nature and Historical Experience: Essays in Naturalism and the Theory of History*, New York 1958.

[56]L. J. Goldstein, *Historical Knowing*, London 1976.

[57]Ibid., p. 9.

[58]Ibid., p. 58. See also Jack Meiland, *Scepticism and Historical Knowledge*, New York 1965. The same kind of point informed German neo-idealism late in the last century; see Georg Simmel, *The Problems of the Philosophy of History*, New York 1977.

[59]E. J. Hobsbawm, 'The Revival of Narrative: Some Comments', *Past and Present* 86, 1980.

[60]C. Behan McCullagh, 'Historical Instrumentalism', *History and Theory*, vol. 12, 1973.

[61]L. O. Mink, 'Narrative Form as a Cognitive Instrument', in R. H. Canary and H. Kozicki, *Literary Form and the Historical Understanding*, Wisconsin 1978, pp. 143-4.

[62]See Hayden White's dissection of one paragraph of A. J. P. Taylor in 'Historicism, History, and the Figurative Imagination', *History and Theory*, Beiheft 14, 1975.

[63]Mink, 'Narrative Form', p. 148.

[64]H. White, *Tropics of Discourse*, Baltimore 1978, p. 22.

[65]H. White, *Metahistory: The Historical Imagination in Nineteenth Century Europe*, Baltimore 1973, p. 29 (modified).

[66]*Metahistory*, p. 315.

[67]Ibid., p. 427.

[68]Ibid., p. 13.

[69]White, *Tropics of Discourse*, p. 133.

[70]Ibid., p. 99.

[71]*Metahistory*, p. 434.

[72]*Tropics of Discourse*, chapter 11.

[73]Ibid., p. 282.

[74]Murphey, *Our Knowledge of the Historical Past*, p. 16.

[75]H. Gilliam, 'The Dialectic of Realism and Idealism in Modern Historiographical Theory', *History and Theory*, vol. 15, 1976.

[76]Urbach, 'Is Any of Popper's Argument Against Historicism Valid?', *British Journal of the Philosophy of Science*, vol. 29, no. 2, 1978.

[77]M. White, *Foundations of Historical Knowledge*, p. 30.

[78]R. F. Atkinson, *Knowledge and Explanation in History*, London 1978, p. 12.

[79]G. D. O'Brien, in *Hegel on Reason in History*, Chicago 1975, makes a case for seeing Hegel as a determinate historical thinker.

[80]J. L. Gorman, Review of Goldstein, *History and Theory*, vol. 16, 1977.

Chapter 5

[1]J. H. Hexter, *Doing History*, London 1971.

[2]T. Parsons, *The Structure of Social Action*, New York 1937.

[3]Boston 1976.

[4]*American Historical Review*, vol. 75, no. 3, 1970.

[5]J. Huizinga, 'The Task of Cultural History', in *Men and Ideas*, London 1960.

[6]Harmondsworth, 1972.

[7]London 1972.

[8]C. Becker, 'Everyman His Own Historian', *American Historical Review*, vol. 37, 1932. 'What is Historiography?', *American Historical Review*, vol. 44, 1938.

[9]See the important United States Social Science Research Council study *Theory and Practice in History*, New York 1946.

[10]C. Beard, 'That Noble Dream', *American Historical Review*, vol. 41, 1935.

[11]L. von Mises, *Theory and History*, London 1958, p. 183.

[12]Sir Charles Oman, *On the Writing of History*, London 1939, p. 257.

[13]See J. G. Renier, *History: Its Purpose and Method*, London 1950.

[14]The critical study of documents, inscriptions, and coins respectively.

[15]C. V. Langlois and C. Seignobos, *Introduction to the Study of History*, London 1926, p. 59, p. 127.

[16]J. Barzun and H. F. Graff, *The Modern Researcher*, New York 1970, p. 55.

[17]V. H. Galbraith, *Introduction to the Study of History*, London 1964.

[18]G. Bachelard, *The Philosophy of No*, New York 1969; A. Koyré, *Metaphysics and Measurement*, London 1968.

[19]Some of these statements are collected in F. Stern (ed.), *The Varieties of History*, London 1970.

[20]Buckle's *History of Civilization in England*, vol. 1, 1861, was a curious combination of materialism and idealism, positivism and realism. A rare defence of his aspirations is conducted by G. A. Wells, 'The Critics of Buckle', *Past and Present* 9, 1956.

[21]Barzun and Graff, *The Modern Researcher*, p. viii.

[22]C. G. Crump, *History and Historical Research*, London 1928, p. 18.

[23]Crump, *History*, p. 60.

[24]Langlois and Seignobos, *Introduction*, p. 172.

[25]*Introduction*, p. 118.

[26]Galbraith, p. 3.

[27]J. M. Vincent, *Aids to Historical Research*, New York 1934, p. 15.

[28]Langlois and Seignobos, *Introduction*, p. 192.

[29]Barzun and Graff, *The Modern Researcher*, p. 55.

[30]T. R. Tholfsen, *Historical Thinking: An Introduction*, New York 1967.

[31]L. Gottschalk, *Understanding History: A Primer of Historical Method*, New York 1951.

[32]G. M. Young, *Victorian England: Portrait of An Age*, G. K. Clark (ed.), Oxford 1978, p. 18. The view of history as 'portraits', to which Young adheres, finds support in the well-known and over-rated article by Berlin, 'The Concept of Scientific History', *History and Theory*, vol. 1, 1960. Berlin endorses the notion of history as amateur, common-sense 'practical judgements founded on observation'.

[33]L. Namier, *Personalities and Power*, London 1955, pp. 1-4.

[34]J. Fortescue, *The Writing of History*, London 1926.

[35]London 1960.

[36]J. Topolski, *Methodology of History*, Boston, Part 4.

[37]J. H. Hexter, *The History Primer*, London 1972, pp. 68-9.

[38]*The History Primer*, p. 260.

[39]Barzun and Graff, p. 239.

[40]H. Trevor-Roper, *History: Professional and Lay*, Oxford 1957.

[41]Langlois and Seignobos, p. 312.

[42]L. Namier, *Avenues of History*, London 1952, p. 6.

[43]G. R. Elton, *The Practice of History*, Sydney 1967, p. 6.

[44]*The Practice of History*, p. 18.

[45]G. Kitson Clark and G. R. Elton, *Guide for Research Students Working on Historical Topics*, Cambridge 1958, pp. 8-9.

[46]G. Kitson Clark, *The Critical Historian*, London 1967, pp. 25, 135.

[47]H. Butterfield, *The Whig Interpretation of History*, Harmondsworth 1973, p. 93.

[48]Butterfield, *History and Human Relations*, London 1951; *Man On His Past*, Cambridge 1955.

[49]Butterfield, 'History and the Marxian Method', *Scrutiny*, vol. 1, no. 4, 1933.

[50]J. H. Plumb, *The Death of the Past*, London 1969.

[51]*History in a Changing World*, Oxford 1955.

[52]*The New History*, New York 1965.

[53]*The Relevance of History*, London 1972.

[54]E. H. Carr, *What is History?*, Harmondsworth 1964, p. 70.

[55]Ibid., p. 87.

[56]Ibid., p. 94.

[57]Elton, *The Practice of History*, p. 53.

[58]M. Bloch, *The Historian's Craft*, Manchester 1954, p. 22.

[59]M. M. Postan, *Fact and Relevance in History: Essays on Historical Method*, Cambridge 1971, p. 51.

[60]*The Historian's Craft*, pp. 14-17.

[61]Ibid., p. 22.

[62]Ibid., p. 45.

[63]Marx, *Grundrisse*, p. 107.

[64]*The Historian's Craft*, p. 11.

[65]Ibid., pp. 50, 55, 147, 189.

[66]Ibid., p. 8, p. 10.

[67]Ibid., pp. 13-14.

[68]Ibid., p. 12.

[69]Ibid., p. 64.

[70]See L. von Ranke, *The Theory and Practice of History*, (eds.) G. G. Iggers and K. von Moltke, New York 1973; Krieger, *Ranke: The Meaning of History*, Chicago 1977.

[71]'Psycho-history', for example, whose advocates are divided as to whether positivist or interpretative methods are appropriate.

[72]N. B. Harte (ed.), *The Study of Economic History: Collected Inaugural Lectures, 1893-1970*, London 1971, p. xxi.

[73]Ibid., p. 13.

[74]Ibid., p. 167.

[75]Ibid., p. 31.

[76]Ibid., p. 68.

[77]G. Unwin, *Studies in Economic History*, 1927, p. 38.

[78]E. Power, in *The Study of Economic History*, p. 112.

[79]A. J. Taylor (ed.), *The Standard of Living in Britain in the Industrial Revolution*, London 1975.

[80]*The Study of Economic History*, p. 147.

[81]E. R. Seligman's *The Economic Interpretation of History*, New York 1903, was an early advocate of the economic interpretation of history. He, too, rather unnecessarily avoided Marxism in an otherwise important theoretical book. Another founding statement—that of J. Thorold Rogers—still overhangs the discussions referred to: 'Political economy, rightly taken, is the interpretation of all social conditions'. (*The Economic Interpretation of History*, vol. 1, London 1905.)

[82]L. Benson, *Towards the Scientific Study of History*, New York 1972.

[83]E. P. Thompson, *The Poverty of Theory*, p. 220.

[84]H. G. Gutman, *Slavery and the Numbers Game*, Urbana 1975.

[85]B. Hindess, *The Use of Official Statistics in Sociology*, London 1973; D. Willer and J. Willer, *Systematic Empiricism: Critique of a Pseudo-Science*, New Jersey 1975.

[86]R. W. Fogel, 'The New Economic History: Its Findings and Methods', *Economic History Review*, series 2, vol. 19, 1966; 'The Limits of Quantitative Methods in History', *American Historical Review*, vol. 80, 1975.

[87]R. Johnson, 'Culture and the Historian' in J. Clarke, C. Critcher, and R. Johnson (eds.), *Working Class Culture*, London 1979.

[88]For example, C. Ware (ed.), *The Cultural Approach to History*, New York 1940.

[89]P. Conkin, 'Intellectual History: Past, Present and Future', in C. F. Delzell (ed.), *The Future of History*, Nashville 1977, p. 114.

[90]Quoted in E. Neff, *The Poetry of History*, New York 1947, p. 183.

[91]J. Burckhardt, *Reflections on History*, London 1943, p. 33.

[92]Neff, *The Poetry of History*, p. 4.

[93]F. E. Manuel, *Shapes of Philosophical History*, Stanford 1965; *Freedom From History and Other Untimely Essays*, London 1972.

[94]E. H. Gombrich, *In Search of Cultural History*, Oxford 1969, pp. 28-9.

[95]E. H. Gombrich, *Art History and the Social Sciences*, Oxford 1975, p. 54.

[96]Ibid., p. 55.

Chapter 6

[1]E. J. Hobsbawm, 'From Social History to the History of Society', in M. W. Flinn and T. C. Smout (eds.), *Essays in Social History*, Oxford 1974, p. 24.

[2]P. Stearns, 'Coming of Age', *Journal of Social History*, vol. 10, no. 2, 1976, p. 252.

[3]Hobsbawm sets out to factually summarize the state of affairs rather than express his own ideas. Paradoxically, this very approach prevents him from making the kind of synthetic statement of which he is eminently capable.

[4]J. R. Berkhofer, *American Historical Review*, vol. 84, no. 5, 1979, p. 1328.

[5]Gutman, *Slavery and the Numbers Game*, p. 8.

250

[6]T. Zeldin, 'Social History and Total History', *Journal of Social History*, vol. 10, no. 2, 1976, p. 244.

[7]E. Genovese and E. Fox Genovese, 'The Political Crisis of Social History: A Marxist Perspective', *Journal of Social History*, vol. 10, no. 2, 1976.

[8]G. M. Trevelyan, *English Social History*, Harmondsworth, 1967, p. 9.

[9]Sally Alexander and Anna Davin, 'Editorial', *History Workshop Journal* 1, 1976.

[10]See Raphael Samuel, 'British Marxist Historians', *New Left Review* 120, 1980. Anne Phillips and Tim Putnam, 'Education for Emancipation. The Movement for Working-Class Education 1908-1928', *Capital and Class* 10, 1980.

[11]G. A. Cohen, *Karl Marx's Theory of History*, pp. 73-7; R. Johnson, 'Edward Thompson, Eugene Genovese and Socialist Humanist History', *History Workshop Journal* 6, 1978; G. McLennan, 'Ideology and Consciousness: Some Problems in Marxist Historiography', CCCS Paper No. 45, University of Birmingham, 1977.

[12]Especially *Whigs and Hunters*, London 1974.

[13]P. Anderson, *Lineages of the Absolutist State*, London, NLB, 1974, p. 11.

[14]R. Johnson, G. McLennan, and B. Schwarz, 'Economy, Culture and Concept: Three Approaches to Marxist Historiography', CCCS Paper No. 50, University of Birmingham, 1978. R. Johnson, 'Culture and the Historians', in Clarke, Critcher, and Johnson, *Working Class Culture*, London 1979. CCCS History Group, *Making Histories*, London 1982.

[15]A. Briggs and J. Saville (eds.), *Essays in Labour History*, vol. 1, London 1971.

[16]J. R. McQueen, *Oral History*, no. 1, 1973.

[17]J. White, 'Campbell Bunk, A Lumpen Community in London Between the Wars', *History Workshop Journal* 8, 1979.

[18]H. P. R. Finberg and V. H. T. Skipp, *Local History: Its Objective and Pursuit*, Newton Abbot 1967. R. Samuel, 'Local History and Oral History', *History Workshop Journal* 1, 1976.

[19]P. Thompson, *Oral History*, London 1978, p. 96.

[20]'Oral History', *History Workshop Journal* 8, 1979.

[21]Thompson, *Oral History*, p. 209.

[22]J. White, *Rothschild Buildings*, London 1980. R. Samuel, *East End Underworld*, vol. 1, *Chapters in the Life of Arthur Harding*, London 1981.

[23]B. A. Carroll, *Liberating Women's History*, Urbana 1976, p. 89.

[24]In M. S. Hartmann and L. S. Banner (eds.), *Clio's Consciousness Raised: New Perspectives on the History of Women*, New York 1974.

[25]J. Mitchell and A. Oakley (eds.), *The Rights and Wrongs of Women*, Harmondsworth 1976.

[26]A. Davin, 'Women in History' in M. Wandor (ed.), *The Body Politic*, London 1973.

[27]S. Alexander, 'Women's Work in Nineteenth Century London: A Study of the Years 1820-50', in *The Rights and Wrongs of Women*.

[28]Veronica Beechey, 'Some Notes on Female Wage Labour in Capitalist Production', *Capital and Class* 3, 1977.

[29]S. Rowbotham, *Women, Resistance and Revolution*, London 1972; *Women's Consciousness, Man's World*, Harmondsworth 1973; *Hidden from History*, London 1977; *A New World For Women: Stella Browne – Socialist Feminist*, London 1977; 'In Search of Carpenter', *History Workshop Journal* 3, 1977; S. Rowbotham, L. Segal, and H. Wainwright, *Beyond the Fragments*, second edition, London 1979.

[30]Gerda Lerner has described feminist history as 'transitional' in the current period: *Liberating Women's History*, p. 365.

[31]S. Rowbotham, 'The Trouble with Patriarchy', *New Statesman*, 23 December 1979; S. Alexander and B. Taylor, 'In Defence of Patriarchy', *New Statesman*, 1 February 1980.

[32]C. Delphy, *The Main Enemy*, London 1977. For a critique, see M. Barrett and M. McIntosh, 'Christine Delphy: Towards a Materialist Feminism?', *Feminist Review* 1, 1979.

[33]Mark Cousins, 'Material Arguments and Feminism', *m/f* 2, 1978.

[34]Michèle Barrett, *Women's Oppression Today*, London, NLB, 1980, pp. 36-7.

[35]J. H. Hexter, 'A New Framework for Social History', *Reappraisals in History*, London 1961.

[36]J. H. Hexter, *Doing History*, p. 21.

[37]Hexter's argument also relies heavily on a reductionist and historicist interpretation of Marxism which will not bear elaboration.

[38]J. Chesneaux, *Pasts and Futures, or What is History For?*, London 1978, p. 15.

[39]Ibid., p. 2.

[40]Ibid., p. 28.

[41]Ibid., p. 45.

[42]J. Henretta, 'Social History as Lived and Written', *American Historical Review*, vol. 84, 1979.

[43]I would endorse Henretta's claim that we should conduct 'a search for a philosophy of historical analysis that combines methodology, social theory and political ideology'. 'Social History . . . ', p. 1295. The need for theory as well as commitment is well expressed in the editorials of *History Workshop Journal* 6, 1978, and *Social History* 1, 1976.

[44]'Social History . . . ', p. 1304.

[45]Ibid., p. 1295.

[46]R. Johnson, 'Edward Thompson, Eugene Genovese, and Socialist Humanist History'. Other contributions to the debate appeared in *History Workshop Journal* 7-10.

[47]E. P. Thompson, *The Poverty of Theory*, p. 396; 'The Politics of Theory', in R. Samuel (ed.), *People's History and Socialist Theory*, London 1981.

[48]Stuart Hall, 'In Defence of Theory', in *People's History and Socialist Theory*. Gavin Kitching, 'A View From the Stalls', Mimeo, 1980.

[49]G. Williams, 'In Defence of History'; K. McClelland, 'Some Comments on Richard Johnson', *History Workshop Journal* 7, 1979. For a critique, G. McLennan, 'Richard Johnson and His Critics', *History Workshop Journal* 8, 1979.

[50]An excellent critique is Perry Anderson's *Arguments Within English Marxism*, London 1980.

[51]G. McLennan, 'The Historian's Craft: Unravelling the Logic of Process', *Literature and History*, vol. 5, no. 4, 1979; 'E. P. Thompson and the Discipline of Historical Context', in CCCS History Group, *Making Histories*, forthcoming.

[52]Thompson, *The Poverty of Theory*, p. 220.

[53]In *The Making*, chapter 10, Thompson vehemently opposed 'the orthodoxy of the empirical economic historian', p. 2.

[54]*Poverty*, p. 220.

[55]Ibid., p. 212.

[56]Ibid., p. 234.
[57]Ibid., p. 237.
[58]Ibid., p. 235.

Chapter 7 and Appendix

[1]*Annales d'Histoire économique et sociale*, founded in 1929, became *Annales: Econo-mies, Sociétés, Civilisations* in 1946. I use '*Annales*' to refer to both.

[2]T. Stoianovich, *French Historical Method: The 'Annales' Paradigm*, Ithaca 1977. A less ambitious, but reliable account of *Annales* is G. G. Iggers, *New Directions in European Historiography*, Middletown 1975, chapter 2.

[3]G. H. Nadel, 'Philosophy of History Before Historicism', *History and Theory*, vol. 3, 1964.

[4]*French Historical Method*, p. 25.

[5]Ibid., p. 39.

[6]Ibid., p. 29.

[7]Ibid., p. 30.

[8]C. W. J. Parker, 'Academic History: Paradigms and Dialectic', *Literature and History*, vol. 5, no. 4, 1979.

[9]D. A. Hollinger, 'T. S. Kuhn's Theory of Science and its Implications for History', *American Historical Review*, vol. 78, 1973.

[10]Stoianovich, *French Historical Method*, p. 38.

[11]L. Febvre, 'History and Psychology', in *A New Kind of History: From the Writings of Febvre*, P. Burke (ed.), London 1973.

[12]*Journal of Contemporary History*, vol. 3, 1968.

[13]J. Le Goff, 'Is Politics Still the Backbone of History?', *Daedalus* 1971.

[14]L. Febvre, *A Geographical Introduction to History*, London 1932.

[15]E. Le Roy Ladurie, *The Territory of the Historian*, Hassocks 1979. Ladurie's out-spoken views on methodology have not influenced his sense of qualitative history, as displayed in *Montaillou*, Harmondsworth 1978.

[16]L. Febvre, *A Geographical Introduction to History*, p. 368.

[17]Febvre, *A New Kind of History*, p. 36.

[18]F. Braudel, *Capitalism and Material Life, 1400-1800*, London 1974, p. xi.

[19]Braudel, *The Mediterranean*, London 1975, p. 21.

[20]F. Furet, 'From Narrative History . . . ', *Diogenes* 89, 1975, p. 109.

[21]Bloch does not seem to merit a grand title of the kind earned by the mor controversial *Annalistes*. Braudel calls Febvre 'the Banker'; Peter Scott (*Times Highe Education Supplement*, 9 December 1977) calls Braudel 'The Master' and Henrett refers to him as 'The Dean'. Burke notes Le Roy Ladurie's recent investiture as 'Th Dauphin'!

[22]Braudel, 'Marc Bloch' and 'Lucien Febvre', *International Encyclopedia of the Socie Sciences*, 1968.

[23]See my Conclusion.

[24]Bloch, 'Toward a Comparative History of European Societies', in F. Lane and Riemersma (eds.), *Enterprise and Secular Change*, London 1953.

[25]Bloch, *The Royal Touch*, London 1973.

[26]S. Lukes, *Emile Durkheim*, London 1974; P. Q. Hirst, *Durkheim, Bernard and Epistemology*, London 1975.

[27]R. C. Rhodes, 'Emile Durkheim and the Historical Thought of Marc Bloch', *Theory and Society*, vol. 5, no. 1, 1978, p. 54.

[28]'Social life is constituted wholly of collective "representation".' Durkheim, *The Rules of Sociological Method*, New York 1964, p. xli.

[29]'Historians and the Social Order', in *The Obstructed Path*, New York 1968, p. 43.

[30]Bloch, *Slavery and Serfdom in the Middle Ages: Selected Essays*, Berkeley 1975, p. 91. Febvre refers to Bloch's method as 'retrospective psychology': 'Marc Bloch', in J. T. Lambie (ed.), *Architects and Craftsmen in History*, Tübingen 1956. See *The Historian's Craft*, p. 194.

[31]Bloch, *French Rural History*, London 1966, pp. 59-62.

[32]Ibid., p. 182.

[33]Ibid., pp. 105, 112, 191, 193, 443; *Feudal Society*, London 1965, pp. xx, 113, 288.

[34]*French Rural History*, p. 67.

[35]H. Berr and L. Febvre, 'History', *Encyclopedia of the Social Sciences*, 1932.

[36]Braudel, *The Mediterranean*, p. 21.

[37]Ibid., p. 20.

[38]Ibid., p. 353.

[39]Ibid., p. 20.

[40]Ibid., p. 20.

[41]R. Forster, 'Achievements of the *Annales* School', *Journal of Economic History*, vol. 38, 1978.

[42]E. J. Hobsbawm, 'Note on Braudel's *Mediterranean*', *Past and Present* 39, 1968.

[43]B. Bailyn, 'Braudel's Geohistory—A Reconsideration', *Journal of Economic History*, 1951. J. H. Elliot, 'Mediterranean Mysteries', *New York Review of Books*, 3 May 1973.

[44]J. H. Hexter, 'Fernand Braudel and the Monde Braudellien', *Journal of Modern History*, vol. 44, 1972.

[45]In 'Comments on Forster', *Journal of Economic History*, vol. 38, 1978, Douglas North pejoratively calls *The Mediterranean* 'a work of art', because in North's view Braudel, like the Marxists, is an *innocente* where price theory is concerned.

[46]J. H. Hexter, 'The Burden of Proof', *Times Literary Supplement*, 7 November 1965.

[47]Braudel, 'History and the Social Sciences', *Social Science Information Bulletin*, vol. 9, 1970, pp. 157-8.

[48]'History and the Social Sciences', p. 169.

[49]Althusser and Balibar, *Reading Capital*, p. 99. See also P. Vilar, 'Marxist History: A History in the Making', *New Left Review* 80, 1973.

[50]*Reading Capital*, p. 101.

[51]'Of course, it is rooted in certain determinate sites, in biological time'. *Reading Capital*, p. 101.

[52]Braudel, *Capitalism and Material Life*, p. xii.

[53]*Capitalism and Material Life*, pp. xii-xiii.

[54]Ibid., p. xiii.

[55]Ibid., p. 308.

[56]Ibid., pp. 239, 235-6.

[57]P. Burke, *Economy and Society in Early Modern Europe: Essays From 'Annales'*, London 1972, Introduction.

[58]R. Mousnier and R. Pillorget, 'Contemporary History and the Historians of the Sixteenth and Seventeenth Centuries', *Journal of Contemporary History*, vol. 3, 1968, p. 105.

[59]H. Stuart Hughes, 'Historians and the Social Order', *The Obstructed Path*, New York 1968.

[60]F. Gilbert, 'Three 20th Century Historians', in J. Higham, F. Gilbert and L. Krieger (eds.), *History*, New Jersey, 1965.

[61]*French Historical Method*, p. 67f.

[62]M. Harsgor, 'Total History: The Annales School', *Journal of Contemporary History*, vol. 13, 1978, p. 7. J. Topolski, *Methodology of History*, p. 593.

[63]Braudel wrote the preface to Kula's important book, *An Economic Theory of the Feudal System*, London 1976.

[64]R. Hilton, 'The Transition From Feudalism to Capitalism', London 1974, p. 10. G. Stedman Jones, 'The Poverty of Empiricism', in R. Blackburn (ed.), *Ideology in Social Science*, London 1972.

[65]Braudel, *Afterthoughts on Material Civilization and Capitalism*, Baltimore 1977, p. 83. Wallerstein is the director of the 'Fernand Braudel Centre for the Study of Economies, Historical Systems, and Civilizations' in Binghampton, New York.

[66]This is partly because, as Braudel is aware, there is a problem in socialist thought about the role of markets in a non-capitalist society. *Afterthoughts*, pp. 113-4.

[67]Braudel speaks favourably of Marx's dictum that men do not choose the circumstances in which they make history, but his somewhat inaccurate rendering is taken from Levi-Strauss's *Structural Anthropology*, not Marx's *Eighteenth Brumaire*. 'History and the Social Sciences', p. 160.

[68]*Capitalism and Material Life*, p. xiii, *Afterthoughts*, p. 46.

[69]'History and the Social Sciences', p. 172.

[70]*Afterthoughts*, p. 64.

[71]*Capitalism and Material Life*, p. 243.

[72]*Afterthoughts*, p. 40.

[73]Ibid., p. 48.

[74]Braudel, cited in Topolski, *Methodology of History*, p. 163.

[75]*Capitalism and Material Life*, p. 444.

[76]*Afterthoughts*, p. 61.

[77]Ibid., pp. 65-72.

[78]Ibid., p. 110.

[79]*Capitalism*, p. 444.

[80]V. Kiernan, 'Reflections on Braudel', *Social History* 4, 1977.

[81]R. Brenner, 'The Origins of Capitalist Development: A Critique of Neo-Smithian Marxism', *New Left Review* 104, 1977, p. 48.

[82]K. Takahashi, 'A Contribution to the Discussion', in Hilton (ed.), *The Transition From Feudalism to Capitalism*, p. 73.

[83]Ibid., p. 69.

[84]Ibid., p. 84.

[85]R. H. Hilton, 'A Comment', *The Transition*, p. 109.

[86]M. Dobb, 'A Reply', *The Transition*, p. 60.

[87]P. Sweezy, 'A Rejoinder', *The Transition*, p. 106.

[88]M. Dobb, *Studies in the Development of Capitalism*, London 1963, p. 11.

[89]Ibid., p. 21.

[90]Ibid., p. 13.

[91]E. Laclau, *Politics and Ideology in Marxist Theory*, London, NLB, 1977, p. 41.

[92]Ibid., p. 34.

[93]'The Origins . . . ', p. 61.

[94]*Politics and Ideology*, p. 42.

[95]R. Brenner, 'Dobb on the Transition from Feudalism to Capitalism', *Cambridge Journal of Economics* 2, 1978.

[96]Hilton, *The Transition*, p. 19, p. 20. Sweezy, *The Transition*, p. 54. I. Wallerstein, *The Modern World System*, New York 1974, pp. 124, 129.

[97]Brenner, 'Dobb on the Transition . . . ', p. 134.

[98]G. McLennan, *Economy and Society*, vol. 7, no. 2, 1978.

[99]J. Banaji, 'Modes of Production in a Materialist Conception of History', *Capital and Class* 3, 1977.

[100]E. J. Hobsbawm, 'Feudalism, Capitalism and the Absolutist State', *Our History* 66, 1976.

[101]Marx, *Grundrisse*, p. 459.

[102]Hindess and Hirst, *Pre-Capitalist Modes of Production*, p. 288.

[103]Wallerstein, *The Modern World System*, pp. 38, 44, 74, 348-9. See also 'Civilization and Modes of Production', *Theory and Society*, vol. 5, no. 1, 1978.

[104]*The Modern World System*, p. 74.

[105]Ibid., p. 77.

[106]Hobsbawm, 'Feudalism, Capitalism and the Absolutist State'.

[107]Hobsbawm, *The Age of Capital*, London 1977. *The Age of Revolution*, London 1977.

[108]A similar view is put by Hans Medick, 'The Transition from Feudalism to Capitalism: Renewal of the Debate', in Samuel (ed.), *People's History and Socialist Theory*.

Chapter 8

[1]Marx and Engels, *Selected Works*, London 1968, p. 35.

[2]*Selected Works*, p. 37.

[3]*Selected Works*, p. 46.

[4]S. Hall, 'The "Political" and the "Economic" in Marx's Theory of Classes', in A. Hunt (ed.), *Class and Class Structure*, London 1977, p. 30.

[5]Marx and Engels, *Selected Works*, p. 44.

[6]*Selected Works*, pp. 46-7.

[7]Marx, *Capital* Volume 1, p. 101.

[8]In the postface to the second edition of *Capital*, Marx cites a reviewer who says that in treating 'the social movement as a process of natural history', 'the facts must be investigated as accurately as possible'.

[9]*Capital* Volume 1, p. 91.

[10]Martin Nicolaus, 'Proletariat and Middle Class in Marx: Hegelian Choreography and the Capitalist Dialectic', *For a New America*, vol. 7, no. 1, 1967.

[11]L. Krieger, 'Marx and Engels as Historians', *Journal of the History of Ideas*, 1953.

[12]Althusser and Balibar, *Reading Capital*, pp. 194-5.

[13]Ibid., p. 195.

[14]Thompson, *The Poverty of Theory*, p. 253.

[15]*Reading Capital*, p. 255.

[16]*Poverty of Theory*, p. 257.

[17]Ibid., p. 258.

[18]*Capital* Volume 1, p. 381.

[19]Ibid., p. 345.

[20]Ibid., p. 346.

[21]Ibid., p. 444.

[22]Ibid., p. 446.

[23]Ibid., p. 348.

[24]Ibid., p. 344.

[25]For example, Marx's description of the baking industry—both of the working day of the bakers and of the contamination of the bread: 'a certain quantity of human perspiration mixed with the discharge of abscesses, cobwebs, dead cockroaches, and putrid German yeast, not to mention alum, sand, and other agreeable mineral ingredients'. *Capital* Volume 1, p. 359.

[26]*Capital* Volume 1, p. 375.

[27]Ibid., p. 377.

[28]Ibid., p. 348, p. 382.

[29]Ibid., pp. 412-3.

[30]Hall 'The "Political" and the "Economic" . . . ', p. 35.

[31]Another interesting feature of the chapter, and the book, is Marx's comparative discursive analysis. For example, 'Let us listen for a moment to the voices of the factory inspectors' (p. 349). Professional public opinion (p. 364) and the press are examined: the *Morning Star* is the 'organ of the free trading gentlemen Cobden and Bright' (p. 365). Lastly, the manufacturers: 'Let us hear how capital itself regards this 24 hour system' (p. 370), or, 'E. F. Sanderson answers in the name of all the Sandersons' (p. 374).

[32]Hall, p. 30.

[33]*Capital* Volume 1, p. 504.

[34]Ibid., p. 519.

[35]Ibid., p. 529.

[36]Ibid., p. 532.

[37]Hall, p. 30.

[38]G. A. Cohen, *Karl Marx's Theory of History*, p. 295.

[39]Also *Grundrisse*, for example pp. 459, 471, 497.

[40]*Capital* Volume 1, p. 926.

[41]Ibid., p. 875.

[42]Ibid., p. 875.

[43]Ibid., p. 876.

[44]Ibid., p. 900.

[45]Ibid., p. 874.

[46]Ibid., p. 928.

[47] Ibid., p. 874.

[48] Ibid., p. 928.

[49] Ibid., pp. 928-9.

[50] Ibid., p. 929.

[51] *Grundrisse*, p. 749.

[52] G. A. Williams, *France 1848-51: Marx and Tocqueville*, Open University Course A231, Units 5-8, 1975.

[53] Marx, *Surveys from Exile*, Harmondsworth 1973, p. 117.

[54] Ibid., p. 89.

[55] Ibid., p. 93.

[56] Ibid., pp. 66, 90.

[57] Ibid., p. 52.

[58] R. Price, *The French Second Republic: A Social History*, London 1972, pp. 165-7.

[59] *Surveys From Exile*, p. 89.

[60] Ibid., p. 41.

[61] Ibid., p. 58.

[62] Ibid., p. 73.

[63] Ibid., p. 123.

[64] Ibid., p. 124.

[65] Ibid., p. 118.

[66] Ibid., p. 130.

[67] Ibid., p. 131.

[68] E. J. Hobsbawm, *The Age of Capital*, p. 140.

[69] L. von Mises, *Theory and History*, London 1958, p. 135.

[70] Lenin, *The State and Revolution*, Peking 1970, pp. 43-4.

[71] Marx, *The Civil War in France*, Moscow 1974, p. 50.

[72] Despite his solidarity with the Commune, Marx initially thought that an insurrection would be 'desperate folly'. *The Civil War in France*, p. 30.

[73] *Civil War*, p. 51.

[74] Marx and Engels, *Selected Correspondence*, London 1936, p. 311.

[75] N. Poulantzas, *Political Power and Social Classes*, p. 202.

[76] *The Civil War in France*, p. 58.

[77] Ibid., pp. 51, 55.

[78] Ibid., p. 36.

[79] David Fernbach, 'Introduction' to *Surveys from Exile*.

[80] *Surveys from Exile*, pp. 152-6.

[81] Ibid., p. 97.

[82] Ibid., p. 173.

[83] Ibid., p. 174.

[84] Price, *The Second French Republic*, p. 41.

[85] *Surveys from Exile*, pp. 222, 225.

[86] Ibid., p. 190.

[87] Marx's comments on the nature of the peasantry as a class are often referred to as an example of his use of criteria that were not purely economic. This is true, but it does not follow that Marx's analysis is free of ambiguity. On the one hand, economic conditions and the cultural identity they enforce provide the criterion for class differentiation. But Marx seems to think that this is inadequate: if a 'feeling of community, national links, or a political organization' is absent, then a class—the

peasantry—cannot be said to have been formed (p. 239). Obviously, Marx proposes two senses of 'class' here, one of which is more directly political than the other (economic) sense. But the condensed descriptions give no clue as to *which* is the more apt in historical analysis, or whether the more 'fundamental' definition can stand without the broader one. My own feeling is that only the fundamental (economic) definition can be used without confusion, though it cannot tell us everything we might want to know.

[88]*Surveys*, p. 175.

[89]Ibid., p. 190.

[90]Ibid., p. 186.

[91]Ibid., p. 237.

[92]Hayden White examines Marx's literary vein to show how Marx, and all historians, could never be 'scientific'. *Metahistory*, chapter 8.

[93]Perry Anderson, *Lineages of the Absolutist State*, p. 23. Gareth Stedman Jones, 'Engels and the Genesis of Marxism', *New Left Review* 106, 1977.

[94]E. J. Hobsbawm, 'Introduction' to Engels, *The Condition of the Working Class in England in 1844*, London 1969.

[95]Engels, *Condition*, p. 50.

[96]Ibid., p. 39.

[97]Ibid., p. 163.

[98]Ibid., p. 133.

[99]Ibid., p. 249.

[100]Ibid., p. 285.

[101]Ibid., p. 262.

[102]Ibid., p. 53.

[103]*Germany: Revolution and Counter-Revolution*, London 1933, p. 11.

[104]*The Role of Force in History*, London 1968, p. 63.

[105]Ibid., p. 91.

[106]*The Peasant War in Germany*, Moscow 1956, p. 156.

[107]Ibid., p. 37.

[108]Ibid., p. 54.

[109]Ibid., pp. 44-5.

[110]Ibid., p. 23.

[111]Ibid., p. 100 ff.

[112]Ibid., pp. 138-9.

[113]Engels, 'Origin of the Family, Private Property and the State', in Marx and Engels, *Selected Works*, p. 590.

[114]E. Terray, *Marxism and Primitive Societies*, New York 1972, p. 88.

[115]Marx and Engels, *Selected Works*, p. 496.

[116]R. Delmar, 'Looking Again at Engels's "Origin of the Family"', in J. Mitchell and A. Oakley (eds.), *The Rights and Wrongs of Women*.

[117]Kathy Sachs, 'Engels Revisited: Women, the Organization of Production, and Private Property', in M. Z. Rosaldo and L. Lamphere (eds.), *Women, Culture and Society*, Stanford 1974, p. 222.

[118]Lucy Bland *et al.*, 'Relations of Production: Approaches Through Anthropology', in CCCS Women's Studies Group, *Women Take Issue*, London 1978, p. 156.

[119]L. Brown, 'The Family and Its Genealogies – A Discussion of Engels's "Origin of the Family"', *m/f* 3, 1979, pp. 6-8.

[120]Ibid., p. 8.
[121]P. Q. Hirst, *Social Evolution and Sociological Categories*, London 1976, p. 36.
[122]Ibid., p. 44.
[123]L. H. Morgan, *Ancient Society*, Calcutta 1958 (written 1877), p. 36.
[124]Ibid., p. 563.
[125]Ibid., p. 509.

Chapter 9 and Appendix

[1]A. Soboul, *The French Revolution*, 2 vols., London 1974, p. 21.
[2]Ibid., p. 110.
[3]Ibid., p. 553.
[4]More precisely, the really revolutionary road is taken when 'the producer becomes a merchant and capitalist'. The merchant may take possession of production, but at best, for Marx, this is a transitional form (*Capital* Volume 3, Chicago 1918, p. 393). Soboul gives 'Way 1' a more total and immediate character than is warranted by Marx's own comments.
[5]*The French Revolution*, pp. 10-11.
[6]Ibid., p. 462.
[7]Ibid., p. 3.
[8]Ibid., p. 22.
[9]Soboul, *A Short History of the French Revolution 1789-1799*, London 1977, p. 87.
[10]*The French Revolution*, p. 611.
[11]Ibid., p. 449.
[12]Ibid., p. 613.
[13]Ibid., p. 609.
[14]Ibid., p. 8.
[15]Ibid., p. 9.
[16]Soboul's term, *The French Revolution*, p. 1.
[17]*The French Revolution*, p. 9.
[18]Ibid., p. 9.
[19]Ibid., p. 610.
[20]Ibid., p. 14.
[21]Soboul, 'The Classic Historiography of the French Revolution and its Critics', *Proceedings of the First Annual Meeting of the Western Society for French History*, New Mexico 1974, p. 456.
[22]Soboul, *A Short History*, p. 1.
[23]*The French Revolution*, p. 557.
[24]Ibid., pp. 561-2.
[25]In a useful recent survey ('The Marxist Interpretation of the French Revolution', *English Historical Review*, vol. 93, 1978, pp. 366-7), G. Ellis reports Furet's accusation that Soboul is a 'vulgar Marxist', and that several Althusserian Marxists have joined with Furet's critique.
[26]A. Cobban, *The Social Interpretation of the French Revolution*, London 1964, p. 25.
[27]Soboul, *The French Revolution*, p. 27.
[28]*A Short History*, p. 3; 'The Classic Historiography', p. 450.
[29]*The French Revolution*, pp. 33-4.

[30]Ibid., p. 43.

[31]Ibid., p. 38.

[32]Ibid., p. 38.

[33]Ibid., p. 35.

[34]Ibid., p. 450.

[35]Ibid., p. 50.

[36]In chapter 47, section V of *Capital* Volume 3, Marx discusses how some forms of rent that involve a share in the crop, as *metayage* does, are typically transitional pre-capitalist rent-forms. Soboul (p. 60) indicates that at least in some richer regions, rent in kind is of the more capitalist feudal sort that Marx referred to as the *metairie* system. (Marx, *Capital* Volume 3, p. 933.)

[37]*The French Revolution*, p. 59.

[38]Ibid., p. 58.

[39]Ibid., p. 35.

[40]Ibid., p. 62.

[41]Ibid., p. 65.

[42]C. B. Behrens, '"Straight History" and "History in Depth": The Experience of Writers on Eighteenth Century France', *The Historical Journal*, vol. 8, 1965, p. 122.

[43]E. L. Eisenstein, 'Who Intervened in 1788?', *American Historical Review*, vol. 71, 1965-6. G. Lefebvre, *The French Revolution*, 2 vols., London 1962, 1964.

[44]Soboul, *The French Revolution*, p. 8.

[45]Ibid., p. 44.

[46]Ibid., p. 51.

[47]Ibid., p. 45.

[48]Ibid., p. 47.

[49]Ibid., p. 48.

[50]Ibid., p. 48.

[51]Ibid., p. 50.

[52]Ibid., p. 51.

[53]Soboul, 'The Classic Historiography', p. 455.

[54]*The French Revolution*, p. 8, p. 23.

[55]Ibid., p. 58. See also G. Lefebvre, *The Great Fear of 1789*, London 1973.

[56]*The French Revolution*, p. 27.

[57]Ibid., p. 7.

[58]B. Moore, jun., 'Evolution and Revolution in France', chapter 2 of *Social Origins of Dictatorship and Democracy*, Harmondsworth 1969.

[59]Marx, *Surveys from Exile*, p. 239.

[60]E. J. Hobsbawm, *The Age of Revolution*, London 1977, p. 84.

[61]*The French Revolution*, p. 11.

[62]Ibid., p. 27.

[63]Ibid., p. 67.

[64]Ibid., p. 75.

[65]Ibid., p. 74.

[66]Ibid., p. 160.

[67]Ibid., p. 161.

[68]Ibid., p. 163.

[69]Ibid., p. 208.

[70]Ibid., p. 225.

[71]Ibid., p. 244.

[72]See F. Furet and D. Richet, *The French Revolution*, London 1970, p. 182. A. Cobban, *Aspects of the French Revolution*, St. Albans 1968, p. 266.

[73]D. Guerin, *Class Struggle in the First French Republic: Bourgeois and Bras Nus 1793-1795*, London 1977.

[74]Soboul, *The French Revolution*, p. 292.

[75]Ibid., p. 276.

[76]Ibid., p. 276.

[77]Ibid., p. 260.

[78]*A Short History*, p. 79.

[79]Ibid., p. 87.

[80]Soboul, 'Some Problems of the Revolutionary State 1789-96', *Past and Present* 65, 1974, p. 67.

[81]*The French Revolution*, p. 277.

[82]Ibid., p. 277.

[83]Ibid., p. 394.

[84]Soboul, *The Parisian Sansculottes and the French Revolution 1793-4*, Oxford 1964, p. 66.

[85]Ibid.

[86]R. Cobb, *The Police and the People: French Popular Protest 1789-1820*, Oxford 1970, p. 120.

[87]Soboul, *The French Revolution*, p. 281.

[88]Ibid., p. 414.

[89]Soboul, 'Robespierre and the Popular Movement 1793-4', *Past and Present* 5, 1954.

[90]*The Parisian Sansculottes*, p. 53.

[91]Ibid., p. 52.

[92]Ibid., p. 412.

[93]Ibid., p. 11 (emphasis added).

[94]'Some Problems . . .', p. 58.

[95]Ibid., p. 68.

[96]*The French Revolution*, p. 490.

[97]*The French Revolution*, p. 491; 'Some Problems . . .', p. 69.

[98]*The French Revolution*, p. 98.

[99]Ibid., p. 612.

[100]G. V. Taylor, 'Non-Capitalist Wealth and the Origins of the French Revolution', *American Historical Review*, vol. 72, 1966-7.

[101]J. M. Roberts, *The French Revolution*, Oxford 1978, p. 148.

[102]C. B. Behrens, ' "Straight History" . . . ', p. 125. Cobban, *The Social Interpretation*, p. 23.

[103]G. Lefebvre, 'What Is the Historical Past?', *New Left Review* 90, 1975.

[104]Soboul, *The Parisian Sansculottes*, p. 10.

[105]Guerin, *Class Struggle*, p. 4.

[106]Kaplow, Shapiro and Eisenstein, 'Class in the French Revolution: A Discussion', *American Historical Review*, vol. 72, 1966-7.

[107]G. V. Taylor, 'Non-Capitalist Wealth . . . ', p. 496.

[108]'Non-Capitalist wealth . . . ', p. 463.

262

[109]Cobban, *The Social Interpretation*, p. 9.

[110]Ibid., p. 13.

[111]Ibid., p. 168.

[112]Behrens, '"Straight History" . . . ', p. 125.

[113]Behrens, 'Professor Cobban and his Critics', *The Historical Journal*, vol. 9, 1966.

[114]Cobban, *Aspects*, p. 65.

[115]Ibid., p. 93.

[116]*The Social Interpretation*, p. 52.

[117]Ibid., pp. 114-115, 154-155.

[118]Ibid., p. 89.

[119]R. Forster, 'The Survival of the Nobility During the French Revolution', in Douglas Johnson (ed.), *French Society and the Revolution*, Cambridge 1976.

[120]B. Moore, *Social Origins*, p. 77.

[121]Cobb, *The Police and the People*, p. 120.

[122]G. Rude, *The Crowd in the French Revolution*, Oxford 1959.

[123]Olwen Hufton, 'Women in Revolution 1789-96', in Johnson (ed.), *French Society and the Revolution*.

[124]R. Cobb, *Reactions to the French Revolution*, Oxford 1972, p. 130.

[125]Ibid., p. 131.

[126]Cobban, *The Social Interpretation*, p. 13.

[127]Hobsbawm, *The Age of Revolution*, chapter 3.

[128]J. Godechot, *France and the Atlantic Revolution of the Eighteenth Century 1770-1799*, New York 1965; R. R. Palmer, *The World of the French Revolution*, London 1970.

[129]Colin Lucas, 'Nobles, Bourgeois and the Origins of the French Revolution', *Past and Present* 60, 1973.

[130]N. Hampson, *The French Revolution: A Concise History*, London 1975, p. 105. See also the 'Aftermath' to Hampson's *A Social History of the French Revolution*, London 1963.

[131]Marx, *Capital* Volume 3, p. 919.

[132]Paul Ginsborg, 'Gramsci and the Era of Bourgeois Revolution in Italy', in J. A. Jarvis (ed.), *Gramsci and Italy's Passive Revolution*, London 1979.

[133]Dobb, in Hilton (ed.), *The Transition From Feudalism to Capitalism*, p. 49.

[134]Sweezy, *The Transition*, p. 52.

[135]Dobb, *The Transition*, p. 52.

[136]Ibid., p. 63.

[137]Hindess and Hirst, *Pre-Capitalist Modes of Production*, pp. 265-6.

[138]Ibid., p. 279.

Chapter 10

[1]H. F. Moorhouse, 'The Marxist Theory of the Labour Aristocracy', *Social History*, vol. 3, no. 1, 1978. John Field, 'British Historians and the Concept of the Labour Aristocracy', *Radical History Review* 19, 1978-9.

[2]The terms 'classic' and 'revisionist' are mainly heuristic. No pejorative attitude is intended in my use of the latter term in particular. But since these debates are related to questions of 'Stalinism' and 'Eurocommunism', it would be an evasion not to retain their political flavour.

[3]Marx, *Capital* Volume 1, p. 342.

[4]Ibid., p. 344. A wonderful example is Marx's sketch of the owner of a glass works who ruthlessly exploits child labour: 'Meanwhile, late at night perhaps, Mr. Glass-Capital, stuffed full with abstinence, and primed with port wine, reels home from his club, droning out idiotically, "Britons never, never shall be slaves!".' (*Capital* Volume 1, p. 375n.)

[5]V. I. Lenin, *Imperialism, The Highest Stage of Capitalism*, Moscow 1975, p. 14.

[6]Ibid., p. 100.

[7]Ibid., p. 14.

[8]Ibid., p. 98.

[9]Ibid., p. 14.

[10]Engels, *Condition*, p. 31.

[11]Ibid., p. 34.

[12]Marx himself does not appear to hold any theory of the political attributes of the labour aristocracy. On one of the rare occasions on which he refers to the matter of a 'superior class of workers', he implies that its development is indeed logical, but 'This division of labour is purely technical'. (*Capital* Volume 1, pp. 545-6.) Elsewhere, Marx illustrates 'how crises have an impact even on the best paid section of the working class, on its aristocracy' (p. 822).

[13]M. Adler, 'Metamorphosis of the Working Class?', in T. Bottomore and P. Goode (eds.), *Austro-Marxism*, Oxford 1978.

[14]Adler, *Austro-Marxism*, p. 233.

[15]Rothstein, *From Chartism to Labourism*, London 1929, p. 264.

[16]*From Chartism to Labourism*, p. 195.

[17]G. Carchedi, *On the Economic Identification of Social Classes*, London 1977, pp. 8-9.

[18]Ibid., p. 94.

[19]Ibid., p. 95.

[20]E. J. Hobsbawm, 'Lenin and the Labour Aristocracy', in H. Magdoff and P. Sweezy (eds.), *Lenin Today*, London 1970, pp. 50-52.

[21]R. Harrison, *Before the Socialists*, London 1965, p. 5.

[22]J. Foster, *Class Struggle and the Industrial Revolution*, London 1974, pp. 203-4.

[23]K. Burgess, *The Origins of British Industrial Relations*, London 1975, p. 308. See also Burgess, *The Challenge of Labour*, London 1980.

[24]E. J. Hobsbawm, 'The Labour Aristocracy in Nineteenth Century Britain', in *Labouring Men*, London 1964, pp. 290-2.

[25]Harrison, *Before the Socialists*, p. 5.

[26]Hobsbawm, *Labouring Men*, pp. 297-8.

[27]Ibid., p. 276.

[28]Ibid., p. 273.

[29]Thompson, 'Artisans and Others', *The Making of The English Working Class*.

[30]*Labouring Men*, p. 289.

[31]J. Foster, 'British Imperialism and the Labour Aristocracy', in J. Skelley (ed.), *The General Strike 1926*, London 1976.

[32]G. Mackenzie, *The Aristocracy of Labour*, Cambridge 1973.

[33]Hobsbawm, *Labouring Men*, p. 287.

[34]S. and B. Webb, *The History of Trade Unionism*, London 1920.

[35]Harrison, *Before the Socialists*, p. 32.

[36]T. Lane, *The Union Makes Us Strong*, London 1974, chapter 2.

[37]A. L. Morton, *A People's History of England*, London 1976, p. 441.

264

[38]*Labouring Men*, p. 21.
[39]Ibid., p. 275.
[40]*Before the Socialists*, p. 29.
[41]Hobsbawm, Review of Pelling, *Bulletin of the Society for the Study of Labour History* 19, 1969.
[42]*Labouring Men*, p. 275.
[43]J. Field, 'British Historians . . . '
[44]J. Hinton, 'The Labour Aristocracy', *New Left Review* 32, 1965.
[45]*Before the Socialists*, p. 5.
[46]Foster, *Class Struggle*, p. 1.
[47]Ibid., p. 131.
[48]Field, 'British Historians . . . ', p. 72.
[49]M. Nicolaus, 'The Theory of the Labour Aristocracy', in Magdoff and Sweezy (eds.), *Lenin Today*.
[50]G. Stedman Jones, 'Class Struggle and the Industrial Revolution', *New Left Review* 90, 1975.
[51]Poulantzas, *Political Power and Social Classes*, p. 146.
[52]Foster, *Class Struggle*, p. 148.
[53]Foster, 'British Imperialism . . . ', p. 24.
[54]G. Crossick, *An Artisan Elite in Victorian Society*, London 1978, p. 16.
[55]G. Stedman Jones, 'Class Struggle . . . ', p. 61.
[56]R. Q. Gray, *The Aristocracy of Labour in Nineteenth Century Britain*, London 1981, p. 38.
[57]Stedman Jones, 'Class Struggle . . . ', p. 65.
[58]R. Q. Gray, *The Labour Aristocracy in Victorian Edinburgh*, Oxford 1976, p. 4.
[59]Crossick, *An Artisan Elite*, p. 15.
[60]Ibid., p. 13.
[61]Ibid., p. 15.
[62]Ibid., p. 19.
[63]Ibid., p. 19.
[64]Ibid., p. 65.
[65]Stedman Jones, 'Class Struggle . . . ', p. 64.
[66]R. Q. Gray, 'Bourgeois Hegemony in Victorian Britain', in J. Bloomfield (ed.), *Class, Hegemony and Party*, London 1977.
[67]Crossick, *An Artisan Elite*, p. 128.
[68]Gray, *The Labour Aristocracy in Victorian Edinburgh*, p. 7.
[69]Ibid., p. 138.
[70]Ibid., p. 188.
[71]Crossick, *An Artisan Elite*, p. 134.
[72]Ibid., pp. 251-2.
[73]Ibid., p. 243.
[74]Ibid., p. 20.
[75]Ibid., p. 128.
[76]Ibid., p. 130.
[77]Ibid., p. 134.
[78]Gray, *The Aristocracy of Labour*, p. 2.
[79]H. A. Turner, *Trade Union Growth, Structure and Policy*, London 1962, p. 119.
[80]T. R. Tholfsen, *Working Class Radicalism in Mid-Victorian England*, London 1976, p. 157.
[81]*Working Class Radicalism*, pp. 269, 278.

[82]*An Artisan Elite*, p. 14.

[83]*Working Class Radicalism*, p. 158.

[84]Ibid., p. 293 (emphasis added).

[85]H. Perkin, *The Origins of Modern English Society*, London 1969, p. 390.

[86]Ibid., p. 406.

[87]But see the criticisms by the Marxist John Saville in his review of Foster, *Socialist Register 1974*.

[88]H. Pelling, 'The Concept of the Labour Aristocracy' in *Popular Politics and Society in Late Victorian England*, London 1968. E. J. Hobsbawm, Review of Pelling.

[89]A. E. Musson, *British Trade Unions 1800-75*, London 1972; *Trade Unions and Social History*, London 1974; 'Class Struggle and the Labour Aristocracy 1830-1860', *Social History*, vol. 1, no. 3, 1976.

[90]J. Foster, 'Some Comments on "Class Struggle and the Labour Aristocracy 1830-1860"', *Social History*, vol. 1, no. 3, 1976, p. 366.

[91]Musson, 'Class Struggle . . . ', p. 344.

[92]M. J. Piva, 'The Aristocracy of the English Working Class: Help for a Debate in Difficulties', *Histoire Sociale − Social History*, vol. 7, no. 14, 1974, p. 204.

[93]R. Samuel, 'Class and Classlessness', *Universities and Left Review* 6, 1959.

[94]Piva, 'The Aristocracy . . . ', p. 284.

[95]G. Stedman Jones, 'Class Expression Versus Social Control? A Critique of Recent Trends in the Social History of "Leisure"', *History Workshop Journal* 4, 1977.

[96]L. A. Coser and B. Rosenberg (eds.), *Sociological Theory: A Book of Readings*, chapter 4, 'Social Control', New York 1967.

[97]A. P. Donajgrodski, Introduction to *Social Control in Nineteenth Century Britain*, London 1977.

[98]R. Johnson in Donajgrodski (ed.), *Social Control*, p. 98.

[99]Gray, 'Politics, Ideology and Class Struggle Under Early Industrial Society: A Critique of John Foster', *Marxism Today*, December 1977.

[100]H. F. Moorhouse, 'The Marxist Theory of the Labour Aristocracy', p. 82.

[101]Moorhouse, 'Attitudes to Class and Class Relations in Britain', *Sociology*, vol. 10, 1976. Moorhouse and W. C. Chamberlain, 'Lower Class Attitudes to Property: Aspects of the Counter-Ideology, *Sociology*, vol. 8, 1974.

[102]Moorhouse, 'The Political Incorporation of the British Working Class: An Interpretation', *Sociology*, vol. 7, 1973.

[103]Gray, 'The Political Incorporation of the Working Class', *Sociology* 9, 1975.

[104]J. M. Cousins and R. L. Davis, 'Working Class Incorporation', in F. Parkin (ed.), *The Social Analysis of Class Structure*, London 1974.

[105]A. Reid, 'Politics and Economics in the Formation of the British Working Class: A Response to H. F. Moorhouse', *Social History*, vol. 3, no. 1, 1978.

[106]Gray, 'The Aristocracy of Labour . . . '.

Conclusion

[1]Alasdair MacIntyre, 'Causality and History', in Manninen and Tuomela (eds.), *Essays on Explanation and Understanding*, p. 141.

[2]G. R. Elton, 'The Historian's Social Function', *Transactions of the Royal Historical Society*, Fifth series, vol. 27, 1977, p. 204. See also Lawrence Stone, 'History and

the Social Sciences in the Twentieth Century', in C. F. Delzell (ed.), *The Future of History*, Nashville 1977, for a slightly less fever-pitched defence of eclecticism.
[3]'The Historian's Social Function', p. 211.
[4]Ibid., p. 209.

Index